The
Carolina
Curriculum
for Preschoolers
with Special Needs

The Carolina Curriculum for Preschoolers with Special Needs

Nancy M. Johnson-Martin, Ph.D.
CHILD Project
Duke University Medical Center
Durham, North Carolina

Susan M. Attermeier, M.A., P.T.
Clinical Center for the Study of Development and Learning
and

Department of Medical Allied Health Professions
University of North Carolina at Chapel Hill
Chapel Hill, North Carolina

and

Bonnie Hacker, M.H.S., O.T.R.
Developmental Consultants
Durham, North Carolina

Baltimore • London • Toronto • Sydney

Paul H. Brookes Publishing Co.
P.O. Box 10624
Baltimore, Maryland 21285-0624

www.brookespublishing.com

Typeset by Brushwood Graphics, Inc., Baltimore, Maryland.
Manufactured in the United States of America by
Sheridan Books, Inc., Fredericksburg, VA.

Seventh printing, November 1999.

The development of *The Carolina Curriculum for Preschoolers with Special Needs* was
partially supported by a demonstration grant to the CHILD Project from Handicapped
Children's Early Education Programs, Office of Special Education Programs, U.S. Department of Education (Grant Number G008730276). The content, however, does not
necessarily reflect the position or policy of ED/SEP and no official endorsement should be
inferred.

Also available as a companion volume is: *The Carolina Curriculum for Handicapped In-
fants and Infants at Risk,* by Nancy Johnson-Martin, Kenneth G. Jens, and Susan M.
Attermeier. It may be ordered from Paul H. Brookes Publishing Co., P.O. Box 10624,
Baltimore, Maryland 21285-0624 (1-800-638-3775).

Library of Congress Cataloging-in-Publication Data
Johnson-Martin, Nancy, 1934–
    The Carolina curriculum for preschoolers with special needs / by Nancy M. Johnson-
Martin, Susan M. Attermeier, and Bonnie Hacker.
      p.   cm.
    ISBN 1-55766-032-8
    1. Handicapped children—Education (Preschool)—United States—Curricula.
2. Handicapped children—United States—Development. I. Attermeier, Susan M.,
1942–   . II. Hacker, Bonnie J. III. Title.
LC4019.2.J64   1990
371.9′0472′0973—dc20   89-39722
                                                                     CIP

Contents

Contents

Acknowledgments

W<small>E ARE GRATEFUL</small> to staffs of the Clinical Center for the Study of Development and Learning, University of North Carolina at Chapel Hill, and the CHILD Project, Duke University, for their encouragement and support in the development of these curricular materials. We especially appreciate the efforts of Constance O'Donnell and Patsy Coleman who helped in the collection of materials for the communication sections of the curriculum, Beth Leiro who devoted hours to playground observations, Sally Robinson whose creativity in developing learning experiences for young children was an inspiration, and Alfreida Stevens who patiently helped print and collate our various drafts.

We also owe a special debt to the children we have encountered at our clinical work and in the day care centers of Durham County and Chapel Hill who helped us understand the needs of young handicapped children and the challenge of meeting those needs in group care settings. Invaluable consultation was provided to our project regarding play activities for young children by Mary Hardin of the Transitional Preschool, and regarding motor skill development by Ann Van Sant of Temple University. Susan Bell gave generously of her valuable time to get pictures for us.

Finally, we give special thanks to Bob, Elisabeth, Ted, Robert, Julia, Daniel, and Erin —members of our families who adapted themselves to our distraction and their disrupted schedules, and provided the emotional support to get us through the project.

The
Carolina
Curriculum
for Preschoolers
with Special Needs

chapter *1*

Introduction

WITH THE PASSAGE OF PL 99-457 (Education of the Handicapped Act Amendments of 1986), the United States made a major commitment to the education of all preschoolers with handicaps. This law represents the culmination of 20–30 years of effort by scientists and practitioners to demonstrate the effectiveness of early intervention in preventing or reducing the effects of handicapping conditions. The early years of this movement were dominated by concerns for the children of poverty who were at risk for school failure and focused on the preschool years (ages 3–5). However, for the latter half of this period, the federal government has provided most of its support to research and service programs for infants who are handicapped and at high risk (ages birth to 3 years). This support gave rise to a proliferation of materials that currently provide a diverse menu for early interventionists of models for incorporating intervention, assessment instruments for evaluating children and programs, and curriculum materials to promote developmental progress. The primary efforts for continuing to provide help to preschoolers were support to: Head Start programs, which serve not only children who are economically disadvantaged but also a certain proportion of children who are handicapped; developmental day programs for children with moderate to severe mental retardation; and projects that focus on specific and relatively severe handicapping conditions (e.g., severe/profound mental retardation, deaf-blind, multihandicapped). As a result of these differences in funding priorities, there is currently a more limited selection of materials available to aid educators and other interventionists who work with preschoolers who are handicapped than there is for those working with infants.

EDUCATIONAL ENVIRONMENTS AND THEIR IMPLICATIONS FOR CURRICULA

Along with PL 94-142 (Education for All Handicapped Children Act of 1975), PL 99-457 requires that children be served in the "least restrictive environment" (i.e., a setting as much like that of nonhandicapped children as possible). In infant interven-

1

tion, the "least restrictive environment" has been viewed as the home. Thus, intervention has focused on helping parents feel competent to provide intervention for their own children who are handicapped, with support from professionals. With the growing number of infants whose mothers work outside the home, this view of intervention has required some modifications. Many early interventionists now work with both parents and day care workers to help them provide appropriate intervention activities for the infants throughout the day. However, the emphasis on adult-child interactions remains the focus of the intervention.

The problem of intervention environments becomes even more complex when the individual reaches the preschool age. Many more preschoolers than infants are cared for in group settings, whether half-day preschools or full-day day care centers. Therefore, the "least restrictive environment" for a preschooler who is handicapped is usually in a group setting with nonhandicapped peers. In such a setting, adults may have relatively little time to devote to the needs of one child. Also, during this period, peer relationships become much more important for the child's development. Peer relationships not only have a direct effect on the development of social skills and self concept, but also an indirect impact on all other areas of development through the effects of imitation and motivation. The curricula models used for infants that focus on adult-child interactions for learning are not as appropriate for this preschool population. Models are needed that make use of both adult and peer interactions.

BACKGROUND OF THE CCPSN

The Carolina Curriculum for Preschoolers with Special Needs (CCPSN) was written to be an extension of the Carolina Curriculum for Handicapped Infants and Infants at Risk (CCHI), which accommodates children who function in the 0–24-month range. Published in 1986, the CCHI was developed for both children with mild delays who are developing slowly but in a normal pattern, and children who are multiply handicapped whose patterns of development are markedly atypical. The CCHI divided the usual five domains of development (e.g., gross motor, fine motor, cognitive, language, social/self-help) into 24 areas or "sequences" in which the order of items was determined by how skills should be taught, not by the mean ages at which normal children learn a skill (the common practice in most other curricula).

Following the publication of the CCHI, there were numerous requests from its users for an extension to accommodate handicapped young children who function beyond the 24-month level. After reviewing other curricula available for the preschool period, and observing both children with handicaps and nonhandicapped children in preschool and day care settings, the authors concluded that such an extension should follow the basic philosophy and format of the CCHI, but should include a greater emphasis on the integration of intervention activities into the daily life of children in group care settings.

THE CCPSN APPROACH

Like the CCHI, the CCPSN divides the five or six major domains of development into teaching sequences. As might be expected, the number of these sequences is greater than in the CCHI so as to accommodate the rapidly expanding skills and learning that are a part of the preschool child's development. The sequences are probably somewhat less ordinal than in the infant curriculum as well, both because the variability of development becomes greater as children get older and because several related skills may be consolidated into one sequence to avoid having an almost infinite number of sequences. Table 1.1 provides a list of the sequences and the developmental domains under which they are organized in this curriculum.

The items included in the sequences were drawn from the clinical experience of the authors, the research literature, and a variety of published assessment instruments (see References, at the end of this chapter). In the process of organizing items

Table 1.1.   Domains and sequences of the CCPSN

Domain	Sequence
Cognition	Attention and Memory Concepts: I. General 　　　　　　 II. Size and number Symbolic Play Reasoning Visual Perception: I. Block designs 　　　　　　　　　 II. Puzzles and matching
Communication	Expressive Vocabulary Interest in Sounds and Language Functions Receptive Skills Conversation Skills Sentence Construction
Social adaptation	Responsibility Self Concept Interpersonal Skills Self-Help Skills: I. Eating 　　　　　　　　 II. Dressing 　　　　　　　　 III. Grooming 　　　　　　　　 IV. Toileting
Fine motor	Fine Motor Skills: Hand use Fine Motor Skills: Manipulation Fine Motor Skills: Bilateral skills Fine Motor Skills: Tool use Visual-Motor Skills: I. Pencil control and copying 　　　　　　　　　　 II. Representational drawing 　　　　　　　　　　 III. Cutting
Gross motor	Locomotion: I. Walking 　　　　　　 II. Tiptoe walking 　　　　　　 III. Galloping/skipping 　　　　　　 IV. Running 　　　　　　 V. Hopping Stairs: I. Up stairs 　　　 II. Down stairs Jumping: I. Jumping up 　　　　　 II. Jumping down 　　　　　 III. Broadjumping Balance: I. Static balance 　　　　　 II. Dynamic balance Balls: I. Throwing balls 　　　 II. Catching balls Outdoor equipment

into sequences and assigning the sequences to the different domains, the authors recognized that their decisions were often arbitrary. There is a significant overlap of skills in the cognitive, language, and fine motor areas. For example, visual-perceptual and visual-motor tasks are included in the fine motor domain in some testing instruments and in the cognitive domain in others; concepts such as *in, under,* and *more* are included both in tests of receptive language and cognitive ability. For the purposes of assessing a child and determining what skills should be targeted for intervention, the domain to which these skills are assigned is irrelevant. However, the domains do become important when one attempts to interpret assessment findings in terms of strengths and weaknesses for the child. For that reason, it is important to recognize the areas of significant overlap. Figure 1.1 shows the most obvious areas of overlap.

The authors have observed that in many programs serving young children with handicaps, there appears to be an underlying assumption that all children, regardless of handicapping conditions, must work through all domains in the developmental curriculum, eventually demonstrating the skills observed in normally developing children. Some modifications may be made for sensory impairments (e.g., a child who is blind is not required to learn colors), but few modifications are considered for other kinds of handicapping conditions. The CCPSN is *not* intended to be used in this fashion. Specific handicapping conditions may make whole sequences inappropriate for some children and others appropriate only with significant modifications. For example, a child with severe athetoid or spastic cerebral palsy will never be able to do most of the items in the fine motor skills and visual-motor skills sections. Instead of spending their time trying to master the motor requirements of sorting small beads, these children should be working on motor activities recommended by the occupational and physical therapists that will be *functional* for self-help or independent play activities. The *cognitive* components of visual-motor tasks (e.g., the form discrimination aspect of copying block patterns) should be worked on through tasks that minimize motor requirements. This curriculum makes an effort to include items in the cognitive sequences that cover most of the cognitive aspects of the visual-motor items.

It is probably both impossible and undesirable to develop a curriculum that has modifications for every kind of handicapping condition. No curriculum can replace the intelligence and creativity of a good teacher. In the CCPSN, the authors have made an effort to describe each sequence in such a way that the teacher will understand the underlying purpose of the series of items and will, therefore, be able to make modifications in the items to accommodate a particular child's needs. For example, the introduction to the Reasoning sequence (4.) concludes with the statement "The purpose of this sequence is to help the child become aware of his or her world, to be curious, to be able to discuss his or her perceptions and conclusions with adults, and to develop both confidence and pleasure in his or her efforts to understand." Many of the items in this sequence require the child to answer questions. If the child is unable to communicate through speech or some form of augmentative communication, it may be necessary to create multiple choice options through pictures so that the child could demonstrate reasoning by pointing or eye gaze. The child can work through the sequence quite well with such modifications and should be encouraged to do so. *It is not necessary that every child demonstrate his or her skills in the same way.*

SEQUENCE	DOMAIN				
	Cognition	Communication	Social adaptation	Fine motor	Gross motor
Attention and Memory	X				
Concept: General	X	X			
Size and number	X	X			
Symbolic Play	X	X			
Reasoning	X	X			
Visual Perception: Block designs	X			X	
Puzzles and matching	X			X	
Expressive Vocabulary	X	X			
Interest in Sounds and Language Functions	X	X			
Receptive Skills	X	X			
Conversation Skills		X			
Sentence Construction		X			
Responsibility	X		X		
Self Concept			X		
Interpersonal Skills			X		
Self-Help Skills: Eating			X		
Dressing			X		
Grooming			X		
Toilet			X		
Fine Motor Skills: Hand use				X	
Fine Motor Skills: Manipulation				X	
Fine Motor Skills: Bilateral skills				X	
Fine Motor Skills: Tool use	X			X	
Visual-Motor Skills: Pencil control and copying	X			X	
Representational drawing	X			X	
Cutting				X	
Locomotion: Walking					X
Tiptoe walking					X
Galloping/skipping					X
Running					X
Hopping					X
Stairs: Up stairs					X
Down stairs					X
Jumping: Jumping up					X
Jumping down					X
Balance: Static balance					X
Dynamic balance					X
Balls: Throwing balls					X
Catching balls					X
Outdoor equipment					X

Figure 1.1. Overlap of domains for the sequences in the CCPSN.

LEARNING AND GENERALIZATION

One of the primary assumptions underlying the CCPSN is that users understand the basic principles of learning; specifically, that learning can procede best if desirable responses are followed by positive reinforcement (e.g., a cheer, a smile, a sticker), if inadequate responses are *shaped* into adequate responses to ensure success, and if those skills that are taught to the child are *functional* (i.e., they are likely to continue to be reinforced by natural consequences in the environment).

A major problem in any kind of education or training program, especially for children with handicaps, is to assure that skills that are taught in one setting (e.g., the classroom) are used in another (e.g., home, grocery store). There is ample evidence that generalization is more likely if the child practices the skill with a variety of materials and in a variety of settings. For this reason, the authors have tried throughout the CCPSN to suggest varied materials for teaching activities and, often, to suggest several teaching activities. It is critical that the user of the curriculum recognize the importance both of making use of the variety suggested by the curriculum and of creating additional activities uniquely suited to the child and his or her environments.

REFERENCES

Almy, M., Chittenden, E., & Miller, P. (1967). *Young children's thinking*. New York: Teachers College Press.

Bayley, N. (1969). *The Bayley Scales of Infant Development*. New York: Psychological Corporation.

Boehm, A.E. (1987). *Boehm Test of Basic Concepts—Preschool Version*. New York: Psychological Corporation.

Bracken, B.A. (1984). *The Bracken Test of Basic Concepts*. Columbus, OH: Charles E. Merrill.

Crabtree, M. (1963). *The Houston Test for Language Development* (Parts I and II). Chicago: Stoelting.

Espenshade, A., & Eckert, H. (1967). *Motor development*. Columbus, OH: Charles E. Merrill.

Folio, R.M., & Fewell, R.R. (1983). *Peabody Developmental Motor Scales* (Revised Experimental Edition). Allen, TX: DLM Teaching Resources.

Gallahue, D.L. (1982). *Developmental movement experiences for children*. New York: John Wiley & Sons.

Hedrick, D., Prather, E., & Tobin, A. (1984). *Sequenced Inventory of Communication Development*. Seattle: University of Washington Press.

Kaufman, A.S., & Kaufman, N.L. (1983). *Kaufman Assessment Battery for Children*. Circle Pines, MN: American Guidance Service.

McCarthy, D. (1970). *McCarthy Scales of Children's Abilities*. New York: Psychological Corporation.

Roberton, M.A., & Halverson, L.E. (1984). *Developing children—their changing movements: A guide for teachers*. Philadelphia: Lea and Febiger.

Santa Cruz County Board of Education. (1988). *Help for Special Preschoolers, Assessment Checklist: Ages 3–6*, Palo Alto, CA: VORT Corp.

Sparrow, S.S., Balla, D.A., & Cicchetti, D.V. (1984). *Vineland Adaptive Behavior Scales*. Circle Pines, MN: American Guidance Service.

Terman, L.M., & Merrill, M.A. (1973). *Stanford Binet Intelligence Scale* (Form L-M). Boston: Houghton Mifflin.

Thorndike, R.L., Hagen, E.P., & Sattler, J.M. (1986). *Stanford Binet Intelligence Scale* (4th ed.). Chicago: Riverside Publishing.

Zimmerman, I.L., Steiner, V.G., & Evatt, R.L. (1979). *Preschool Language Scale* (rev. ed.). Columbus, OH: Charles E. Merrill.

chapter **2**

Group Settings for Preschoolers with Handicaps

As previously noted, the least restrictive environment for most preschoolers with handicaps is with a group of other preschool children, most of whom are not handicapped. Providing these environments may be difficult in public schools where there are not yet programs for nonhandicapped preschoolers. Some school systems are making use of existing public and private preschool and day care settings in the community by providing money to support the additional time and the special services required for the special needs of each child with a handicap.

The characteristics that define the best preschool settings for children with special needs are the same as those that define the best preschool settings for normally developing children. In the sections that follow, the authors discuss some of those characteristics.

GROUPING CHILDREN FOR OPTIMAL LEARNING

Many preschool settings separate children by chronological age rather rigidly, and maintain that separation throughout the day. Even within the normal population of children, there is considerable variability in the emergence of particular social, cognitive, motor, and language skills. While a well-structured classroom and a creative curriculum will reduce the frustrations of children who are on "the slow side of normal" within these age groups, the effects on self-esteem can be significant. The problem is magnified when children with special needs are integrated into normal settings. Because their delays or unusual patterns of skills prevent them from participating in many activities with peers, they may end up being more isolated from other children in an integrated setting than they would be in a self-contained program for youngsters who are handicapped.

One solution to this problem is to have multi-age groups throughout the child care setting, making it more like a family where different aged members are expected to have different skills and to help each other learn. While this solution has merit, it is also fraught with problems due to licensing laws that require different teacher/child ratios for younger and older children, and may specifically forbid mixing of very young children because of safety concerns.

Another solution is to have flexible groupings where children move from one small group to another within the same classroom or between classrooms in order to assure that groups of children have similar skill levels when tackling the learning of something new. This also provides opportunities for children to be together who share a particular interest. Flexible grouping is a particularly helpful strategy when one is integrating children with moderate to severe delays or children with special handicapping conditions such as cerebral palsy. Preschoolers with moderate to severe mental retardation often function quite well in settings with children who are 1, 2, or even 3 years younger than themselves. They should not require special modifications, but will not progress as rapidly as normal children, and may need extra practice.

Children with cognitive ability in the normal range but who have mild orthopedic or neurological handicaps may be able to participate in all activities with their same-age peers; consultation with physical and occupational therapists will help clarify this, as well as assist the provider to adapt activities, if necessary.

Children with unusual patterns of skills also require flexible grouping strategies. Some children with cerebral palsy who cannot talk are still quite capable of learning some age-level preacademic skills by being with other children their age who are asking the questions they cannot ask themselves. They may need major modifications in activities to allow them to *demonstrate* what they know (e.g., matching rather than naming), but are still able to learn at a normal rate and should be with their peers for this kind of learning. However, for gross motor activities, they may need to be grouped with a few other children who need specific therapies or interventions or to have specially designed activities that they do with support on the playground.

For children with severe motor impairment, a variety of devices are available that can provide proper positioning and mobility, both indoor and outdoor. However, there may be a limit to the amount of *independent* mobility possible. In such cases, it is up to the care providers to spend extra effort to move the children from place-to-place, to physically assist them in games, and to include them in the activities.

PHYSICAL SETTING

The preschool classroom should be designed to engage the child in play and learning. In most cases, this works best when the area is divided into a number of learning areas designed to accommodate and facilitate different types of play. Typical areas include:

1. Pretend play (e.g., play kitchen with dishes, dress-up clothes for boys and girls, puppets, playhouse, small vehicles, dolls, clothing)
2. Messy play (e.g., an area with washable flooring that might include a sandbox, water table, paint, and easels)
3. Quiet play (e.g., a carpeted area with large pillows to lie or sit on; a place to look at books, do puzzles, or daydream)
4. Constructive play (e.g., a place to play with blocks of different shapes, sizes, materials [For older preschoolers, a carpentry area is popular.])

5. Manipulative play (e.g., tables or trays with pegboards, popbeads, Play-Doh, stringing beads, small toys)
6. Visual-motor play (e.g., child-sized tables and chairs for drawing, coloring, cutting)
7. Active play (e.g., low slides and climbing frames, crawling tunnels, trampolines)

There are many ways in which these areas can be set up to accommodate children with different handicapping conditions. Allowing space for a wheelchair to fit under a table, providing dress-up clothes that slip easily over the shoulders, and adapting toys for children with poor motor skills are a few examples of such adaptations. Physical, occupational, and speech-language therapists can provide consultation on adaptations for specific children. The goal of the adaptations is always to allow the child with a handicap free access to areas, and to promote play with the other children.

STRUCTURE OF THE DAY

One of the biggest challenges for preschool teachers who serve children with special needs is the provision of individualized instruction. The needs will vary from child-to-child, and frequently, the very nature of a child's problem makes it easy to overlook his or her instructional needs in a busy classroom. For example, the child who talks very little does not attract the attention of others and therefore receives less of the conversational interaction he or she needs. Also, many children who are not independently mobile are also content to remain where they are placed and, therefore, miss out on interactions with their mobile peers.

While it is clearly not possible to tend to each child's needs all the time, there are a number of strategies that can be used to maximize learning. One is to use structured times, such as circle time or story time, for individualized purposes. One child may need to say the names of objects, another may be working on counting, and another may need praise for just sitting still! Another strategy is to subtly manipulate the interactions between normal children and children with special needs so that they relate with each other as much as possible. Perhaps a child who does not speak much can be given a favorite toy or game that can be used by more than one child at once. This strategy may attract other children to him or her. A nonmobile child may have to be physically moved from place-to-place, but there may be a way for the other children to participate in the process. Consult the therapists who are working with the children for specific ideas. Finally, work on specific concepts or activities can and should take place throughout the day, in as many different situations as possible. This will not only hasten the child's ability to perform the skill, but will also help the child to generalize it (i.e., use it spontaneously in a new situation).

In order to keep in mind what each child is working on, it is very helpful to create charts that display items from each child's individualized education program (IEP) (see Chapter 4, this volume), and hang them on the wall. Having these charts in clear view throughout the day will remind all those who are interacting with the children to work on the needed skills whenever they would naturally occur.

Most children with special needs will need some individual instruction during the day, and this requires setting aside time, as well as private space. Some preschools have a small room that can be used for that purpose. Other preschools simply partition off a corner with a curtain or book case for such activities.

OPTIMIZING LEARNING AND GOOD BEHAVIOR

The optimal learning environment for children with special needs has the same basic characteristics as the optimal learning environment for normally developing children. The National Association for the Education of Young Children (NAEYC; 1986) has summarized what is known about the way in which preschoolers learn in their position statement, *Good Teaching Practices for 4- and 5-year-olds*. This statement suggests that teachers of young children are more like guides or facilitators than like teachers in the more traditional sense. The teacher's role is to prepare the environment for children to learn through active exploration and interaction with adults, other children, and materials. Concrete learning activities should be provided to the children with materials and people relevant to their own life experiences. The teacher should view each child as a unique person with an individual pattern and timing of growth and development. Thus, learning activities are developed to accommodate differences in ability and interests.

In addition, the instructional program should be "child led." That is, the children should be allowed to make choices throughout the day that demonstrate their own interests and preferences. The teacher should then introduce learning through those activities that the child has chosen. For example, if there are centers in the classroom, each child should be able to choose where to go and what to do when he or she gets there. Within each center, there should be materials that accommodate different levels of ability and learning styles. As the child participates in the center, the teacher can walk by and insert some comment or question to enhance the learning. If the child is avoiding activities that need to be included in his or her learning, it is the teacher's job to make those activities truly interesting and rewarding to the child so that he or she will choose them. By being allowed to choose, children learn to take responsibility for themselves and learn how to negotiate turn-taking with other children.

Most behavior problems in the preschool period arise from an environment that does not provide the child with adequate experiences of success and approval. Inappropriate developmental demands, whether too high or too low, are almost certain to promote either withdrawal or disruptive behavior.

One of the primary tasks of preschool education is to help children develop self-control—to deal appropriately with their emotions, to share, to negotiate, and to demonstrate respect for others. Teachers facilitate this self-control by providing good examples for the children, redirecting them, and setting clear limits that match and respect their understanding and needs. Self-control *is not taught* by rigid enforcement of rules, punishment, lecturing, or attempts to make children feel ashamed.

Probably the most important attributes a teacher or caregiver of young children can possess is a sense of humor and an ability to both see and respond to what is "good" in each child. Children need and thrive on attention. If they do not get the caregiver's attention by doing something "good," they will get it by doing something "bad." A caregiver in a group setting rarely has quite enough attention to go around. This makes it all the more important that the positive be emphasized both when dealing with behavior and when dealing with learning activities. "Bad" behavior can often be dealt with very effectively by ignoring it, while giving a lot of attention to another child who is engaging in desirable behavior.

THE IMPORTANCE OF BOOKS AND READING ALOUD

Storytime is an important part of every preschooler's day because it develops a vital set of prereading skills. By having stories read to them, children develop a rich store of language concepts and vocabulary. They are stimulated to develop their imagination and creativity and learn to extend their attention span. Most importantly, they learn from the example of the teacher that reading is pleasurable, and develop the desire to read by themselves. With this background, they are prepared for success in school and are ready to develop a lifetime habit of reading for information and enjoyment.

Reading aloud takes on special importance for the child who is limited in the ability to move independently; such children rely on others to bring the world to them in order to learn about it. The following is a list of how to provide the most benefits from reading aloud to a child:

1. Schedule at least one storytime every day. There are many children who do not get read to at home, so school may be their only opportunity to have the experience.
2. Preview all books to see if there are sections that need to be shortened, expanded upon, or eliminated. Select books with an appropriate storyline for the age group. Reading slightly above the child's cognitive level is all right, but do not choose stories that are beyond their emotional level.
3. Avoid controlled-vocabulary books that are designed for new readers. The concepts and vocabulary of preschoolers are far beyond that level, so those books will not challenge them. Remember that the purpose of reading aloud is not to teach the children how to read for themselves; rather, it is to feed them new ideas and to instill a love of reading.
4. For younger children, choose books with simple colorful pictures or pop-up pages.
5. Seat the children in a semicircle around you. Read slowly and expressively, changing voices to match different characters in the story. Run your finger under the words as you read, and hold the book so that it is facing the children.
6. Seat children with vision or hearing handicaps close to you and make sure they get the maximum amount of information.
7. Children with mobility handicaps do not need preferential seating to see and hear, but if any body movement or manipulation is being included in storytime, make sure that they participate, even if that means having somebody help them move.
8. Welcome the children's questions about the story and take time to answer them. This is a good time to elaborate on the theme of the story or to relate it to the children's direct experiences. Avoid "quizzing" the children about the story.

9. If some of the children have trouble sitting still, give them paper and crayons to use as you read. Don't require them to sit in a particular position, but do make sure they are not crowded too close together.

10. Have plenty of books in the classroom and allow the children to have free access to them. Keep a special basket of picture books for the youngest children.

HELPFUL READINGS

Biber, B. (1984). *Early education and psychological development.* New Haven, CT: Yale University Press.

Elkind, D. (1986, May). Formal education and early childhood education: An essential difference. *Phi Delta Kappa,* pp. 631–636.

Forman, G., & Kuschner, D. (1983). *The child's construction of knowledge: Piaget for teaching children.* Washington, DC: National Association for the Education of Young Children.

Kamii, C. (1985). Leading primary education toward excellence: Beyond worksheets and drill. *Young Children, 40*(6), 3–9.

National Association for the Education of Young Children. (1986). *Good teaching practices for 4- and 5-year-olds.* Washington, DC: Author.

Seefeldt, C. (Ed.). (1987). *Early childhood curriculum: A review of current research.* New York: Teachers College Press.

Spodek, B. (1985). *Teaching in the early years* (3rd ed.). Englewood Cliffs, NJ: Prentice-Hall.

Trelease, J. (1979). *The read aloud handbook.* New York: Viking-Penguin, Inc.

chapter 3

Selected Handicapping Conditions and Their Effects

T HERE ARE MANY different kinds of conditions that may result in a child having special needs. This chapter discusses the most common conditions that can be encountered by preschool teachers, the effects that these conditions have on classroom function, classroom tips for coping with these conditions, and information on which specialists can be of help. At the end of this chapter is a supplementary list of written resources, along with a list of organizations to contact for information about particular conditions.

It is recommended that teachers read through all of the descriptions in this chapter, even if they do not have children in their class who are diagnosed with all of the conditions. Teachers may encounter children who display the characteristics listed, but who have not been diagnosed as having a problem. If this happens, the teacher may want to ask the permission of the parents to have the appropriate professional do an informal observation of the child to determine if there is a need for further evaluation.

PROBLEMS IN COMMUNICATION: SPEECH AND LANGUAGE

Communication problems are probably the most common concern that leads preschoolers to be referred to professionals for evaluation and intervention. It is important that caregivers recognize that communication problems may be a symptom of other disabilities such as mental retardation or autism (discussed later in this chapter). It is also important to recognize that within the communication domain itself there are different kinds of impairments. Normal communication depends on both *speech* and *language*. Speech is the ability to produce sounds that can be understood as words and sentences. Language includes both the comprehension of what others say and the ability to formulate one's thoughts in symbolic form (i.e., in words or gestures that stand for words). Communication difficulties may arise from speech problems, from language problems, or from both. The careful observations of a parent, teacher, and/ or other caregivers will be an invaluable aid to professionals who will try to determine the nature of a communication problem.

Speech Disorders

Disorders of speech affect the way children sound. Every child has a unique voice, but differences in the way a child talks become problematic when a child's speech is not easily understood by a variety of listeners, or when a child's manner of talking distracts listeners from what he or she is trying to say. Sometimes children have speech disorders without having any other problems. Other children have speech disorders as part of another condition (e.g., children with cerebral palsy, cleft palate, hearing impairment, or oral dyspraxia often exhibit speech disorders). Finally, a normal child can cause damage to the vocal cords through specific behaviors. There are four main categories of speech disorders in the preschool population: articulation disorders, phonological disorders, voice quality disorders, and fluency disorders (i.e., stuttering).

The following can be used as general guidelines in determining whether or not a child has a speech disorder:

By the age indicated, a child should be able to produce the sound indicated, regardless of where in the word the sound occurs:

3 years:	m,n,ng,p,f,h,w
3½ years:	y
4 years:	k,b,d,g,r
4½ years:	s, sh
6 years:	t,v,l,th (*th*in)
7 years:	z,zh (mea*s*ure), th (fa*th*er), j

As this process of acquiring sounds occurs, there are typical errors that children make:

2 years:	There will be a lot of substitution and omission of final consonants
3 years:	There will still be some distortion and substitution of consonants
4 years:	There should be very few omissions and distortions
5 years:	There may be continued errors in blends; consonants may not be mastered in all contexts

Characteristics

The following is a breakdown of the four main categories of speech disorder and the characteristics of each category as they relate to a child with such a disorder:

1. Articulation/phonological disorders:
    a. Delay in the ability to produce sounds and to use them in words, beyond the ages listed above
    b. Disorders, such as omissions and substitutions, in the manner and placement of speech sounds within words, beyond the ages listed above
2. Voice disorders:
    a. Harsh, raspy voice when child doesn't have a cold

    b.   The child tries to talk and can't get sounds out

    c.   Nasal voice, in which it sounds like the air is coming out of the nose, not the mouth

    d.   Denasal voice, which sounds like the child has a stuffy nose, but doesn't have a cold

3. Fluency disorders (i.e., stuttering):

    a.   The child repeats a part of a word more than three times

    b.   The child has ten or more repetitions for every 100 words

    c.   The child substitutes "uh" for the vowel in the word (e.g., "tuh, tuh, tuh, table")

    d.   The child tries to speak but no sound comes out, or the voice gets turned off between repetitions

    e.   The dysfluencies sound strained and the child seems frustrated by the inability to get the word out

Effects of Speech Disorders in the Classroom

A child's inability to clearly communicate wants, needs, and feelings will hamper learning and interaction in the classroom. When children have difficulty making themselves understood, they often become frustrated and may tantrum or display other forms of acting-out behavior. Children who have speech problems are often ignored by teachers and peers because it is difficult to understand them; this can lead to secondary language delay, especially in social and interaction skills, because of the lack of opportunities for successful communication. Therefore, it is very important that such children get help to improve communication abilities so that other areas of development will not be affected.

Classroom Tips

The following are a few classroom tips that can be used to better understand children with speech disorders:

1. If you are concerned about a child, arrange for screening with a speech/language pathologist.
2. Try talking at a slower rate, especially to the child with dysfluent speech.
3. Give the child with dysfluent speech plenty of time to complete a message. Do not finish words or sentences for the child, and do not ask him or her to stop and start over when stuttering occurs.
4. If a child is engaging in voice-damaging screaming during play, encourage him or her to make sounds with the lips or tongue rather than the voice.
5. Encourage the child with dysfluent speech and the child engaging in vocal abuse to use an "easy voice," one that is softer and slower.
6. If you are having difficulty understanding a child, ask to be told in another way, to be shown a picture, or to be shown an object that will help you understand. Try to teach the child not to "give up" when having difficulty.
7. Give all children with speech difficulties ample opportunities to interact with children whose speech is clearer and more developed.

8.   Give the child opportunities to successfully communicate by talking when there is a high probability of success (e.g., answering specific questions, verbalizing a choice from a known selection, naming a friend while pointing at him or her).

Specialists Who Help

Speech/language pathologists are trained to deal with all of the problems and disorders in this area.

Language Impairment

Impairments in language may occur in receptive language (the ability to understand and remember what is said by other people), in expressive language (the ability to express ideas in words or other symbols), or in both areas. In either the receptive or expressive areas, language impairments may be characterized as either language delays or language disorders. With a language delay, skills are developing slowly but at a relatively even pace in a normal sequence in the various language areas (e.g., sentence construction, conversation, understanding). With a language disorder, either the order in which skills are learned is unusual or there are significant differences in development among the different language areas. For example, one language disorder might be characterized by the child's use of relatively long and complex sentences but an inability to sustain a meaningful conversation with another person. Another disorder might be characterized by excellent understanding of language but extreme difficulty in "finding" the words to express even simple ideas.

Many language delays are related to limited opportunities for learning. Some home environments do not provide support for the development of good language skills. Unfortunately, neither do some preschool and day care settings! Other language delays may be a result of generally slow development. However, if a child is very slow in all areas of development, it is likely that he or she may have mental retardation rather than a language delay. Still other language delays will occur without evidence of limited stimulation or delays in other areas. The cause for these is often unknown. Language disorders appear to be related not to environmental conditions but to developmental factors in the child that are, as yet, poorly understood.

Characteristics

Under the two distinct categories of language impairments—language delay and language disorder—a child with apparently normal skills in other developmental domains may have symptoms such as:

Language delay:
   a.   Speech sounds like that of a younger child—the sentences are shorter and simpler and the grammar immature
   b.   Difficulty in following instructions at an age-appropriate level
Language disorder
   a.   Statements that bear little relationship to the ongoing conversation or inappropriate replies to questions
   b.   Unusual grammatical constructions

c.   More than usual difficulty in remembering the correct names of things

d.   Frequent dysfluency or "losing" a thought in midsentence

Effects of Language Delays and Language Disorders in the Classroom

Particularly in group settings, adults depend on speech to direct the behavior and activities of children and to understand their needs and desires. Children who cannot follow instructions or who cannot understand explanations are at a serious disadvantage and may appear to have behavioral problems. Likewise, children who cannot express themselves at an age-appropriate level are apt to develop problems in relating to both the teacher and peers.

Classroom Tips

It is important that a teacher work with children at their level of understanding to ensure success and avoid behavioral problems. The most effective teacher will be one who is aware of the particular skills of the child who is language impaired and will provide support in the form of gestures, manual signs, pictures, and demonstration to help the child understand and communicate. Instructions will need to be given at different levels for different children in the classroom.

Specialists Who Help

Speech/language pathologists are the primary specialists who assist with language delays or language disorders.

HYPERACTIVITY/ATTENTION DEFICIT DISORDERS

Another common problem identified by parents and teachers in preschool children is "hyperactivity." It is normal for young children to be active and to have relatively short attention spans. However, a major developmental change that occurs between infancy and school age is a gradual increase in the amount of time a child can remain interested in an activity, and a gradual change from fairly continuous motor activity to alternating periods of activity and quiet in response to the environment (e.g., high levels of activity outdoors and low levels when looking at television or a book). The child who is hyperactive or has an attention deficit disorder may not show this developmental progression, or may show it to a lesser degree than other children of the same age.

When identifying children as hyperactive, inattention and nonconformity to school routine are more pertinent than actual activity levels. Some hyperactivity may be a result of organic dysfunction and be associated with other signs of neurological immaturity or impairment. Other hyperactivity is due to temperamental characteristics and lack of opportunities to learn self-control. In some cases, the hyperactivity is caused by environmental demands that conflict with the child's abilities. A normally active 3-year-old may become "hyperactive" (i.e., wiggly, silly, bothering children next to him or her) if required to sit and engage in passive learning activities for long periods of time (e.g., 20 minutes or more). Similarly, a 5-year-old child with mental retardation who is functioning on a 3 year level may appear hyperactive in a kindergarten class, whereas he or she would not appear so in a class of 3-year-olds where the behavioral demands would be more appropriate.

Characteristics

Compared to other children of the same age or developmental level, the child shows symptoms of:

1. Inattention
    Fails to finish projects
    Doesn't seem to listen
    Has difficulty sticking to an activity
2. Impulsivity
    Often acts before thinking
    Shifts from one activity to another
    Has difficulty organizing activities
    Needs a lot of supervision
    Has difficulty awaiting turn
3. Hyperactivity
    Runs about or climbs on objects or furniture excessively
    Has difficulty sitting or fidgets excessively
    Moves about excessively during sleep
    Always on the go, acts as if "driven by a motor"

Effects of Hyperactivity/Attention Deficit Disorders in the Classroom

Children who are hyperactive or have an attention deficit disorder are very disruptive to classroom routine and require an unusual amount of attention from the teacher or caregiver. There is a risk that these children and their caregivers will get involved in highly negative interactions in which the children get attention primarily when engaging in disruptive behavior. This attention reinforces and increases the amount of disruptive behavior.

Classroom Tips

Hyperactive children need a more consistent environment than do other children in order to learn rules and self-control. It is especially important for adults to be highly specific about the behaviors that are acceptable and unacceptable and to concentrate on "catching the child being good" so that desirable behaviors can be rewarded through praise, privileges, or awarding stickers. It is also critical to recognize the limits of the child's ability to sit still so that the demands of the classroom are modified to maximize success. For example, there is no reason that every child should have to be seated with both feet on the floor for art or other activities. Some children will accomplish the tasks with much less disruption if allowed to stand, walk, or wiggle. The rule should be to avoid disrupting the children's activities rather than to meet an adult's idea of attentive behavior.

Specialists Who Help

A diagnosis of hyperactivity is usually made by a psychologist or physician after careful observations, interviews with parents and other caregivers, and a general developmental evaluation. These professionals will then guide the classroom teacher and parents in proper techniques to be used with the child.

MENTAL RETARDATION

Children with mental retardation have both below-average intelligence and below-average ability to cope with tasks of everyday living. There are many causes of mental retardation, including maternal infections, defects in metabolism, diseases of the brain, and abnormalities of the chromosomes. Environmental problems, which could include lack of stimulation, poor diet, and inadequate medical care can also cause mental retardation. However, in many cases, the cause of the retardation cannot be determined.

Characteristics

The following are a few characteristics of children with mental retardation:

1. Some children with mental retardation have a normal appearance, while others do not. Children with mental retardation may also have additional problems such as visual or hearing problems, medical problems, behavioral problems, or difficulty with motor skills.
2. It is very important to realize that children with mental retardation are capable of learning; however, they will progress at a slowed rate. Mental retardation is classified into four degrees of severity: mild, moderate, severe, or profound.

    Most children with mental retardation are in the *mild mental retardation* range. They can be expected to learn about 9 months' worth of information over a 12-month period. With adequate education and vocational training, they have the potential to become relatively independent adults.

    Children with *moderate mental retardation* learn at a slower rate, about 6 months' worth over a 12-month period. These children will have difficulty with abstract thinking and will need more repetition to learn new concepts. As adults, they will need assistance but may be partially independent.

    Children with *severe mental retardation* may learn 3 to 4 months' worth over a 12-month period. They will continue to learn new skills, but will need a great deal of repetition. They will not have independent living skills as adults.

    Children with *profound mental retardation* will learn only 1 or 2 months' worth over a 12-month period, and may function primarily as reactors to stimuli. They will require custodial care as adults.

Effects of Mental Retardation in the Classroom

Children with mild mental retardation in the 2–5-year-old range can generally function well in groups with children without mental retardation who are 1 or 2 years younger. These children may require no particular classroom adaptations. Children with moderate and severe mental retardation will need specialized instruction for at least part of the day in order to learn new material. The greater the degree of retardation, the more repetitions will be necessary in order for the child to learn. Children with mental retardation sometimes develop behavior problems that require input from a specialist.

Classroom Tips

The following are helpful classroom tips to use when teaching children with mental retardation:

1. Use simple, clear verbal instructions. Sometimes it helps to use gestures as well.
2. Break tasks down into parts that can be easily accomplished. If necessary, physically guide the child through the task, and then gradually withdraw your help.
3. Pay special attention to building self-esteem by praising desirable behavior and calling attention to attractive traits. If the child with mental retardation is in a group with children of normal intelligence, take care that the child is included in all group activities. Often, assigning a buddy will help.

Specialists Who Help

Psychologists provide diagnosis as well as classroom consultation and behavior management strategies. Speech/language pathologists frequently work with children who have mental retardation, both directly and in consultation with teachers.

AUTISM

Autism is a disorder characterized by a severe disruption of communication and social skills that is present before 30 months of age. Autistic children are often very confusing to caregivers because they look quite normal but demonstrate very unusual behaviors and patterns of development. Most autistic children also have mental retardation; however, there is a great deal of variability in this. Visual-motor skills may be delayed, or they may be average or even superior; they are generally more advanced than other skills. Speech may be absent, consist only of echoing what others have said, or be self-initiated but have little relationship to what others have said or are doing. The children may avoid touch or other contact with people or they may cling indiscriminately. Neither speech nor social skills are simply delayed; they are atypical for children of any age. The causes of autism are not understood, but it is generally believed to be an inborn disorder.

Characteristics

Compared to other children of the same age or developmental level, the child with autism shows symptoms of:

1. Delayed or unusual language development
2. Social development that is impaired beyond what would be expected from the child's cognitive abilities

3. An insistence on sameness as shown by stereotyped play, abnormal preoccupa-
   tions, or resistence to change

Related Behaviors/Characteristics

The following are a few related behaviors or characteristics of a child with autism:

1. Mental retardation
2. Self-stimulatory behaviors (e.g., noises, hand flapping)

Effects of Autism in the Classroom

Many of the problems that arise in working with children with autism in the classroom
result from the disruption of normal social interactions. Children with autism will
interact little with their peers and may unpredictably engage in disruptive behavior
such as destroying block constructions of other children. Discipline is often difficult
because these children are influenced very little by praise or other social reinforce-
ments. "Time out" will usually be an ineffective means of decreasing undesirable
behaviors since they may prefer to be left alone. Children with autism may become
extremely upset by changes in established routines.

Classroom Tips

Children with the more severe forms of autism may need to be in self-contained
classes, perhaps integrated for parts of the day with nonhandicapped peers. However,
there are children with autism who can be mainstreamed effectively. The teacher will
need to identify reinforcers (e.g., raisins, crackers, other edibles; time with a particular toy) to supplement praise, and the other usual social reinforcers used to maintain
learning and good behavior in a preschool classroom. It is also important to maintain
a regular schedule, making the environment as predictable as possible for the child.
When changes are necessary, the teacher should be prepared for the child to become
upset, but also to try to prepare him or her for the change. Communication may be
enhanced by the use of gestures and standard "signs" used for deaf communication.

Specialists Who Help

The diagnosis and treatment of autism is done by either a psychologist or a psychia-
trist. Sometimes speech/language therapists are involved in setting up communication systems.

CEREBRAL PALSY

Cerebral palsy is a condition that causes abnormal movement and postural patterns. It
is a result of damage to an immature brain. Most of the time, the actual cause of the
cerebral palsy is unknown but the damage is considered to have occurred before the
time of birth, either because the brain did not develop properly or because something
occurred to damage a brain that was developing properly. Bleeding in the brain could

cause cerebral palsy, as could an infection. Sometimes children are normal at birth but have an infection of the brain or trauma to the head that results in cerebral palsy. Whatever the cause, the damage is a one-time occurrence, and does not get worse over time. However, if children are severely involved, they may appear to get worse because they cannot keep up with the rapidly increasing expectations for movement.

Characteristics

The term "cerebral palsy" covers a wide range of disabilities. In order to describe any particular child with cerebral palsy, the authors use terminology related to the *type* and *distribution* of the motor involvement, as well as its *severity*.

The following are the three main *types* of motor disorders, and their typical patterns of *distribution*:

1. The most common type of motor disorder is usually referred to as "spastic." Children with spastic motor disorders move in stereotypical patterns, generally bending and straightening their limbs as a unit, and having difficulty using variety in movement. They have control over whether or not they will move their limbs. If they are relaxed and you try to move their limbs for them, you encounter an abnormal amount of resistance or stiffness.

    Some children have spastic motor disorders only in an arm and leg on one side of the body. This is called "hemiplegia." Some children are involved primarily in the legs and only a little in the arms and trunk. This is called "diplegia." Some children are involved in all parts of the body. This is called "quadriplegia."

2. Athetosis is another type of cerebral palsy. Children with athetosis show movement patterns that are wide ranging and difficult for them to control. Some have normal muscle tone, some have athetosis combined with spasticity (muscle stiffness), and some have athetosis combined with hypotonia (floppy muscles).

    These children always have total body involvement, but frequently have more difficulty with head, mouth, and arm movements than with leg movements. Another trait often seen in children with athetosis is over-reaction to sensory stimuli.

3. Ataxia is a less common form of cerebral palsy. Children with ataxia have normal movement patterns but will have difficulty in accurately aiming their arm toward a target. When walking, they have poor balance, and often weave from side to side. Children with ataxia usually have muscle tone in the low normal or mildly hypotonic range. They always have whole-body involvement.

Severity of involvement is more important in terms of classroom activities. Children are described as having *mild, moderate, or severe* involvement.

Effects of Cerebral Palsy in the Classroom

Mildly involved children will have little difficulty in the classroom. They will not require much in way of adaptations to the classroom or to class routine; however, therapists will recommend activities that will help them develop better motor skills. These children will be at an age-appropriate level, or nearly so, in walking and self-care.

Moderately involved children will require more time and effort on the part of the teacher to make sure that they can participate in classroom activities. These children may gain the ability to walk but it may be much later than normal children, and may require the use of special equipment such as braces or a walker. In the meantime, they will make use of adaptive equipment such as wheelchairs and standing tables.

Severely involved children need help with all daily activities. Because their mobility is so limited, they must have their position changed for them many times during the day. As a rule, these children will not gain the ability to walk or otherwise care for themselves, and may not be able to speak. For these children, the primary mode of learning will be watching and listening to others. The inability to talk can be at least partially compensated for with an augmentative communication system.

Classroom Tips

The following are a few classroom tips that can be used to better assist children with cerebral palsy:

1. The fact that children with cerebral palsy are not able to move normally, or perhaps speak, does not necessarily mean that they have mental retardation. Although it is generally true that as the degree of brain damage increases, the likelihood of mental retardation also increases, there are children with severe involvement who have average or above-average intelligence. If you are unsure about the cognitive abilities of a nonspeaking child, it is safer to assume that he or she can understand you, and to talk to him or her as you would to a child of the same age. It is very important to develop communication systems for such children.
2. Cerebral palsy is not a painful condition. If a child with cerebral palsy is complaining of pain, this should be investigated immediately.
3. Besides the motor disorder, children with cerebral palsy can have a variety of other problems. They could have a seizure disorder, visual problems, hearing problems, or learning disabilities. Each child is different, and the teacher needs to know what each one's specific problems are in order to provide a beneficial classroom experience.

Specialists Who Help

Physical and occupational therapists are involved with almost all children with cerebral palsy. If the child's impairment is mild the therapists may simply consult with the teacher on ways to help him or her improve on motor skills. If the child's impairment is moderate or severe, the therapists will need to be more directly involved. They will show the teacher how to position the child for function, safely lift and carry the child, and if necessary, help him or her eat.

For children who cannot talk, it is very important to obtain an augmentative communication system. This is done by having the child examined by a team of professionals that generally includes a speech/language pathologist, a psychologist, an occupational therapist, and a physical therapist. This team will decide what type of communication system is best. Communication systems can range from simple picture boards to electronic devices.

All children with cerebral palsy should be followed by a pediatrician who can monitor all health issues, including monitoring by an orthopedist, if necessary.

SPINA BIFIDA

Spina bifida is a condition in which the child's spinal column does not close properly before birth. Because of this, the spinal cord bulges out, and does not develop below the level of the lesion. The result is paralysis of muscles innervated below the level of the lesion, as well as loss of sensation below that level. The cause is not known.

Characteristics

The following are characteristics displayed by children with spina bifida:

1. Muscle paralysis or weakness below the level of the lesion (The higher the lesion is on the spine, the more problems the child will have. If the lesion is above the waist, the legs will be completely paralyzed. The child may learn to walk with braces and crutches or a walker, but eventually will use a wheelchair. If the lesion is below the waist, he or she can be taught to walk with braces and crutches and may be able to function without a wheelchair.)
2. Lack of sensation below the level of the lesion (This includes sensation from the skin, as well as the inside of the body.)
3. Lack of control over bowel and bladder function (The extent of this will again depend on the level of the lesion, but all children with spina bifida have problems in this area.)
4. Deformities of the spine, legs, and feet resulting from the uneven pull of muscles, as well as malformations of the bones
5. Hydrocephalus, a condition that involves excessive accumulation of fluids in the brain (This is present in most children with spina bifida. It is treated by placing a shunt tube that drains off the excessive fluid from the brain into either the heart or the abdomen.)
6. Mental retardation and language disorders (These are sometimes present in children with spina bifida.)

Effects of Spina Bifida in the Classroom

Children with spina bifida can talk and use their arms well. Depending on the level of the lesion and how long they have been receiving therapy, they may be walking with a walker or using a wheelchair. If so, the classroom should be arranged so that there is enough space for these children to maneuver. There should be no loose rugs on the floor if a walker is being used. Children who are not walking must be positioned carefully according to the instructions of the therapists. Toilet training may be impossible, and special procedures may have to be carried out at school.

Classroom Tips

The following are a few classroom tips used in the care of children with spina bifida:

1. It is very important to prevent or minimize skin breakdown. The most common problem areas are the back, elbows, hips, heels, and ankles. Any skin area that receives pressure or rubbing from braces, clothing, or furniture can break down.

The child's parents will show you how to check for pressure or irritation. If serious skin breakdown occurs, the child may have to be taken out of school until it heals.

2. If the child cannot control urine, it is very important to keep the diaper area clean and dry in order to prevent skin breakdown.

3. Because of the lack of skin sensation, the child is unable to detect cuts, abrasions, and even fractures. If the child is actively moving around on the floor, protective clothing such as thick pants should be worn to prevent injury.

4. If a child has a shunt to control hydrocephalus, you do not need to worry about fluid going back into the brain, even if the child is held upside down, since the shunt has a one-way valve to prevent that from happening. However, sometimes the shunt system develops problems and the child would need immediate medical attention. If you see vomiting, irritability, drowsiness, confusion, or muscle stiffness, notify the parents and make sure the child is seen by a doctor.

Specialists Who Help

All children with spina bifida need expert medical attention, and are usually followed by orthopedists and neurologists. Physical therapists work with the children to get them as mobile as possible, and also work closely with parents and teachers to prevent deformities and skin breakdown as much as possible. If the child is showing cognitive or language deficits, psychologists and speech/language pathologists will work with the child directly and consult with the teacher.

DEVELOPMENTAL DYSPRAXIA

Praxis, or motor planning, is the ability to mentally plan out and smoothly execute a coordinated motor act. Difficulty with motor planning is referred to as dyspraxia. The child with developmental dyspraxia generally knows what he or she wants to do, but cannot figure out how to get his or her body to cooperate. Learning new motor skills is very difficult, particularly if complex motor patterns are involved. Therefore, children with dyspraxia demonstrate both motor delays and poorly coordinated movement.

Characteristics

The following are a few characteristics commonly seen in children with developmental dyspraxia:

1. Clumsiness, poor coordination
2. Delays in fine, gross, and/or visual-motor skills
3. Ability to understand directions, but inability to carry out the task
4. Difficulty learning new motor skills
5. Poor motor imitation
6. Difficulty transferring skills learned in one situation to a new situation
7. In some children, speech difficulties due to oral dyspraxia

The following are related behaviors sometimes seen in children with dyspraxia:

1. Avoidance of motor tasks
2. Need to be in control of situations
3. Desire for predictable, stable routines
4. Wide fluctuations in abilities from day to day
5. Silly, clowning behavior

Effects of Developmental Dyspraxia in the Classroom

Children who are dyspraxic may experience problems in a number of areas in the classroom due to their motor delays and difficulty in learning new and complex motor skills. They are likely to have problems with such fine motor and visual-motor tasks as coloring, cutting, drawing, and pasting. Poor imitation skills result in difficulty with action songs and rhythm activities.

Gross motor skills are often quite delayed. As a result, children may avoid playground activities and outdoor equipment. Children with dyspraxia are often delayed in achieving independence in self-help skills such as dressing and undressing; buttons, zippers, and snaps pose particular problems. They may also be messy eaters relative to their same-age peers.

Classroom Tips

Complex tasks need to be broken down into smaller, easily accomplished tasks. When teaching a new skill, physically guide the child through the movement several times, then gradually fade the assistance. Provide verbal cues about the required movements. Simple obstacle courses and creative movement programs offer opportunities for these children to learn more about body movement in space. For children with severe difficulty, materials and expectations may need to be adapted to allow them to participate in learning without being penalized for poor motor coordination. Precut pictures for art activities, use of stencils for drawing, and placing Velcro closures on clothing are examples of such adaptations.

Specialists Who Help

Pediatric occupational therapists are skilled in the evaluation and treatment of children with developmental dyspraxia. They can also provide consultation on integration of these children into the classroom.

TACTILE DEFENSIVENESS

The term "tactile defensiveness" refers to discomfort with or negative response to light or unexpected touch. The tactile system provides two ways of responding to tactile input. The first is protective—a "fight or flight" reaction, which should be fairly well integrated in the preschooler. The second is a discriminitive response that provides information on the characteristics of what is being felt (e.g., a rough or smooth surface). Children who demonstrate tactile defensiveness tend to overreact to light or unexpected touch, responding with a protective (defensive) reaction rather than a discriminatory response.

Characteristics

The following are a few general characteristics commonly seen in children with tactile defensiveness:

1. Dislike being touched
2. Dislike hairbrushing or washing
3. Dislike having teeth brushed, face washed or wiped
4. Avoid certain textures (e.g., gritty, fuzzy, scratchy, slimy) and related activities (e.g., walking in grass, fingerpainting, playing with Play Doh)
5. Dislike certain foods due to their texture
6. Dislike certain clothing because of the texture or the presence of rough seams or tags

The following are related behaviors that are sometimes seen in children with tactile defensiveness:

1. Restless behavior, sometimes hyperactivity
2. Very low frustration tolerance
3. Peer difficulties (e.g., striking a child after an accidental touch)

Effects of Tactile Defensiveness in the Classroom

Difficulties often arise concerning behavior when the child with tactile defensiveness is lightly touched, often accidentally, by another child. The child with tactile defensiveness immediately respond with a protective reaction such as jumping up, fleeing, disrupting the group, or hitting the child that he or she perceived as doing the hitting.

Children with tactile defensiveness often avoid classroom activities involving messy materials such as fingerpaint, sand, or glue.

Classroom Tips

It is important to remember that these children react to light or unexpected touch as if it were painful or uncomfortable. Avoid touching them unexpectedly. When you do touch, use a firm rather than light approach (e.g., a hug will be tolerated better than a pat on the back or head). Let these children stand at the beginning or end of lines in order to reduce the chance of negative contact with peers. Do not seat them too close to other children; allow adequate space at circle time or have children sit on separate squares of carpet. Do not force these children to interact with materials perceived as unpleasant; however, do continue to offer opportunities for the interaction.

Specialists Who Help

Pediatric occupational therapists are skilled in the evaluation and treatment of children with tactile defensiveness. They can also provide consultation regarding integration of these children into the classroom.

GRAVITATIONAL INSECURITY

Gravitational insecurity is a fear or discomfort with movement or heights. Children with gravitational insecurity are often described as "earthbound." They prefer to maintain their feet in contact with the ground at all times.

Characteristics

The following are a few characteristics commonly seen in children with gravitational insecurity:

1. Avoidance of activities involving movements or heights (e.g., climbing, swinging)
2. Difficulty with stairs, often placing both feet on each step
3. Poor balance
4. Possible secondary delays in gross motor skills
5. Possible oversensitivity to movement, becoming carsick easily or nauseated after carnival rides

Effects of Gravitational Insecurity in the Classroom

Children with gravitational insecurity are often very hesitant on the playground, and may be particularly fearful about being on equipment with other children. They may also be hesitant on stairs.

Classroom Tips

Offer children with gravitational insecurity support, without pushing them to attempt activities that are frightening. Encourage them to explore movement on low equipment, allowing them to be in control of the movement. If steps pose a particular problem for a child, let him or her come down the stairs last so that other children won't bump into him or her.

Specialists Who Help

Pediatric occupational therapists are skilled in the evaluation and treatment of children with gravitational insecurity. They can also provide consultation regarding integration of these children into the classroom.

VISUAL IMPAIRMENT

Visual impairment refers to limitations in vision that are not correctable. These limitations range from low vision to near or total blindness. For educational purposes, most states use the criterion of "visual impairment, significant enough to interfere with learning." Visual impairment in children is often congenital (e.g., from cataracts or glaucoma). Other visual impairments are acquired, caused by: high concentrations of oxygen used to save premature babies, injury, degenerative diseases, or tumors. In some cases of congenital visual impairment, there is no identifiable cause.

Characteristics

In general, there are three types of visual impairments:

Acuity problems, with "blindness" defined as visual acuity of 20/200 or less in the better eye with correction, and "low vision" defined as visual acuity better than 20/200 but less than 20/70 in the better eye with correction.

Visual field problems (e.g., tunnel vision, other field restrictions).

Cortical visual impairment, a condition in which the visual apparatus is functioning but the child is not processing visual information. This is generally associated with significant mental retardation, and will often improve over time and/or with developmental intervention.

Effects of Visual Impairment in the Classroom

Children with visual impairment have lost or limited use of a major learning mode, and will need extra support and attention to gather information about the environment. Special instruction in orientation and mobility may be required. Extra effort will be required to instill language concepts; incidental concepts may be fragmented or erroneous. General motor skill development may also be delayed. Young children who are significantly visually impaired often present feeding problems, primarily refusing to accept textured food.

Classroom Tips

Familiarize children who are visually impaired with the classroom at a time when other children are not present. Keep furniture and other objects in a constant place so that these children can learn how to maneuver around the room and avoid obstacles. Marking these children's chairs and cubbyholes with textured materials may be helpful. Make sure the room is well lit, to allow use of any residual vision. Additional direct illumination of materials may also help.

Use simple, concrete verbal cues to describe actions, objects, and events in the immediate environment. Minimize discussion of subjects with which these children have no direct experience. Avoid vague words like "here," "there," and "this," which assume a visual orientation. During visually oriented activities, provide appropriate materials to handle; do not require these children to sit passively during those activities. Encourage learning through other sensory modes and/or through motor activities.

Read to children with visual impairment often, describing pictures, providing real objects that correspond to the story, and acting out the story. For children who are blind, obtain braille/print books and allow them to explore them casually.

Some children engage in "blindisms" such as rocking or eye-poking. If this occurs, engage these children in other interesting activities. Minimize periods of inactivity by providing a full and highly structured daily schedule. Provide clear verbal and tactile signals for upcoming transitions from one activity to another.

Specialists Who Help

Children with suspected visual loss should be evaluated by an ophthalmologist. Depending on the type and severity of visual loss and associated handicaps, children who are visually impaired would need services from an ophthalmologist, a teacher of the visually impaired, an orientation and mobility instructor, a low-vision optometrist, and/or an occupational therapist.

HEARING IMPAIRMENT

Hearing impairments range from mild loss of hearing to profound deafness. These impairments can be either congenital due to hereditary disorder or maternal infection, or acquired through disease or head injury. Excessive exposure to loud noises causes hearing loss, but this is not generally found in the preschool population. In some cases of congenital hearing impairment, there is no identifiable cause.

Characteristics

There are two major categories of hearing impairment:

1. "Conductive" impairment is due to dysfunction in the middle or outer ear. This type can be helped with amplification.
2. "Sensorineural" impairment is due to dysfunction of the inner ear or the pathway to the brain. Even with amplification, sounds are very unclear.

Hearing impairment is also classified according to the severity of loss, as follows:

1. *Mild:*   20–35 dB loss
2. *Moderate:*   40–60 dB loss
3. *Severe:*   70–90 dB loss
4. *Profound:*   Greater than 90 dB loss

Effects of Hearing Impairment in the Classroom

Communication skills are often very limited in the preschool children with hearing impairments. Even those with a mild to moderate loss may exhibit significant delays in both receptive language (i.e., understanding what is said to them) and expressive language (i.e., communicating thoughts and desires to others). As a result, these children may be isolated from their peers in the classroom. Behavioral management is often more challenging because of limitation in the teacher's ability to use verbal cues, particularly at a distance.

Classroom Tips

Coordination between the speech pathologist and the classroom teacher is imperative for facilitation of communication. Children who are hearing impaired will often be using total communication that combines the use of manual signs with speech. Therefore, it is important for the teacher to learn and use the signs.

Most children with hearing impairments will be wearing some type of hearing aid, and the teacher will need to know how each child's operates.

When talking to children who are hearing impaired make sure you have their attention and have them watch your face and hands. During circle time, place these children near you, but directly across rather than beside you.

Specialists Who Help

Children with suspected hearing loss should be evaluated by an audiologist. If hearing loss is confirmed, they will need to have periodical follow-up checkups by the audiologist, as well as evaluation and intervention by a speech/language pathologist. Children with severe or profound hearing loss may need service from a teacher of the hearing impaired.

DOWN SYNDROME

Down syndrome is caused by a chromosomal abnormality and is a common cause of mental retardation. Children with Down syndrome are identified at birth because of their physical appearance. The diagnosis is then confirmed by an analysis of the chromosomes. The cause of the chromosomal abnormality is unknown.

Characteristics

The following are characteristics displayed by children with Down syndrome:

1. Almost all children with Down syndrome have mental retardation, usually in the mild to moderate range.
2. These children have a typical facial appearance, with skin-folds called "epicanthic folds" at the inner side of the eyes, rather flat faces, and, sometimes, protruding tongues. They are usually shorter than normal children of their age.
3. Many children with Down syndrome have heart defects that limit their energy. As a rule, the defects can be corrected surgically.
4. Gross and fine motor skills will be achieved at a delayed rate, but will be functional.
5. Almost all children with Down syndrome have difficulty speaking. They may start talking very late, use short sentences, and have difficulty articulating their words. Their ability to speak is usually more delayed than their cognitive abilities.
6. Children with Down syndrome have a tendency to put on weight.

Effects of Down Syndrome in the Classroom

There are no major differences between children with Down syndrome and children with other forms of mental retardation. However, the delay in speech production often makes these children appear to have a more severe form of mental retardation.

Classroom Tips

The following are a few classroom tips found to be beneficial when teaching children with Down syndrome:

1. Use the same general instructional guidelines as for other children with mental retardation.
2. Make it a point to talk to these children and to give plenty of time for a response. This will require special attention on your part since it is very natural to speak less to children who do not speak to you.

3. Teach them to use gestures and signs for words that they understand but are not able to express. This will *not* delay speech.

4. Make sure that these children engage in physical activity, and watch their food intake.

Specialists Who Help

Psychologists perform the same types of services as with other children with mental retardation. Speech/language pathologists provide both direct and consultative services, and assist in the selection of signs for communication, if that is appropriate. Physical and occupational therapists often work with children with Down syndrome to improve motor skills. If you see a child becoming obese, suggest that the parents consult a nutritionist.

ADDITIONAL RESOURCES

Publications

Achenbach, T.M. (1982). *Developmental psychopathology* (2nd ed.). New York: John Wiley & Sons.

This book provides a sophisticated review of disorders in children and current related research.

Ayres, A.J. (1979). *Sensory integration and the child.* Los Angeles: Western Psychological Services.

This introduction to the concept of sensory integration includes information on dyspraxia, tactile defensiveness, and gravitational insecurity. The treatment procedures discussed are often used by physical and occupational therapists. The book can be helpful to parents and teachers in understanding the treatment.

Barkley, R.A. (1981). *Hyperactive children: A handbook for diagnosis and treatment.* New York: Guilford Press.

Although written for professionals who treat hyperactive children and their families, this book is not difficult to read and provides extremely helpful advice for the management of these children.

Batshaw, M., & Perret, Y. (1986). *Children with handicaps: A medical primer* (2nd ed.). Baltimore: Paul H. Brookes Publishing Co.

This is a good source for medical, genetic, nutritional, and dental information. All of the major developmental disabilities are described, along with treatment approaches. This book has very good illustrations, a glossary of medical terms, and an appendix that describes common, as well as unusual, syndromes.

Broughton, B. (1986). *Creative experiences: An arts curriculum for young children—including those with special needs.* Chapel Hill, NC: Chapel Hill Training-Outreach Project, Lincoln Center.

Creative movement, drama, music, and visual arts activities are presented, along with suggestions for modifying activities for students with hearing impairments, mental impairments, physical handicaps, speech impairments, or visual impairments. An audiotape of songs is included. The activities are all cross-referenced to items on the Learning Accomplishment Profile, which is also included.

Corn, A.L., & Martinez, I. (1986). *When you have a visually handicapped child in your classroom: Suggestions for teachers.* New York: American Foundation for the Blind.

Teachers will find this pamphlet very helpful because it contains information on classroom adaptations and other resources as well as basic information on visual impairment.

Exceptional Parent is a monthly magazine for parents of children with physical or mental disabilities. It contains a wealth of information and is recommended reading for parents, teachers, and therapists. To subscribe, contact: *Exceptional Parent,* P.O. Box 3000, Dept EP, Denville, NJ 07834.

Ferrell, K.A. (1984). *Parenting preschoolers: Suggestions for raising young blind and visually impaired children.* New York: American Foundation for the Blind.

Parents will find this pamphlet useful for basic information concerning the development of children with visual impairments, and for acquainting themselves with terminology and programs.

Ferrell, K.A. (1985). *Reach out and teach: Meeting the training needs of parents of visually and multiply handicapped young children.* New York: American Foundation for the Blind.

This is a two-volume set of books that integrates general information on the development of children with visual impairments, with specific activities that can be done at home or at school. The books are very well written and illustrated, and cover infancy, as well as the preschool years.

Finnie, N. (1975). *Handling the young cerebral palsied child at home.* New York: E.P. Dutton.

Anyone who works with children who have cerebral palsy will find this book useful. Along with descriptions of the characteristics of the children, there are extensive explanations of practical methods for helping them learn basic skills. Methods of lifting, carrying, and transporting the children are also covered. This book is well known to physical and occupational therapists, and comes highly recommended.

Flemming, B.M., Hamilton, D.S., & Hicks, J.D. (1977). *Resources for creative teaching in early childhood education.* San Diego: Harcourt Brace Jovanovich.

This book contains a wealth of resources and ideas. It begins with a general description of resources that are needed in a preschool setting as well as procedural guidelines. The bulk of the book consists of seven sections of activities, arranged around themes and presented so that the activities can be integrated throughout the day. The theme areas are: self-concept, families, family celebrations, seasons, animals, transportation, and the world in which we live.

Gordon, I., Guinagh, B., & Jester, R. (1972). *Child learning through child play.* New York: St. Martin's Press.

This book contains descriptions of learning activities with sections on sorting and matching, understanding patterns, recognition games, word play, physical coordination, imaginative play, and creative activities. It is well-illustrated and emphasizes the use of common materials.

Hacker, B. (1988). *Hands on*. Durham, NC: Boundries Unlimited.
For children who need specific teaching on development of fine motor skills, this manual provides step-by-step instructions. Activities cover the 3–6-year-old developmental period and use everyday materials.

Hacker, B. (1989). *Draw 1, cut 2*. Durham, NC: Boundries Unlimited.
For children who need specific teaching of visual-motor skills, this manual provides objectives, individual activities, and related activities. The activities cover the 3–6-year-old developmental period.

Lorton, M.B. (1972). *Workjobs: Activity-centered learning for early childhood education. Menlo Park, CA: Addison-Wesley.*
A wide variety of manipulative activities that can either be incorporated into activity centers for use by individual children or used as group activities are described. The activities are divided into language (perception, matching, classification, sounds, letters) and math (sets, number sequences, combining and separating groups, relationships). Although intended for nonhandicapped children, the activities could easily be adapted for children with handicaps.

Mainstreaming Preschoolers. (1986). Washington, DC: Head Start Bureau, Administration for Children, Youth, and Families, Office of Human Development Services, U.S. Department of Health and Human Services.
This is an 8-volume set, with each volume containing an introduction to mainstreaming, followed by mainstreaming suggestions for a specific disability. There are separate volumes for children with orthopedic handicaps, mental retardation, health impairments, emotional disturbance, learning disabilities, speech and language impairments, visual handicaps, and hearing impairments. They were written specifically to assist in integrating these children into a preschool setting. They are practical as well as informative. The set is currently out of print, but may be reissued. Until that occurs, contact your local Head Start program; each program was issued a set of the books.

Marcus, E., & Granovetter, R. (1986). *Making it easy: Crafts and cooking activities. Skill building for handicapped learners*. Palo Alto, CA: VORT Corporation.
A wide variety of clever ideas for activities are contained in this book. Emphasis is on use of free or inexpensive materials, using crafts and cooking to teach conceptual, as well as practical, skills. There are suggestions for adapting activities for handicapped learners; however, they are not extensive.

Materials update: Current listing of audio-visual and print materials for early childhood. Chapel Hill, NC: Training-Outreach Project, Lincoln Center.
This resource is published in newspaper format and is available at no charge from: Training-Outreach Project, Lincoln Center, Merritt Mill Road, Chapel Hill, NC 27514. *Materials Update* may be helpful in locating curriculum materials for your particular needs.

New friends: Mainstreaming activities to help young children understand and accept individual differences. (1983). Chapel Hill, NC: Chapel Hill Training-Outreach Project, Lincoln Center.

These materials are very useful in teaching nonhandicapped children about handicapping conditions. The "New Friends" training program includes a book of classroom activities and simulation exercises, accompanied by a teacher's manual.
There are units on vision, hearing, moving, communication, learning, and emotions. Each unit concludes with a list of further resources.

Taylor, B.J. (1985). *A child goes forth* (6th ed.). New York: Macmillan.
Many preschool teachers will find this book useful, as it can serve as an overall
curriculum guide. There are chapters on planning the curriculum; creative ex-
pression; language, stories, and books; music, movement, sound, and rhythm; sci-
ence; prestory activities; excursions; special occasions; outdoor equipment; food
experiences and recipes; and math. Each chapter concludes with tips for parents
and a pertinent bibliography.

Associations

This is a partial listing of organizations that provide information and support services
for children with particular disabilities. More listings can be found in the *Exceptional
Parent* magazine that publishes an annual Directory of Organizations. This directory
also includes a state-by-state listing of parent coalitions. The American Association
of University Affiliated Programs (8605 Cameron Street, Suite 406, Silver Spring,
Maryland 20910) also publishes an annual Resource Guide, available at a nominal
price.

American Foundation for the Blind
1615 M Street, NW
Suite 250
Washington, DC 20036
(202) 457–1487

Association for Children and Adults
    with Learning Disabilities
3115 North 17th Street
Arlington, VA 22201
(703) 243–2614

Association for Retarded Citizens
    of the U.S.
2501 Avenue J
Arlington, TX 76011
(817) 640–0204
(800) 433–5255

Cornelia de Lange Syndrome
    Foundation
60 Dyer Avenue
Collinsville, CT 06022
(203) 693–0159
(800) 223–8355

Cri du Chat
The 5p-Society
11609 Oakmont
Overland Park, KS 66210
(913) 469–8900

Cystic Fibrosis Foundation
6931 Arlington Road
Bethesda, MD 20814
(301) 951–4422

Epilepsy Foundation of America
4351 Garden City Drive
Suite 406
Landover, MD 20785
(301) 459–3700

National Down Syndrome Society
141 Fifth Avenue
Seventh Floor
New York, NY 10017
(212) 460–9330
(800) 232–6372

National Fragile-X Foundation
Post Office Box 300233
Denver, CO 80203
(800) 835–2246, ext. 58

National Mental Health Association
1021 Prince Street
Alexandria, VA 22314
(703) 684–7722

National Society for Children and
    Adults with Autism
1234 Massachusetts Avenue, NW
Suite 1017
Washington, DC 20005
(202) 783–2825

Spina Bifida Association of America
1700 Rockville Pike
Suite 450
Rockville, MD 20852
(301) 770–7222

Support Organization for Trisomy
18/13 (SOFT)
5030 Cole
Pocatello, ID 83202
(208) 237–8782

United Cerebral Palsy
    Association, Inc
1522 K Street, NW
Suite 1112
Washington, DC 20005
(202)842–1266

chapter **4**

How to Use the CCPSN

Although the CCPSN is intended for use in home, preschool, and daycare settings, this use should be under the guidance of a specialist in early intervention or preschool special education. This specialist is responsible for evaluating the child, developing an individualized education program (IEP), and monitoring the child's progress. In this capacity he or she must work closely with the family, the teacher, and/or other care providers and the professional specialists involved with the child. The early interventionist or educational specialist will use the CCPSN for assessment and program planning. Teachers and/or daycare providers will use the curriculum for reference in working with the special children in their classes but may also use it as a guide to group and individualized activities for all children in their care.

ASSESSMENT FOR CURRICULUM ENTRY

The first step in planning any educational program is to determine what skills a child has mastered and what skills he or she should learn next. The CCPSN has an Assessment Log (see pp. 44–63) on which all of the items in the curriculum are listed. When you are not yet thoroughly familiar with the curriculum, you should read quickly through all of the sequences on the log several times prior to beginning an assessment on a child. When you are ready to assess, give yourself some time to watch the child while playing alone with toys and then while playing with either a parent or other children. After no more than 20 minutes of observation, you will find that you are able to score many items that the child has passed and will have a sense of the levels at which you should begin a more formal assessment. If you have the opportunity to have the child in a classroom for several days before filling out the Assessment Log, you may find that you can score most on the log without ever having directly administered an item.

The CCPSN is not a test that requires the use of specified materials. Therefore, use of the CCPSN does not require a special kit for its implementation. Neither is a kit desirable for it will create a tendency to teach to the materials included in the kit rather than teaching skills with the necessary variety of materials to assure generalization.

All of the materials that you will need for an assessment are commonly found in a preschool classroom. They are listed in Table 4.1. Note that on the Assessment Log, there are four columns to allow four different assessments on the same form. Mark the date of your assessment at the top of the column. Work through the Assessment Log with a child, beginning each sequence at the level where you have observed the child accomplishing many skills but have not observed some others. If you have not observed the child demonstrating the skills of any of the items of a sequence, try a sampling procedure whereby you begin with the first item in the sequence and then move up to the first item in each of the next age levels until the child fails. At that point, work backward until you feel comfortable that the child has all of the preceeding skills, and forward until you feel that there are no more items he or she could pass. There are no rigid rules for determining whether you have a "complete" assessment. For most children, it will be quite adequate to have passes on all the items listed for one age level and failures on all items at a higher age level.

The time necessary to complete the Assessment Log will depend on the characteristics of the child and the opportunities that you have had to observe him or her before filling out the log. If you do an assessment without any prior observation, it may take up to 2 hours. If you have had ample observation time, it may take no more than 30 minutes. Since the assessment is essentially criterion referenced, it does not matter whether it is done in 1 day or over several weeks.

Table 4.1. Materials necessary for CCPSN assessment

Manipulables
  Form boards
  Puzzles (e.g., 2 pc.–20 pc. interlocking)
  Pop beads
  Peg boards (e.g., 1/4 inch)
  Tools (e.g., tongs, hammer, nails, clothespins)
  Blocks of various sizes, shapes, and colors
  Jars with screw-on lids
  Bottles with small necks with raisins or other
    small objects inside

Art Materials
  Play-Doh
  Fingerpaints
  Crayons
  Markers
  Construction paper
  Scissors

Housekeeping/pretend
  Dolls
  Stuffed animals
  Doll furniture
  Cooking and eating utensils
  Rolling pin
  Pitcher or teapot
  Clothes with various fasteners (e.g., small and
    large buttons, zippers)
  Shoes with laces
  Comb and brush

Games
  Playing cards
  Old Maid cards
  Dice
  Candyland
  Animal Lotto cards
  Dominoes

Books and pictures
  Nursery rhymes
  Stories
  Pictures (e.g., colored and line drawings to
    name, match, and sort)

Outdoor equipment
  Large and small balls
  Jungle gym or other climbing equipment
  Balance beam
  Wheel toys

Other
  Coins (e.g., penny, nickel, dime, quarter)
  Variety of small toys of different sizes, shapes,
    and colors (e.g., vehicles, plastic animals)

CHARTING ASSESSMENT RESULTS

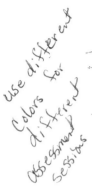

Once the items on the Assessment Log have been assessed, a Developmental Progress Chart (see pp. 64–65) can be completed to reveal a profile of skills. (Additional copies of the chart, available with the Assessment Log, may be procured from Paul H. Brookes Publishing Company.) Each item on the log is represented by a blank on the chart. If an item is passed, the corresponding space should be colored in completely with a highlighter or reference marker. If the skill in question appears to be inconsistent or emerging, the space should be colored in only partially (e.g., ◪). If the assessment and charting procedures are employed at regular intervals, using different colors to complete the charting with each new assessment, a visual display is provided of the youngster's progress through the curriculum sequences.

SELECTING CURRICULAR ITEMS FOR AN INDIVIDUAL CHILD'S INTERVENTION PROGRAM

Within the body of the CCPSN, there is a teaching activity that corresponds to each item in the Assessment Log and that is depicted on the Developmental Progress Chart. Caregivers should select activities for a given child on the basis of the first item the child failed or the item that was judged to be emerging *in each sequence*, unless a particular handicapping condition makes this strategy inappropriate. However, this may produce an intervention plan including up to 40 items that will be unwieldy for most children and most programs. Therefore, a decision must be made regarding which sequences will be worked on at a given time. In making this decision, it is important to consider several factors:

1. The child's parents and other caregivers (e.g., a day care provider) should be "major players" in deciding what is most important for the child. They will be more committed to working on those skills that they feel are important and more committed, overall, to an intervention plan that they have helped to develop. The educational specialist has the responsibility of exploring the caregivers' concerns and interpreting their curriculum goals. The description of each sequence, which is placed at the beginning of the items for that sequence, will help the specialist explain why these particular skills are important and how they relate to the caregivers' long-term goals for the child.
2. It is frequently possible to combine the goals from two sequences into one intervention activity. For example, spatial concepts are readily taught through gross motor and fine motor activities. In fact, combining motor and cognitive or language activities often aids in the learning of both. One might, for example, combine the goals of crossing the midline (item 15.e) and sorting colors (item 2-I.a) by having the child pick up colored blocks and place them in matching cans.
3. It is important to include sequences that both emphasize a child's strengths and highlight his or her weaknesses when planning the intervention program. Working in an area of strength is more likely to bring success and to enhance motivation. Furthermore, strengths can often be used to overcome the deficits created by weaknesses.

4. Since all of the sequences are important, a plan should be developed to change the sequences targeted for instruction at given intervals in order to assure that all are given equal attention. For children who are developing very slowly, it may be appropriate to change the plan only once every 6 months. For children who are developing rapidly, it may be appropriate to change every 2 or 3 months.

5. In developing an intervention plan, it is critical to remember that *you are working on sequences, not simply on items*. This means that when a child masters an item in the sequence, you immediately move on to work on the next item in that sequence. Thus, although the plan may be to change the program every 6 months, the child's activities may change much more frequently. He or she may, for example, work through 4 items in the Expressive Vocabulary sequence, 2 items in the Fine Motor Skills: Bilateral Skills sequence, and 3 in the Concept: General sequence.

DEVELOPING AN IEP

The IEP provides a systematic way of ensuring that those professionals who are working with children who have special needs have a clear idea of the nature of that child's needs and the activities that should be planned to meet those needs. An IEP should: 1) focus on the individual child, 2) be the result of careful assessment and planning, and 3) enumerate specific changes that are expected to occur in development and behavior as a result of intervention. It is generally expected that an adequate IEP will contain at least the following:

1. A statement about a youngster's present level of performance/development
2. Long-term goals (e.g., 6–12 months) and short-term objectives (e.g., 1 month)
3. A description of specific developmental and treatment services that are to be provided
4. The date on which programmatic services are expected to be initiated and the expected duration of services
5. A statement about the setting(s) in whichs the child will receive services
6. Evaluation procedures to be used
7. A schedule of and procedures for review

The CCPSN lends itself readily to supplying information necessary for several components of the IEP. The child's level of performance/development is described in the Assessment Log and Developmental Progress Chart Section. Short-term objectives are the mastery of specific items chosen for intervention from the sequences. Long-term goals may be identified either from items further ahead in the sequence or from the general description of the sequences chosen for intervention. The items within each sequence provide the specifics about activities that will be included to facilitate the mastery of the objectives.

For preschoolers who are being served in a variety of settings, formats for IEPs may need to be different than those for children in regular public settings. The IEP may need to be written to indicate activities that will take place in several different settings, including: 1) individual activities that will be a part of one-on-one intervention provided by a "resource teacher," 2) activities that will be embedded in group experiences in a day care setting, and/or 3) activities that parents or other caregivers can use to facilitate development at home. The inclusion of both individual and group activities for the curriculum items in the CCPSN should aid in the development of more comprehensive IEPs.

In addition to information provided by the curriculum, the IEP should include a description of other treatment services (e.g., physical and/or occupational therapy, medical follow-up) that will be required, and the evaluation procedures that will be used. There is general agreement among practitioners that a review of a program for preschoolers should occur more frequently than the annual review required for school-aged children, perhaps every 3 to 6 months. If a careful record is kept on the Assessment Log of items mastered during the course of intervention, it will take a relatively short period of time to update the Assessment Log on those sequences currently not included in the intervention plan, and to fill in the Developmental Progress Chart. At the point of review, a new IEP should be developed including some or all of the sequences that were not included in the previous IEP.

IMPLEMENTING THE IEP

When the IEP has been developed, the intervention process can begin. Careful planning will be necessary to assure that all of the objectives in the IEP are included regularly in the child's schedule. This is particularly true when the child is being served in more than one setting and/or by more than one service provider. If the child is in a mainstreamed group setting, the teacher (or day care provider) should develop a daily or weekly plan that will integrate the intervention activities into the classroom routine. Having a list of the objectives to review quickly each morning will alert the teacher to facilitate work toward the objectives as he or she interacts with the child throughout the day. If a resource teacher is also working with the child individually, it is important that he or she consult regularly with the teacher/day care provider to assure generalization and a sharing of the child's problems or concerns. Regular contact with parents to determine if the same kind of progress is being observed at home and in the group program is equally important.

How do you know when an item has been mastered? Each curriculum item lists a criterion to help you determine if an item has been mastered sufficiently enough to move on to the next item in the sequence. Such criteria are fairly arbitrary and should serve only as a guide. The critical issues in determining item mastery are whether the child can do the item consistently and whether the child can demonstrate the skill with different materials and/or in different settings (i.e., the skill has been generalized sufficiently to be useful).

Record keeping is an important part of determining whether or not a child has mastered the IEP objectives (or curriculum items). Trial-by-trial records are extremely useful in demonstrating the child's progress toward mastery. When the child is working with a resource teacher, such records should be kept. However, this form of record keeping becomes problematic in a group setting. The teacher/day care provider should be encouraged to keep at least a weekly log on the child's progress. If he or she has a list of the objectives and the settings in which they are most likely to be taught or observed (see example in Figure 4.1), it is relatively simple to check off each day which ones were worked on. At the end of the week, the progress can then be observed. As the care provider interacts with the child, he or she can check on specific skills.

Activity	Opportunity to observe					Mastered (date)
	M	Tu	W	Th	F	
General play activities Pretend (i.e., assume different roles, takes difference voices) Asks Wh—questions Shows pride in achievement Helps with adult activities Uses toys appropriately						
Circle and/or book activities Identifies objects by function Names 3 elements in picture						
Block center Builds tower of 8–10 blocks						
Manipulative center Strings small beads Hammers golf tees in styrofoam						
Housekeeping center Unscrews lids Puts on clothes						
Art center Copies a circle Cuts straight line						
Playground or indoor motor games Walks on rough surfaces—no falling Gallops Up 10 steps, 2 feet/tread, railing Jumps up 2 inches Throws small ball 7 feet Climbs jungle gym then drops to ground Understands fast and slow						
Self-care Toilet trained Washes and dries hands						

Figure 4.1.   Sample classroom checklist for IEP objectives.

When it becomes evident, through whatever method(s) of record keeping, that the child has mastered one of the objectives in the IEP, it is critical to create a new objective from the next item in that sequence. This may require a minor modification in the teacher's/caregiver's plan for classroom activities, however, it will frequently only require alerting him or her to give a slightly different emphasis to the activities that have been used.

Assessment Log
and
Developmental Progress Chart

ASSESSMENT LOG

Insert the date of your assessment at the top of the column and insert a + in the box for each mastered item.

Age (Years)		Curriculum Sequences	Date: ___	Date: ___	Date: ___	Date: ___
	1.	**Attention and Memory**				
	a.	Anticipates parts of rhymes or songs				
	b.	Repeats 2-digit sequences or 2 unrelated words				
	c.	Points to the hand that is hiding a toy				
(2.5)	d.	Joins in saying nursery rhymes—repeats parts of them				
	e.	Tells the name of an object or picture shown briefly in a group of 2 and then hidden				
	f.	Remembers incidental information (e.g., "What did you see at the zoo?")				
	g.	Repeats 3-word sentences				
(3)	h.	Says or sings at least 2 nursery rhymes or songs in a group or with an adult				
	i.	Identifies from 4 or more pictures 1 seen only briefly				
	j.	Names 1 of several (e.g., 4 or more) objects or pictures, shown, named, and then hidden				
	k.	Repeats a sequence of 3 digits or 3 unrelated words				
(3.5)	l.	Repeats 4-word sentences including adjectives				
	m.	Remembers and names which of 3 objects has been hidden				
	n.	Describes familiar objects without seeing them				
	o.	Recalls 1 or 2 elements from a story just read (no prompts)				
(4)	p.	Matches both color and shape of an object (or picture) seen only briefly				
	q.	Sings songs or says rhymes of at least 30 words (words may be repeated)				
	r.	Recalls 3–4 elements from a story without prompts				
	s.	Matches both color and shape of 2 objects (or pictures) seen only briefly				

Age (Years)	Curriculum Sequences	Date: ___	Date: ___	Date: ___	Date: ___
(4.5)	t. Describes events that happened in the past (e.g., yesterday, last week)				
	u. Recalls most of the essential elements in a story				
	v. Repeats 5–6-word sentences, maintaining the grammatical structure				
	w. Repeats sequence of 4 numbers or unrelated words				
(5)	x. Remembers the place in an array where a picture was seen only briefly (e.g., 5 seconds)				
	2-I. Concepts: General a. Sorts objects by color, form, or name				
(2.5)	b. Follows directions including *in, out,* and *on*				
	c. Identifies *soft* and *hard*				
	d. Identifies *red, blue,* and *yellow*				
(3)	e. Identifies *square* and *round*				
	f. Understands *up, down, top,* and *bottom*				
	g. Understands *under, over, next to,* and *beside*				
	h. Understands *fast* and *slow*				
	i. Understands *empty* and *full*				
(3.5)	j. Answers questions or makes statements indicating an understanding that different activities occur at different times of the day (e.g., breakfast in morning, sleep at night)				
	k. Selects "the one that is different" or "the one that is not the same"				
	l. Understands *heavy* and *light*				
	m. Understands *around, in front of, in back of, between, high,* and *low*				
	n. Completes 2 analogies (i.e., sentences involving opposites)				
(4)	o. Groups by 2 characteristics (e.g., size and color, shape and color)				
	p. Understands *fat, skinny, thick,* and *thin*				
	q. Understands *rough* and *smooth*				

45

Age (Years)		Curriculum Sequences	Date: ___	Date: ___	Date: ___	Date: ___
	r.	Understands *backward* and *forward*				
	s.	Understands materials and can tell of what material common objects are made				
(4.5)	t.	Sorts by categories (e.g., foods, clothes, toys, mother's belongings)				
	u.	Labels all primary colors (e.g., red, yellow, blue, green, black, white)				
	v.	Labels *square, triangle,* and *circle*				
	w.	Names examples within a category (e.g., animals, objects in a kitchen, clothes)				
	x.	Compares sizes of familiar objects not in view				
	y.	Completes sentences involving analogies (at least 5)				
(5)	z.	Identifies an object that does not belong in a set and finds the one that does belong using up to 3 characteristics (e.g., size, shape, color, number, object class)				
		2-II. Concepts: Size and number				
	a.	Uses or understands size words (e.g., big, little)				
(2.5)	b.	Selects *"just one"*				
	c.	Answers number questions involving *one* and *two*				
	d.	Gives/selects *two* and *three*				
(3)	e.	Follows instructions including *all* and *none* or *not any*				
	f.	Matches a picture with 2 objects to the correct picture in a set that includes 1, 2, 3, and 4 objects				
	g.	Understands *tall, short, more,* and *less*				
	h.	Matches pictures containing different configurations of objects up to 6				
(3.5)	i.	Gives *one more*				
	j.	Counts up to 6 objects in a row				
	k.	Answers addition questions involving + 1 up to 5				
	l.	Identifies (or correctly uses) *bigger* and *biggest, smaller* and *smallest, larger* and *largest*				

Age (Years)		Curriculum Sequences	Date: ___	Date: ___	Date: ___	Date: ___
(4)	m.	Counts 10 objects in a row				
	n.	Understands *same number* and can sort a set into halves				
	o.	Identifies *penny, nickel,* and *dime* when named				
	p.	Counts correctly to 20				
(4.5)	q.	Matches 3-part sequences of pictures or objects depicting quantities up to 6				
	r.	Gives the correct number of objects when asked—all numbers from 4 to 10				
	s.	Tells current age, how old he or she was last year, and how old he or she will be next year				
	t.	Answers addition questions involving $+2$ up to 10				
(5)	u.	Recognizes repeating pattern in a sequence and can continue it				
	3.	**Symbolic Play**				
	a.	Engages in adult role-playing (e.g., cooks, hammers, talks on play telephone)				
(2.5)	b.	Pretends that objects are something other than what they are (e.g., blocks are food)				
	c.	Assumes different roles in playing house or other activities				
(3)	d.	Represents more complex events in play (e.g., plays doctor with doll or animal, goes shopping using baby carriage or wagon as a shopping cart)				
	e.	Pretend play includes a 3–4-part logical sequence that evolves as play proceeds				
(3.5)	f.	Uses materials to construct other objects				
	g.	Uses dolls, stuffed animals, or puppets as participants in play—gives dialogue to them				
(4)	h.	Describes own activities during play				
	i.	Builds large structures from blocks or chairs and centers play around them				
(4.5)	j.	Involves others in pretend play—discusses roles				
	k.	Uses toy animals or dolls to act out "what would happen if"				

Age (Years)		Curriculum Sequences	Date: ___	Date: ___	Date: ___	Date: ___
(5)	l.	Engages in complex adult role-playing (e.g., plays house with other children, solving problems as adults would solve them)				
	4.	**Reasoning**				
	a.	Experiments with cause and effect in play				
(3)	b.	Answers at least 1 "why do" question correctly (e.g., "Why do we have [or use] stoves?", "Why do we use umbrellas?")				
	c.	Identifies *silly* or *wrong* pictures or events				
(3.5)	d.	Answers 2 or more "what do you do when" questions (e.g., hungry, tired, thirsty)				
	e.	Describes simple absurdities seen in pictures or in real life (e.g., an adult sucking his or her thumb, going to bed with clothes on)				
(4)	f.	Responds appropriately to "Tell me how" or "how do you" questions (e.g., "Tell me how [how do] you make a sandwich?")				
	g.	Describes what "will happen next"				
	h.	Finds "one to go with this" (e.g., nail with hammer, thread with needle, shoe with sock)				
(4.5)	i.	Reasons about experiences and asks and answers questions (e.g., "Why can't I . . . ?"; "What will happen if . . . ?"; "Why doesn't it . . . ?"; "Why did ___ do ___ ?")				
(5)	j.	Reasons about future events (e.g., "If ___ happens, I will . . . ")				
	5-l.	**Visual Perception: Block designs**				
	a.	Imitates block train				
	b.	Imitates block building				
(3)	c.	Imitates block bridge				
(3.5)	d.	Copies horizontal bridge				
	e.	Imitates 5-block gate				
(4.5)	f.	Copies horizontal block patterns (Group 1)				
(5)	g.	Copies horizontal block patterns (Group 2)				

48

Age (Years)	Curriculum Sequences	Date:	Date:	Date:	Date:
	5-II. Visual Perception: Puzzles and matching				
	a. Places *round, square,* and *triangular* forms in form board (same orientation)				
(2.5)	b. Places *round, square,* and *triangular* forms in reversed form board				
	c. Puts together 2 kinds of two-piece puzzles				
(3)	d. Puts together a puzzle with 4 or 5 interconnected pieces				
(3.5)	e. Matches geometric forms (orientation irrelevant)				
	f. Matches at least 8 geometric shapes				
(4)	g. Completes 8–10-piece interconnected puzzles				
(4.5)	h. Imitates construction of a simple visual pattern using parquetry blocks				
	i. Completes a 12–20+-piece interconnected puzzle				
	j. Matches letters and numbers				
(5)	k. Matches name and short words				
	6. Expressive Vocabulary				
	a. Names most common objects when seen				
	b. Names objects that are heard				
	c. Names objects touched or handled				
	d. Names 2 or more pictures of common objects				
	e. Names 6 or more pictures of common objects				
(2.5)	f. Uses at least 50 different words				
	g. Names 8 or more line drawings of common objects				
(3)	h. Names most pictures of familiar objects				
(3.5)	i. Names pictures of objects seen primarily in books (e.g., farm animals or tractors for city children)				
(4)	j. Defines 2 or more simple words (e.g., "What do we mean by _____?", "What is a _____?")				
(4.5)	k. Defines 5 simple words				
(5)	l. Defines 10 simple words				

Age (Years)		Curriculum Sequences	Date: ___	Date: ___	Date: ___	Date: ___
	7.	**Interest in Sounds and Language Functions**				
	a.	Identifies objects, people, and events by their sounds				
	b.	Listens carefully to new words, may ask for repetition				
(3)	c.	Repeats new words to self				
(3.5)	d.	In play, uses different voices for different people				
(4)	e.	In play or conversation, uses statements such as, "He said . . . "				
	f.	Asks word meanings or otherwise indicates awareness that words mean something				
(4.5)	g.	Makes rhymes to simple words				
(5)	h.	Soon after hearing the meaning of a new word, uses it in his or her own speech				
	8.	**Receptive Skills**				
	a.	Understands *look*				
	b.	Identifies pictures of familiar objects				
	c.	Follows 1-step commands related to 2 objects or an object and a place (e.g., "Put the ____ on/in the ____"; "Take the ____ to the ____")				
(2.5)	d.	Identifies 6 body parts				
	e.	Identifies 10 or more line drawings of objects when the objects are named				
	f.	Identifies 5 or more objects by usage (e.g., "Show me what we drink out of")				
	g.	Responds appropriately to "where" questions				
(3)	h.	Responds appropriately to "why" questions				
	i.	Responds to "yes/no" questions with appropriate words or gestures (e.g., "Do you want ____?"; "Is that your ____?")				
	j.	Responds appropriately to "who" and "whose" questions				
(3.5)	k.	Identifies pictures of objects by function (e.g., "Show me the one that ____")				

Age (Years)		Curriculum Sequences	Date: ___	Date: ___	Date: ___	Date: ___
	l.	Follows 2-step commands involving sequence (e.g., "Put the doll on the shelf and then bring me the ball")				
	m.	Responds appropriately to "which" and "how many" questions				
(4)	n.	Names objects by function (e.g., "What cuts the grass?")				
	o.	Follows 3-step instructions in sequence involving 2–3 different objects (e.g., "Put the doll on the shelf, put your shirt in the hamper, and bring me the ball")				
	p.	Responds appropriately to statements or questions involving regular plurals				
(4.5)	q.	Understands statements or instructions involving negations (e.g., "The dog is not big"; "Do not take the red one")				
	r.	Responds appropriately to "how far" questions				
(5)	s.	Responds appropriately to questions involving time concepts (e.g., before, after, today, tomorrow, tonight)				
	9.	**Conversation Skills**				
	a.	Requests objects or activities with words or signs				
	b.	Greets familiar people with word or sign				
	c.	Asks simple questions (e.g., "What doing?"; "Where going?")				
(2.5)	d.	Asks "yes/no" questions with appropriate inflection				
	e.	Comments on appearance or disappearance of objects or people				
	f.	Requests assistance (e.g., "Help!"; "You do it.")				
	g.	Requests permission (e.g., "Johnny go out?"; "I turn it?")				
(3)	h.	Sustains conversation for several turns				
	i.	Changes speech depending on listener (e.g., talks differently to babies and adults)				
	j.	Talks on telephone, waits his or her turn to respond				

Age (Years)		Curriculum Sequences	Date: ___	Date: ___	Date: ___	Date: ___
	k.	Uses words to describe attributes of toys or foods (e.g., shape, size, color, texture, spatial relationships)				
	l.	Completes incomplete sentences begun by an adult (e.g., analogies, words in familiar stories)				
(3.5)	m.	Describes what is happening or what he or she is seeing				
	n.	When asked to "tell all about" a picture, names 3 or more elements or describes what is happening				
	o.	Responds correctly to "what do you do" and "why do we" questions				
	p.	Tells a story by looking at pictures				
	q.	Describes functions of objects				
(4)	r.	Answers "what is," "whose," "who" and "how many" questions appropriately (if not correctly)				
	s.	Communicates cause-and-effect relationships (e.g., "It is broken and it doesn't work any more.")				
	t.	Uses contingent queries to maintain a conversation (e.g., "Why did he do that?"; "Then what happened?")				
(4.5)	u.	Creates interest in a listener by indirect references (e.g., "I have a new toy in my room.")				
	v.	Communicates knowledge about the world to peers and adults				
	w.	Makes statements about cause and effect (e.g., uses such words as "because" and "since"—"I can play because I am not sick any more.")				
(5)	x.	Tells 2 familiar stories without pictures for help—includes all important parts				
	10.	**Sentence Construction**				
	a.	Uses 2-word utterances to indicate: possession (e.g., "Mommy's sock."; "My doll.") and action (e.g., "Eat cookie."; "Find shoes.")				
	b.	Uses 2-word utterances to indicate: nonexistence (e.g., "No juice."; "Daddy bye-bye.") and recurrence (e.g., "More juice.")				
	c.	Uses 2-word utterances to indicate: specificity (e.g., "This toy."; "That box.") and characteristics (e.g., "Hot stove."; "Pretty bunny.")				

Age (Years)	Curriculum Sequences	Date: ___	Date: ___	Date: ___	Date: ___
	d. Uses "s" on the ends of some words to form plurals				
(2.5)	e. Uses auxiliary verbs, usually shortened (e.g., gonna, wanna, hafta)				
	f. Uses "ing" on verbs (e.g., "I helping")				
	g. Uses negative terms (e.g., can't, don't)				
	h. Uses personal pronouns (e.g., me, you, mine, your)				
	i. Uses prepositional phrases (e.g., in house, on table)				
(3)	j. Uses 3-word phrases to specify (e.g., "That big one."; "This finger hurt."), to indicate rejection (e.g., "No scary book."; "No want that."), and/or to describe (e.g., "The big dog.")				
	k. Uses 3–4-word complete sentences that include subject-verb-object (e.g., "Mommy open that."; "Mommy make big mess.")				
	l. Asks "wh" questions (e.g., why, what, where)				
	m. Uses "I" instead of given name				
(3.5)	n. Uses "s" or "es" on ends of words to indicate possession				
	o. Uses prepositional phrases in sentences (e.g., "Put it *on my lap*.")				
	p. Uses most irregular past tense verb forms correctly				
(4)	q. Uses quantity terms (e.g., some, many, most, few, all)				
	r. Uses "and," "but," "or," and "because" to connect 2 sentences into one (e.g., "It hit me but it didn't hurt.")				
	s. Uses "ing" words other than as verbs (e.g., "Hitting is not nice."; "He got hurt running fast.")				
(4.5)	t. Correctly differentiates past, present, and future verbs; regular and irregular verbs				
	u. Correct word order in "wh" questions (e.g., "Why is John here?")				

Age (Years)		Curriculum Sequences	Date: ___	Date: ___	Date: ___	Date: ___
	v.	Uses endings on verbs or nouns to indicate the activity of a person or thing (e.g., driver, painter, guitarist)				
(5)	w.	Uses comparatives (e.g., big, bigger, biggest; small, smaller, smallest; sad, sadder, saddest)				
		11. Responsibility				
(2.5)	a.	Avoids common dangers (e.g., broken glass, high places, busy streets, big animals)				
(3)	b.	Knows what toys can and cannot do and uses them appropriately				
	c.	Puts toys away neatly when asked (may have to be reminded)				
(3.5)	d.	Follows rules given by adults for new activities or simple games				
	e.	Answers questions related to self-care (e.g., "Why shouldn't you play with knives?"; "Why should you look before crossing the street?")				
(4)	f.	Shows care in handling small animals or potentially breakable objects				
	g.	Responds appropriately to instructions given in a small group				
(4.5)	h.	Plays in own neighborhood without constant adult supervision				
	i.	Buys simple objects in store without help (i.e., gets object or tells clerk what he or she wants, provides money, and waits for change)				
(5)	j.	Answers telephone appropriately and delivers message				
		12. Self-Concept				
	a.	Expresses feelings of *interest, pleasure, surprise, excitement, warning,* and *complaint* (4 or more)				
(2.5)	b.	Knows age (e.g., tells or holds up fingers)				
	c.	Makes positive statements about self				
	d.	Tells own first name				
	e.	Shows pride in achievements				
(3)	f.	Answers correctly when asked if he or she is boy or girl				

Age (Years)		Curriculum Sequences	Date: ___	Date: ___	Date: ___	Date: ___
	g.	Tells own first and last name				
	h.	Calls attention to own performance				
(3.5)	i.	Expresses enthusiasm for work or play				
	j.	Identifies own feelings				
(4)	k.	Can tell what eyes, ears, and nose are used for				
	l.	Talks about own feelings in relation to events				
(4.5)	m.	Shows interest in own body—asks questions about its functions				
	n.	Answers questions about grooming or self-care (e.g., "Why comb hair?")				
(5)	o.	Seeks activities that challenge skills				
	13.	**Interpersonal Skills**				
	a.	Greets familiar adults spontaneously				
	b.	Shares food or toys with familiar adults				
	c.	Plays alongside other children without disruption for 15 minutes				
(2.5)	d.	Helps adults with activities such as picking up, dusting, or wiping the table				
	e.	Expresses affection and/or preference for some peers				
(3)	f.	Expresses regret when another child is hurt or experiences unpleasantness				
	g.	Converses with peers				
	h.	Takes turn most of the time if reminded				
	i.	Responds appropriately to social contact made by familiar adults				
(3.5)	j.	Separates easily from parent in familiar surroundings				
	k.	Tries to comfort peers in distress				
	l.	Plays group games with other children such as tag, hide-and-seek, without constant adult supervision				
(4)	m.	Plays simple board or card games with other children with adult supervision				

Age (Years)	Curriculum Sequences	Date: ___	Date: ___	Date: ___	Date: ___
	n. Asks permission to use other's belongings				
	o. Shows awareness of others' feelings (e.g., "He's mad."; "Are you sad?")				
	p. Uses such terms as "Thank you," "Please," and "You're welcome" appropriately				
	q. Recognizes another's need for help and gives assistance				
(4.5)	r. Plays cooperatively with peers for extended periods without requiring adult intervention				
	s. Identifies special friends				
	t. Spontaneously takes turn and shares				
(5)	u. Asserts self in socially acceptable ways				
	14-I. Self-Help: Eating a. Independently eats entire meal with spoon				
	b. Begins to use fork				
	c. Drinks from a small glass held with one hand				
(2.5)	d. Gets drink unassisted (e.g., turns tap on and off)				
	e. Pours liquid from one container into another				
	f. Spreads with a knife				
(3)	g. Cuts with edge of fork				
(3.5)	h. Swallows food in mouth before taking another bite				
	i. Fixes bowl of dry cereal with milk independently				
(4)	j. Holds fork in fingers				
(4.5)	k. Drinks from water fountain independently				
(5)	l. Fixes sandwich independently				
	14-II. Self-Help: Dressing a. Removes shoes				
	b. Removes coat				
(2.5)	c. Puts on simple clothing (e.g, hat, pants, shoes, socks)				

Age (Years)	Curriculum Sequences	Date:	Date:	Date:	Date:
	d. Puts on all clothes unaided, except for fasteners				
(3)	e. Undoes fasteners (e.g., large buttons, snaps, shoelaces)				
(4)	f. Buttons coat or dress				
(4.5)	g. Dresses and undresses with little assistance				
(5)	h. Zips front-opening clothing such as jacket				
	14-III. Self-Help: Grooming				
(2.5)	a. Dries hands				
(3)	b. Washes own hands				
(3.5)	c. Washes and dries hands and face without assistance				
(4)	d. Brushes teeth				
(4.5)	e. Runs brush or comb through hair				
(5)	f. Blows nose independently upon request				
	14-IV. Self-Help: Toileting				
(2.5)	a. Usually indicates need to toilet; rarely has bowel accidents				
(3)	b. Uses toilet by self, except for cleaning after a bowel movement				
(3.5)	c. Seldom has toileting accidents; may need help with difficult clothing				
(4)	d. Cares for self at toilet (may need assistance wiping after bowel movement)				
(4.5)	e. Tears toilet tissue and flushes toilet after use				
(5)	f. Wipes self after bowel movement				
	15. Fine Motor Skills: Hand use				
	a. Plays with messy materials such as clay—patting, pinching, and fingering				
(2.5)	b. Demonstrates a hand preference (typically in eating)				
	c. Identifies an object by feeling it				
(3)	d. Builds a tower of 8–10 blocks				
(3.5)	e. Demonstrates hand preference by picking up most materials with the same hand; will cross midline in body				

57

Age (Years)	Curriculum Sequences	Date: ___	Date: ___	Date: ___	Date: ___
(4)	f. Places ¼″ pegs in a pegboard				
(4.5)	g. Places 10 pellets in a bottle in 30 seconds				
	16. Fine Motor Skills: Manipulation a. Turns doorknob with forearm rotation				
(2.5)	b. Unscrews cap from small bottle				
	c. Unbuttons large buttons (e.g., ¾″)				
(3)	d. Screws on lids				
	e. Makes simple forms with Play-Doh (e.g., balls, snakes)				
	f. Turns wind-up key 90° in one turn				
(3.5)	g. Removes bottle cap in 30 seconds				
(4)	h. Holds one small object in palm of hand and then moves forward to pincer grasp without assistance from other hand				
(4.5)	i. Buttons ½″ buttons				
(5)	j. Places paper clips on paper				
	17. Fine Motor Skills: Bilateral skills a. Strings large beads				
	b. Pulls apart large popbeads				
(2.5)	c. Holds bowl and stirs				
(3)	d. Strings small beads (e.g., ½″)				
(3.5)	e. Ties single knot				
(4)	f. Laces 2 holes in shoes				
(4.5)	g. Does simple sewing on lacing card or cloth				
(5)	h. Folds 8½″ × 11″ paper in half (no demonstration)				
(2.5)	**18. Fine Motor Skills: Tool use** a. Transfers material with a spoon				
(3)	b. Uses small wooden hammer to pound in objects				
(3.5)	c. Uses rolling pin to flatten material				
(4)	d. Uses wooden tongs to transfer materials				
(4.5)	e. Uses hammer and pegs or nails				
(5)	f. Uses clothespin to transfer small objects				

Age (Years)		Curriculum Sequences	Date:	Date:	Date:	Date:
		19-I. Visual-Motor Skills: Pencil control and copying				
	a.	Makes a crayon rubbing				
	b.	Imitates vertical stroke				
(2.5)	c.	Imitates horizontal stroke				
(3)	d.	Copies a circle with a circular scribble				
	e.	Copies a circle				
(3.5)	f.	Copies a cross				
	g.	Traces a $6'' \times {}^1/_4''$ line with no more than one deviation				
(4)	h.	Holds marker with fingers in tripod position				
(4.5)	i.	Copies a square				
	j.	Traces outline of simple stencil				
(5)	k.	Copies asterisk (*)				
		19-II. Visual-Motor Skills: Representational drawing				
(3.5)	a.	Draws a person with a head and 1 feature				
(4)	b.	Draws a person with a head and 4 features				
	c.	Draws simple pictures of things seen or imagined				
(4.5)	d.	Draws a person with a head and 6 features				
(5)	e.	Draws a person with a head and 8 features				
		19-III. Visual-Motor Skills: Cutting				
	a.	Snips with scissors				
(3)	b.	Makes continuous cut across paper				
(3.5)	c.	Cuts straight line, staying within $^1/_2''$ of guideline				
(4)	d.	Cuts a $5''$ circle (at least three-fourths of the circle)				
(4.5)	e.	Cuts a $5''$ square				
(5)	f.	Cuts out pictures following general shape				
		20-I. Locomotion: Walking				
	a.	Walks backward 10 feet				
(2.5)	b.	Walks on all types of surfaces, rarely falling				
(3)	c.	Uses heel-toe walking pattern, arms swinging at side or free to carry objects				

Age (Years)	Curriculum Sequences	Date:	Date:	Date:	Date:
	20-II. Locomotion: Tiptoe walking				
(2.5)	a. Walks 3–4 steps with heels off the ground				
(3)	b. Walks 5 steps on tiptoes with hands on hips or carrying an object with both hands				
(3.5)	c. Walks 10 feet on tiptoes on a 1″ line				
	20-III. Locomotion: Galloping/skipping				
(3.5)	a. Gallops 5 cycles				
(4)	b. Skips 5 steps				
(4.5)	c. Skips 5–10 steps, with coordinated step-hop				
(5)	d. Skips 10 + steps with rhythmical weight transfer, landing on toes				
	20-IV. Locomotion: Running				
(2.5)	a. Runs 5–10 feet without falling				
(3)	b. Spontaneously avoids large obstacles when running				
(3.5)	c. Runs with some periods of flight (i.e., both feet off ground)				
(4.5)	d. Runs fast				
(5)	e. Runs, changing direction 180° within 4–8 steps				
	20-V. Locomotion: Hopping				
(3.5)	a. Hops once in place				
	b. Hops up to 3 times on preferred foot				
(4)	c. Hops forward 6″ on preferred foot				
	d. Hops 5 times on preferred foot; 3 times on non-preferred foot				
(4.5)	e. Hops forward 8 times with each foot				
(5)	f. Hops forward 16″ on preferred foot; 12″ on non-preferred foot				
	21-I. Stairs: Up stairs				
	a. Walks up 3 steps, using same-step placement, holding railing				
	b. Walks up 10 steps, using same-step placement, holding railing				
(2.5)	c. Walks up 4 steps, using alternate-step placement, holding railing				

60

Age (Years)	Curriculum Sequences	Date: ___	Date: ___	Date: ___	Date: ___
	d. Walks up 10 steps, using alternate-step placement, holding railing				
(3)	e. Walks up 3 steps, using alternate step placement, without holding railing				
(3.5)	f. Walks up 10 steps, using alternate-step placement, without holding railing				
(2.5)	**21-II. Stairs: Down stairs** a. Walks down 3 steps, using same-step placement, holding railing				
(3)	b. Walks down 3 steps, using same-step placement, without holding railing				
(3.5)	c. Walks down 10 steps, using same-step placement, without holding railing				
(4)	d. Walks down 3 steps, using alternate-step placement, holding railing				
	e. Walks down 10 steps, using alternate-step placement, holding railing				
(4.5)	f. Walks down 3 steps, using alternate-step placement, without holding railing				
(5)	g. Walks down 10 steps, using alternate-step placement, without holding railing				
	22-I. Jumping: Jumping up a. Jumps off floor with both feet				
(3)	b. Jumps 2″ off ground or over 2″ hurdle				
(3.5)	c. Jumps 8″ off ground or over 8″ hurdle				
	d. Jumps rope for 2 cycles				
(4)	e. Jumps over several 8″ obstacles in succession				
(4.5)	f. Jumps up 3″ beyond arms' reach				
(5)	g. Jumps, completing a half-turn in 1 jump				
	22-II. Jumping: Jumping down a. Jumps from 8″ height, 1 foot leading				
(3)	b. Jumps from 16″–18″ height, 1 foot leading				
(3.5)	c. Jumps from 18″–24″ height with feet together on take-off and landing				
(4)	d. Jumps from 24″–30″ height with feet together on take-off and landing				

61

Age (Years)	Curriculum Sequences	Date:	Date:	Date:	Date:
(4.5)	e. Jumps from 32″ height, possibly leading with 1 foot				
	22-III. Jumping: Broadjumping				
(3)	a. Broadjumps 4″–14″				
(3.5)	b. Broadjumps 14″–23″				
(4)	c. Broadjumps 24″–35″				
(4.5)	d. Broadjumps 36″ or more				
	23-I. Balance: Static balance				
	a. Stands on 1 leg for 1–2 seconds				
(2.5)	b. Stands with both feet on balance beam				
(3)	c. Balances on preferred leg, with hands on hips and opposite knee bent for 3 seconds				
(3.5)	d. Balances on preferred leg, with hands on hips and opposite knee bent for 5 seconds				
	e. Stands on tiptoes, with arms overhead for 2 seconds				
(4)	f. Stands on each leg, with hands on hips and opposite knee bent for 6 seconds				
(4.5)	g. Stands on tiptoes, with hands overhead for 8 seconds				
(5)	h. Stands on each leg, with hands on hips and opposite knee bent for 10 seconds each				
	23-II. Balance: Dynamic balance				
	a. Walks along 10′ line in a general direction				
	b. Walks with 1 foot on balance beam, other foot on floor				
(2.5)	c. Kicks a ball a few feet				
	d. Walks 3 steps on balance beam with both feet				
	e. Walks along a 10′ line, keeping feet on line				
(3)	f. Kicks a ball 4′–6′				
(3.5)	g. Kicks a ball 6′–12′				
(4)	h. Kicks a ball 12′–15′				
	i. Walks 4–5 steps on balance beam				

62

Age (Years)		Curriculum Sequences	Date: ___	Date: ___	Date: ___	Date: ___
	j.	Does 1 somersault				
(4.5)	k.	Walks full length of balance beam				
	l.	Walks full length of balance beam while carrying something in both hands or with hands on hips				
	m.	Does 2 somersaults in a row				
(5)	n.	Kicks ball 6'–12' in the air				
	24-I.	**Balls: Throwing balls**				
	a.	Throws 8″ ball to an adult, underhand, 5'				
(2.5)	b.	Throws 3″ ball to an adult, underhand, 7'				
(3)	c.	Throws 3″ ball to an adult, underhand, 9'				
(3.5)	d.	Throws 8″ ball to an adult, 2-handed underhand, 9'				
(4)	e.	Throws 3″ ball to an adult, overhand, 10'				
(4.5)	f.	Throws 8″ ball to an adult, overhand, 10'				
	24-II.	**Balls: Catching balls**				
(3)	a.	Catches 8″ ball from 5', arms straight in front of body				
(3.5)	b.	Catches 8″ ball from 5', elbows bent				
(4)	c.	Catches 3″ ball from 5', elbows bent				
(4.5)	d.	Catches 8″ ball from 6', elbows bent and arms held at sides				
(5)	e.	Catches 3″ ball from 7', elbows bent and arms held at sides				
	25.	**Outdoor Equipment**				
	a.	Propels riding toy with feet, 10'				
(2.5)	b.	Climbs ladder on low slide (e.g., 3'–6')				
(3)	c.	Climbs on low jungle gym bars and will drop several inches to ground				
(3.5)	d.	Pedals tricycle at least 10'				
(4)	e.	Enjoys unsteady surfaces and tries to make them move				
(4.5)	f.	Pumps swing				
(5)	g.	Rides bicycle with training wheels				

Developmental Progress Chart

Child: _____

Tester: _____

Dates of Testing (Fill in circle with color used on the chart):

○ **1:** _____
○ **2:** _____
○ **3:** _____
○ **4:** _____

	Curriculum Sequences		2–2.5 years	2.5–3 years	3–3.5 years	3.5–4 years	4–4.5 years	4.5–5 years
Cognition	1. Attention and Memory		a b c d	e f g h	i j k l	m n o p	q r s t	u v w x
	2. Concepts	I.	a b	c d e	f g h i	j k l m n o	p q r s t	u v w x y z
		II.	a b	c d e	f g h i j	k l m n	o p q	r s t u
	3. Symbolic Play		a b	c d	e f	g h	i j	k l
	4. Reasoning		a	b	c	e	f	g
	5. Visual Perception	I.	a	b	c	d	e	g
		II.	a b c d e f	g	h	i	j	k
Communication	6. Expressive Vocabulary		a b c d	e f g	h i j k	l m n o	p q	r s
	7. Interest in Sounds and Language Functions		a b c d e f	g	e		f g	h
	8. Receptive Skills		a b c d	b c	d	e	g	h
	9. Conversation Skills		a b c d e	f g	h i j k	l m n o p q r	s t u	v w x
	10. Sentence Construction		a b c d e f g h i j	k l	k l m n o	p q r s	t u	v w

Domain	#	Skill	Subsection	Items
Social Adaptation	11.	Responsibility		a b c d e f g h i j
	12.	Self Concept		a b c d e f g h i j k l m n o
	13.	Interpersonal Skills		a b c d e f g h i j k l m n o p q r s t u
	14.	Self-Help Skills	I.	a b c d e f g h i j k
			II.	a b c d e f g h
			III.	a b c d e f
			IV.	a b c d e f
Fine Motor	15.	Fine Motor Skills: Hand Use	I.	a b c d e f g
			II.	a b c d e f g h i j
			III.	a b c d e
	16.	Fine Motor Skills: Manipulation	I.	a b c d e f g h
			II.	a b c d e f g
	17.	Fine Motor Skills: Bilateral skills		a b c d e f g h
	18.	Fine Motor Skills: Tool Use		a b c d e f
	19.	Visual-Motor Skills	I.	a b c d e f g h i j k
			II.	a b c d e
			III.	a b c d
Gross Motor	20.	Locomotion	I.	a b c
			II.	a b c d
			III.	a b c d e
			IV.	a b c d e
			V.	a b c d e f
	21.	Stairs	I.	a b c d e f
			II.	a b c d
	22.	Jumping	I.	a b c d e f
			II.	a b c d e
			III.	a b c
	23.	Balance	I.	a b c d e f g h
			II.	a b c d e f g h
	24.	Balls	I.	a b c d e f
			II.	a b c d
	25.	Outdoor Equipment		a b c d e f g

65

Curriculum
Sequences

1.

Attention
and Memory

ITEMS FOR ATTENTION and memory are joined together in this sequence because these skills are so closely related. This sequence includes items that tap visual memory, auditory memory, and both visual and auditory memory. Some of the items require visual-spatial memory and others require sequential memory. Children may have specific deficits that interfere with one form of memory and not another. Thus, a child may have very scattered successes with this sequence. In these cases, teach to both the child's strengths and weaknesses. For example, if a child has 2½–3-year-old skills in auditory sequential memory (i.e., repeating numbers, words, and sentences) but has visual-spatial memory skills at the 4–4½-year level (i.e., matches both color and shape of 2 objects seen only briefly), intervene with items of both kinds at the 2 different levels. Also, think about how one kind of memory might aid the other. In the above instance, provide visual cues to assist in auditory memory (e.g., hold up the correct number of fingers as you say each number).

Children with special handicaps (e.g., a nontalker) may not be able to do many of the items in this sequence. It will be necessary to make modifications to give them opportunities to improve attention and memory skills. For example, although a child cannot speak, he or she may be able to listen to a sequence of numbers and then reproduce that sequence with number cards or with magnetic letters that can be moved on a board. A creative teacher can begin with whatever skills the child presently possesses and create tasks that will expand auditory, visual-sequential, and visual-spatial memory. However, when new or modified items are developed, it is important to remember that they cannot be interpreted as representing the same developmental levels that are associated with the standard items in this sequence. For example, one cannot assume that arranging magnetic numbers in a sequence is equivalent to repeating the numbers. In fact, it is probably a much more difficult task.

69

1. Attention and Memory

a.   Anticipates parts of rhymes or songs

b.   Repeats 2-digit sequence or 2 unrelated words

c.   Points to the hand that is hiding a toy

d.   Joins in saying nursery rhymes—repeats parts of them

e.   Tells the name of an object or picture shown briefly in a group of 2 and then hidden

f.   Remembers incidental information (e.g., "What did you see at the zoo?")

g.   Repeats 3-word sentences

h.   Says or sings at least 2 nursery rhymes or songs in a group or with an adult

i.   Identifies from 4 or more pictures 1 seen only briefly

j.   Names 1 of several (e.g., 4 or more) objects or pictures, shown, named, and then hidden

k.   Repeats a sequence of 3 digits or 3 unrelated words

l.   Repeats 4-word sentences including adjectives

m.   Remembers and names which of 3 objects has been hidden

n.   Describes familiar objects without seeing them

o.   Recalls 1 or 2 elements from a story just read (no prompts)

p.   Matches both color and shape of an object (or picture) seen only briefly

q.   Sings songs or says rhymes of at least 30 words (words may be repeated)

r.   Recalls 3–4 elements from a story without prompts

s.   Matches both color and shape of 2 objects (or pictures) seen only briefly

t.   Describes events that happened in the past (e.g., yesterday, last week)

u.   Recalls most of the essential elements in a story

v.   Repeats 5–6 word sentences, maintaining the grammatical structure

w.   Repeats sequence of 4 numbers or unrelated words

x.   Remembers the place in an array where a picture was seen only briefly (e.g., 5 seconds)

AREA: **1. Attention and Memory**
BEHAVIOR: 1a. Anticipates parts of rhymes or songs

Materials: Normal home or classroom environment

Procedure	Group activities
Tell the child nursery rhymes, jingles, or songs that involve some action (e.g., "Itsy, Bitsy Spider"; "This Little Piggy"; "Two Little Blackbirds Sitting on a Fence"). After the child becomes familiar with a rhyme, slow down on parts of it to see if he or she will do the actions before the words are actually said (You may also see this without slowing down. Young children get excited and move ahead.).	Do nursery rhymes, jingles, and songs in the group. It is often useful to use 1 song every day for a week or even a month to help the children learn it. A good beginning song is one that uses the children's names. For example, "Where is _____, where is _____, Here I am (child raises his or her hands or points to him- or herself). Here I am. How are you today, sir? Very well, I thank you. Clap your hands. Clap your hands (Sung to the tune of "Are you sleeping, Are you sleeping, brother John"). Another easy song is "If you're happy and you know it, clap your hands" (other verses: wear a smile, stomp your feet).

Criterion: The child anticipates parts of a rhyme, jingle, or song either by doing the actions before the words tell him or her to do them, by laughing before the funny part, by saying the next word, or by some other clear indication that he or knows what is coming next. This must be done 5 or more times and at least 2 different rhymes, jingles, or songs should be involved.

AREA: **1. Attention and Memory**
BEHAVIOR: 1b. Repeats 2-digit sequence or 2 unrelated words

Materials: Normal home or classroom environment

Procedure	Group activities
Play games with the child that involve repeating what each other says. Most children at this age love words and will try to imitate almost anything. Always start easy, that is, with only 1 number or a short word. Then move on to a 2-word or number sequence (e.g., "Say apple," "Say Daddy," "Now say apple, Daddy"). If the child gets a 2-word sequence correct after having repeated each word alone first, try a new 2-word sequence.	Play a memory game in the group where you say one word and point to a child who repeats it after you. Move on to two-word or two-number sequences. Young children may have trouble waiting their turn and several will call it out. Do not be critical of this in young children, just say, "You all remembered it, now let's see if Mary can do the next one all by herself."

Criterion: The child repeats 5 or more 2-word or 2-number sequences.

2.5

AREA: **1. Attention and Memory**
BEHAVIOR: 1c. Points to the hand that is hiding a toy

Materials: Several small toys that can be enclosed completely in your hand

Procedure	Group activities
Show the child 1 small toy and then show him or her that you are picking it up with 1 hand. Put both hands behind you momentarily. Bring them back out and ask, "Which hand is it in?" After he or she points, open the hand so that the child can see if he or she was correct. If he or she is not correct, open the other hand and let him or her see the toy. Try again. Alternate hands so that the child does not always find the toy in the same hand. Let the child be the one who hides the toy in his or her hand. Make errors sometimes so the child can have the fun of "fooling you."	Do the activity in the "Procedure" section in a group, having the children take turns guessing which hand has the toy and having them take turns being the one who hides the toy.

Criterion: The child correctly points to the hand hiding the toy 5 out of 6 consecutive times.

2.5

AREA: **1. Attention and Memory**
BEHAVIOR: 1d. Joins in saying nursery rhymes—repeats parts of them

Materials: Normal home or classroom environment

Procedure	Group activities
Recite or sing nursery rhymes and songs with the child. It is a good way to entertain him or her in the car, when having to wait, or when you are busy with household chores. If he or she does not spontaneously begin to say them along with you, help him or her by saying only short phrases and seeing if he or she can imitate them. Then ask the child to sing along with you.	Use short group times to recite nursery rhymes and to sing songs. *As much as possible,* have pictures or actions to go with the rhymes to help the children see that the rhymes have meaning. They will learn them much faster if they perceive some meaning.

Criterion: The child joins in with an adult or with a group of children saying nursery rhymes, repeating at least one 3-word phrase in 2 different rhymes or songs.

3

AREA: **1. Attention and Memory**

BEHAVIOR: 1e. Tells the name of an object or picture shown briefly in a group of 2 and then hidden

Materials: A collection of interesting objects and pictures

Procedure	Group activities
Play a game in which you show the child 2 objects or pictures briefly and then put one behind your back, under a box, or somewhere else out of sight. Ask him or her, "What did I hide?" Let the child also be the one to hide something and you tell what is hidden.	Play the game as in the "Procedure" section but in a group. Try to get the children to take turns guessing what is hidden as well as taking turns hiding a toy.

Criterion: The child names one object or picture shown briefly in a group of 2 and then hidden. He or she should be able to do this on several different occasions, rarely making errors.

3

AREA: **1. Attention and Memory**

BEHAVIOR: 1f. Remembers incidental information (e.g., "What did you see at the zoo?")

Materials: Normal home or classroom environment

Procedure	Group activities
Talk to the child about his or her experiences. When the child goes with one parent to do something, the other parent should ask, "What did you see?" or, "What happened?" If the child is unable to recall, the adult who was present with the child should prompt with leading questions (e.g., "Did you see a firetruck?"). Always act very interested in the child's report of his or her experiences.	Plan brief field trips for the children or invite someone in to show them something interesting. Afterwards, talk about the experience to see what the children recall. Begin with very general questions, such as "What did we see at the fire station?" Then, ask more specific questions to help the children remember more of their experiences.

Criterion: On at least 3 occasions, the child remembers and tells about 2 or more objects, events, or experiences *when asked a general question* about a recent occurrence.

AREA: **1. Attention and Memory**
BEHAVIOR: 1g. Repeats 3-word sentences

Materials: Normal home or classroom environment

Procedure	Group activities
Listen to the child. Many children repeat things they hear without being asked to do so. If he or she does not, see if you can get the child to repeat by starting with a 2-word phrase he or she is already saying. For example, you might say, "Say, 'big boy.' " Then, "Now say, 'Daddy's big boy.' " Once the child readily says the phrase, try a 3-word sentence, "Now say, 'Daddy is home.' " Repeating sentences also works well when you are reading simple books. Read a short sentence and then, "Now you read it." Prompt as necessary by providing the first word, or the first 2 words.	Tell the children you are playing a game in which they have to say what you say. Start with 1-word, then 2-word phrases, and then 3-word sentences.

Criterion: The child repeats 5 different 3-word sentences without prompts.

AREA: **1. Attention and Memory**
BEHAVIOR: 1h. Says or sings at least 2 nursery
rhymes or songs in a group or with an adult

Materials: Normal home or classroom environment

Procedure	Group activities
Say rhymes and sing songs when playing with the child. Ask him or her to say or sing them with you. Use actions with the songs or rhymes or show the child pictures to increase the meaningfulness of the words.	Use group time for saying rhymes and singing songs. Select those that have actions for the children to do and/or for which you have pictures to increase the meaning. Encourage each child to participate.

Criterion: The child says or sings at least 2 nursery rhymes or songs in a group or with an adult, getting most of the words correct.

3.5

AREA: **1. Attention and Memory**
BEHAVIOR: 1i. Identifies from 4 or more pictures 1 seen only briefly

Materials: 8–10 identical pairs of pictures (e.g., cut from magazines, cards from Animal Lotto games)

Procedure	Group activities
Play a game with the child in which you show him or her a picture (e.g., a horse). Take the picture away and show him or her 4 pictures (e.g., a horse, a chair, a dog, a pencil). Ask him or her to find the picture that was just shown. If the child cannot do it, show him or her the picture again. Have him or her point to the one just like it. Hide it again and ask the child to point to the one that was just shown. Then try with another picture and a different set of pictures for choices. Let him or her do the hiding occasionally if he or she wants.	Play the game to the left in a group, having the children take turns identifying the correct picture.

Criterion: On several different occasions, after being shown a picture briefly, the child identifies it in an array of 4 or more pictures.

3.5

AREA: **1. Attention and Memory**
BEHAVIOR: 1j. Names 1 of several (4 or more) objects
or pictures, shown, named, and then hidden

Materials: A collection of interesting objects and pictures

Procedure	Group activities
Place 4 objects or pictures in front of the child, naming each 1 as it is placed. Immediately cover the objects or pictures with the cloth or hide them by placing a cardboard screen in front of them. Ask the child, "What did you just see?" If she can't remember any of them, show them to the child again for a few seconds. Cover them and ask again. Try with several different groups of items. Let the child also hide a group and you remember what is hidden. Make it fun!	Do the activity described in the "Procedure" section with a group of children, letting them take turns telling what they remember and doing the hiding.

Criterion: On 5 occasions, the child names 1 of 4 or more objects or pictures, shown, named, and then hidden.

AREA: **1. Attention and Memory**

BEHAVIOR: 1k. Repeats a sequence of 3 digits or 3 unrelated words

Materials: Normal home or classroom environment

Procedure	Group activities
Proceed as in item 1b.	See item 1b.

Criterion: The child repeats a sequence of 3 digits or 3 unrelated words, at least 2 times (different sequences) on several occasions.

3.5

AREA: **1. Attention and Memory**

BEHAVIOR: 1l. Repeats 4-word sentences including adjectives

Materials: Normal home or classroom environment

Procedure	Group activities
Proceed as in item 1g., using sentences that include adjectives (e.g., "Johnny is a big boy," "Mary has a pretty baby").	See item 1g.

Criterion: The child repeats 5 different 4-word sentences including adjectives.

4

AREA: **1. Attention and Memory**

BEHAVIOR: 1m. Remembers and names which of 3 objects has been hidden

Materials: Small toys and/or other familiar objects

Procedure	Group activities
Place 3 toys on the table. Call the child's attention to each one and name it. Then put a screen (e.g., piece of cardboard, paper, book) between the child and the toys. Cover 1 toy or take it away. Ask the child, "What is under the cover?" or "Which one is gone?" If the child does not know or guesses incorrectly, let him or her see the toy and play with all 3 toys briefly. Then hide the toys again, cover (or take away) one, and ask the child to guess which one is missing again. Let the child also have turns hiding the toys and having you guess.	Arrange one of the classroom centers for memory games. Let children play the game described in the "Procedure" section with each other.

Criterion: The child remembers and names which of 3 objects has been hidden on 3 or more occasions, and rarely makes errors.

4

AREA: **1. Attention and Memory**
BEHAVIOR: 1n. Describes familiar objects without seeing them

Materials: Normal home or classroom environment

Procedure	Group activities
Ask the child questions to encourage him or her to think about and describe objects that cannot currently be seen. It is particularly useful to do this when the child has mentioned the object, indicating an interest in talking about it. For example, if the child said, "Grandma gave me a new teddy bear." You might say, "Tell me about it. What does it look like?" Then, if necessary, ask, "What color is it? Is it bigger than your red puppy?" Ask only as many questions as necessary to help him or her describe the object.	Use "show and tell" and other group sharing times to encourage children to talk about things that they have at home or have seen somewhere else. You can also begin a simple form of the "20 Questions Game" where you say, "I am thinking of something that is . . . (e.g., round and red). Can you guess what it is? After someone guesses correctly, ask one of the children to think of something. Show the children how to ask appropriate questions such as, "Is it bigger than this block?" or "Is it in this classroom?" Asking these kinds of questions will teach the other children how to ask questions to get more information and will teach the child who is thinking of the object to visualize and talk about it more precisely.

Criterion: The child describes at least 5 familiar objects that are no longer in view, using at least 3 accurate descriptive terms. These may be used in response to questions.

AREA: **1. Attention and Memory**
BEHAVIOR: 1o. Recalls 1 or 2 elements from a story just read (no prompts)

Materials: Books with simple stories and a lot of pictures

Procedure	Group activities
Read a story to the child holding the book so that the child can see all of the pictures. If the child wants you to stop so that he or she can look at the pictures and discuss them, do so. At the end of the story, close the book and say, "Now, let's see if you can tell that story to me. What do you remember?" Let the child tell as much as he or she can. Then ask questions until you have elicited most of the story.	Do the activity described in the "Procedure" section. It is particularly important in a group *to hold the book facing the children* while you read and to select books with fairly big pictures so that the children can see them easily. It helps to learn to read upside down but you can also do it by reading from one side.

Criterion: The child recalls 1 or 2 elements from a story just read without any prompting questions.

4

AREA: 1. Attention and Memory
BEHAVIOR:　1p. Matches both color and shape of an object (or picture) seen only briefly

Materials:　A collection of pairs of objects or pictures that vary by shape and color (e.g., blocks that are different shapes and colors, toy vehicles of different colors [e.g., cars, trucks, motorcycles], pictures of geometric shapes that vary in color, pictures of vehicles of different colors)

Procedure	Group activities
Place a box containing 8-10 objects in front of the child (or line up 8-10 pictures in front of him or her). Show the child one object (or picture) for a few seconds. Put it behind your back and ask the child to find the one that is just like the one you showed him or her. The box (or row of pictures) should contain objects that are the same shape but a different color than the sample, objects that are the same color but a different shape, and 1 or more objects that are identical to the sample. For example, you may show the child a red cylinder block. In his or her box should be red, green, and blue cylinders; red, green, and blue square blocks, and red, green, and blue oblong blocks. Or, you may show the child a red car. In his or her box should be 2 cars that are identical except that they are green and blue, a truck and a bicycle that are red, and trucks and bicycles that are green and blue.	Do the activity described in the "Procedure" section in a group, having the children take turns matching the object from memory and choosing the object to hide.

Criterion:　The child matches both color and shape of an object or picture seen only briefly at least 5 times with no errors.

AREA: 1. Attention and Memory
BEHAVIOR:　1q. Sings songs or says rhymes of at least 30 words (words may be repeated)

Materials:　Normal home or classroom environment

Procedure	Group activities
Sing a lot of songs with the child. Choose ones that have movements to them or funny sounds (e.g., "Old MacDonald"—one verse, "Itsy, Bitsy Spider"). Occasionally ask the child to sing a song for you. Help the child get started if necessary.	Sing a lot of songs in the group. Singing 1 or 2 songs at the beginning of group time every day will be fun for the children. Let the children take turns choosing a song and leading the group in singing it. Occasionally ask a child to sing for the other children. If a child is shy or unsure of him- or herself, help him or her to sing while the other children listen. Gradually decrease the amount of help you give.

(continued)

Criterion: The child sings a song or says a rhyme of at least 30 words (the words may be repeated). Examples of such rhymes or songs could include: one verse of "Old MacDonald"; the whole "Itsy, Bitsy Spider" song; "Jack and Jill"; or "Humpty Dumpty."

AREA: **1. Attention and Memory**
BEHAVIOR: 1r. Recalls 3–4 elements from a story without prompts

Materials: Books with simple stories and a lot of pictures

Procedure	Group activities
Proceed as in item 1o.	See item 1o.

Criterion: The child recalls 3–4 elements of a story without being asked questions or having other prompts.

4.5

AREA: **1. Attention and Memory**
BEHAVIOR: 1s. Matches both color and shape of 2 objects (or pictures) seen only briefly

Materials: A collection of pairs of objects or pictures that vary by shape and color (e.g., blocks that are different shapes and colors, toy vehicles of different colors [e.g., cars, trucks, motorcycles], pictures of geometric shapes that vary in color, pictures of vehicles of different colors)

Procedure	Group activities
Proceed as in item 1p., however, show the child 2 objects (or pictures) at a time.	Proceed as in item 1p. This activity readily accommodates children of different abilities. You can ask 1 child to remember only 1 item and another to remember 3 or 4, depending on their capabilities.

Criterion: On 5 of 6 trials, the child matches both color and shape of 2 objects (or pictures) seen only briefly (e.g., 5-10 seconds).

4.5

AREA: **1. Attention and Memory**
BEHAVIOR: 1t. Describes events that happened in the past (e.g., yesterday, last week)

Materials: Normal home or classroom environment

Procedure	Group activities
Talk to the child about things you have done together in the past. Ask the child questions about what he or she did in the past (e.g., "What did you do at Mary's house yesterday?") Also tell the child about activities that you have done alone or with someone	After the children have had a holiday or a weekend away from the group, devote a circle time to their sharing their experiences. Ask each one to tell about one activity that they did.

(continued)

Procedure	Group activities
else. The child will especially enjoy hearing about things you did when you were his or her age. In this way you will model talking about things in the past. Listen for the child to share his or her experiences. Always act interested and ask questions to encourage the child to talk more.	

Criterion: On 5 or more occasions, the child describes an event that occurred in the past, including 2 or more elements in the description without being asked questions.

AREA: **1. Attention and Memory**

BEHAVIOR: 1u. Recalls most of the essential elements in a story

Materials: Books with stories that are easily understood by a child this age and that include some pictures

Procedure	Group activities
Read stories frequently and discuss them afterwards, asking the child questions and listening to his or her comments about the stories. Occasionally ask the child to tell a story back to you that has just been read. Ask questions as necessary to help the child recall all of the essential elements in the story.	As in the "Procedure" section, but in a group.

Criterion: The child recalls most of the essential elements of a story just read without being prompted by questions.

AREA: **1. Attention and Memory**

BEHAVIOR: 1v. Repeats 5–6 word sentences, maintaining the grammatical structure

Materials: Normal home or classroom environment

Procedure	Group activities
Play a game with the child in which he or she says something and you try to repeat it and then you say something and he or she tries to repeat it. Begin with short sentences and phrases or brief sequences of numbers or unrelated words. Work up to longer sentences and sequences. Insert nonsense words, bits of nursery rhymes, or funny sounds both to keep it fun and to sharpen the child's listening skills.	Do the activity described in the "Procedure" section with small groups of children. Have them try to imitate one another.

Criterion: The child repeats at least 5 different 5–6 word sentences, maintaining the grammatical structure.

5

AREA: **1. Attention and Memory**
BEHAVIOR: 1w. Repeats sequence of 4 numbers or unrelated words

Materials: Normal home or classroom environment

Procedure	Group activities
Proceed as in item 1b.	As in item 1b.

Criterion: The child repeats at least 5 different sequences of 4 numbers or unrelated words.

AREA: **1. Attention and Memory**
BEHAVIOR: 1x. Remembers the place in an array where
a picture was seen only briefly (e.g., 5 seconds)

Materials: Two decks of regular playing cards, Old Maid cards, or Animal Lotto cards that have at
least 16 matched pairs of cards

Procedure	Group activities
Play "Concentration" with the child. Place 16 different cards face down on the table, four rows of 4 cards each. Have 16 matching cards in a pile. You take 1 card from the pile and place it on the table. Select 1 card in the array of 16 and turn it over. If it matches the card from the pile, remove it and make a pair that you keep. If it does not match, turn it face down again and place the card you drew on the bottom of the pile. Then the child takes a turn. The object is for the players to remember where the cards are that they have seen so that they can find those cards again to make pairs. If the child has no success, reduce the number of cards in the array to 9 and give the child hints to help him or her remember.	Play the game described in the "Procedure" section with a group of children (no more than 4).

Criterion: Ten different times the child finds the card in the array that matches the card he draws (after having seen the card—chance matchings do not count). This may take only 2 games (with an array of 16) or may take as many as 5 games (two correct trials a game).

2-I.

Concepts: General

A SIGNIFICANT PART OF cognitive ability is the capacity to understand relationships between objects and ideas and to apply information learned in a specific situation to other similar situations. For example, the child first learns that his or her own dog is a dog, then that there is a group of creatures that are dogs; then the characteristics that distinguish dogs from cows, pigs, or horses; then that all creatures sharing certain characteristics are animals. Understanding the characteristics that place a creature in the dog or animal category allows the child to draw conclusions about new experiences, to predict the behavior of new creatures that he or she encounters, and to share his or her experiences with others. Success in school is highly related to a child's mastery of concepts. Therefore, learning basic concepts is one of the primary tasks of the preschool years.

Most children appear to absorb these basic concepts without a deliberate effort by adults to teach them. However, learning will be more efficient if adults are more attentive to teaching the concepts. This is especially true for the child who generally learns information more slowly or has a handicapping condition that interferes with the kind of environmental exploration that reinforces the development of associations between different kinds of experiences.

For this curriculum, there has been a somewhat arbitrary division of the many concepts that are learned in the preschool years into two categories: General and Size and Number. Particularly in the General category, the items are probably not ordinal for any one child. They are ordered roughly by the age levels that are suggested by the various tests of concept development. The user of the curriculum should assess the child through at least 2 age levels at which all items have been failed and teach in an order that makes sense in terms of a classroom curriculum or the kinds of items that the child has failed, rather than adhering strictly to the order listed.

All concepts are learned most readily if they are reinforced throughout the day rather than simply being the focus of one learning exercise. They are also learned more readily if embedded in an activity that *the child has chosen to do*. For example, talk to the child about *in, out,* or *under,* when he or she is getting dressed, dressing a doll, playing with trucks or blocks, or in almost any other activity (e.g., "Your arm goes in the sleeve."; "The truck is going under the bridge."; "Take your arm out of the sleeve."). Think about the concepts that you are teaching and build them into many activities (e.g., story time, outdoor play, art work).

Children with special handicaps are at a disadvantage in learning some concepts. For example, children who are physically handicapped who cannot manipulate objects or move through space may have difficulty with concepts related to spatial relationships. The teacher will need to be creative in determining a way to demonstrate such concepts to the child. Talking about what is going on becomes even more important for the child whose handicaps interfere with the more direct experience of the meaning of various concepts.

2. Concepts
I. General

a. Sorts objects by color, form, or name
b. Follows directions including *in, out,* and *on*
c. Identifies *soft* and *hard*
d. Identifies *red, blue,* and *yellow*
e. Identifies *square* and *round*
f. Understands *up, down, top,* and *bottom*
g. Understands *under, over, next to,* and *beside*
h. Understands *fast* and *slow*
i. Understands *empty* and *full*
j. Answers questions or makes statements indicating an understanding that different activities occur at different times of the day (e.g., breakfast in morning, sleep at night)
k. Selects "the one that is different" or "the one that is not the same"
l. Understands *heavy* and *light*
m. Understands *around, in front of, in back of, between, high,* and *low*
n. Completes 2 analogies (i.e., sentences involving opposites)
o. Groups by 2 characteristics (e.g., size and color, shape and color)

p. Understands *fat, skinny, thick,* and *thin*
q. Understands *rough* and *smooth*
r. Understands *backward* and *forward*
s. Understands materials and can tell of what material common objects are made
t. Sorts by categories (e.g., foods, clothes, toys, mother's belongings)
u. Labels all primary colors (e.g., red, yellow, blue, green, black, white)
v. Labels *square, triangle,* and *circle*
w. Names examples within a category (e.g., animals, objects in a kitchen, clothes)
x. Compares sizes of familiar objects not in view
y. Completes sentences involving analogies (at least 5)
z. Identifies an object that does not belong in a set and finds the one that does belong using up to 3 characteristics (e.g., size, shape, color, number, object class)

2.5

AREA: **2-I. Concepts: General**
BEHAVIOR: 2-Ia. Sorts objects by color, form, or name

Materials: Blocks of different colors and shapes, household objects that could be easily sorted such as laundry (e.g., socks, pants) or silverware (It is important that there is a big difference in the colors or shapes to be sorted. Children at this age often do not know color names and may have trouble distinguishing between blue and purple, but can readily distinguish a dark color like red or purple from a light one like white or yellow.)

Procedure	Group activities
Mix up the objects to be sorted (e.g., red and yellow blocks, table knives and spoons, apples and oranges). Have 2 boxes and say something like, "The red blocks go in this box (place one red block in the box) and the yellow blocks go in this box (place a yellow block in the box)." Leave the examples in the boxes to serve as a guide to the child. Then say, "Now you put a red block in this box (wait for the child to put one in; assist him or her if not done), and a yellow one in this box (again waiting for the child to do it and helping if he or she does not). Now let's see if you can put all the yellow ones in this box and the red ones in this box." Correct errors as they occur by showing the child how the 2 blocks look alike that go in the same box. (At this level, many children do not know color names but can match easily. Continue to label the colors for the child but expect them to match on the basis of the way it looks, not on the basis of knowing the name of the color.)	1. The same as in the "Procedure" section. You can vary the task by promoting cooperative sorting—having everyone sort the blocks as they clean up or assigning two children to a task (e.g., one to pick up the napkins and another to pick up the cups). 2. Sorting tasks are also easy to incorporate into "center activities." The items to be sorted can be in a tub or other large container along with separate boxes with pictures or other marks on them that indicate which item goes in which box.
At home, good activities include sorting silverware, putting away toys, or sorting laundry. Do not ask the child to make more than 2 choices at the beginning. That is, "Give me spoons and knives." or "Give me spoons and forks." not knives, forks, and spoons. Also, begin with relatively few objects to be sorted (e.g., no more than six) so that the child does not get tired of the task. Work up to 10–16, depending on the child's attention span. At first, comment on every correct choice; gradually reduce comments about correctness until you have made only one comment at the completion of the task. It is always appropriate, however, to make comments like "I like the way you are working." or "You're a good helper." while the child is doing the sorting.	

Criterion: The child can sort 10 or more objects into 2 groups, without assistance, after being given an example of what belongs in each group.

AREA: **2-I. Concepts: General**
BEHAVIOR: 2-Ib. Follows directions including *in, out,* and *on*

Materials: Normal household or classroom objects or containers

Procedure	Group activities
Think about the direction words as you give children instructions. Give special emphasis to these words (e.g., "The blocks go in the box and the books go on the shelf", "Please take the book out of the box"). Use these words to talk about what you are doing and play games with the child that will involve these words. For example, hide something and say, "Can you find the ____? Look in the drawer; look on the table."	In addition to the activities above, set up simple obstacle courses that require the children to go into, crawl out of, and climb onto various pieces of furniture or play equipment. As they are doing this ask, "Hey everybody, where is Ned? There he is in the tunnel. Now he's coming out!" Give instructions including these words to individual children as well as to the group to assess whether each has mastered the concepts.

Criterion: The child follows instructions that require an understanding of *in, on,* and *out.* He or she must have demonstrated an understanding of each word in at least 2 different instructions (e.g., "Put the block in the box," "Put the spoon in the drawer," "Put the book on the shelf," "Climb on the chair").

AREA: **2-I. Concepts: General**
BEHAVIOR: 2-Ic. Identifies *soft* and *hard*

Materials: Normal home or classroom environment

Procedure	Group activities
Use the words *soft* and *hard* when describing objects (e.g., "Feel this nice soft pillow."; "This is a hard chair.") Encourage the child to feel various *hard* and *soft* objects, and then ask, "Is that soft?" Try to set up contrasts for the child to experience (e.g., soft cooked eggs versus hard cooked eggs, soft mashed potatoes versus hard carrots, soft grass versus hard stones).	The same as in the "Procedure" section. You may also do an activity on *soft* and *hard* where you bring in many materials and have the children feel them one-by-one and talk about softness and hardness.

Criterion: With three different pairs of objects that differ significantly in softness and hardness, the child can point to, give, or tell which is *soft* and which is *hard.*

3   AREA: **2-I. Concepts: General**
BEHAVIOR: 2-Id. Identifies *red, blue,* and *yellow*

Materials: Objects of different colors

Procedure	Group activities
Always include color names when describing objects. Many children learn color names from hearing them talked about and do not need any specific teaching. Others may not attend to color as an important characteristic. To make color more important, it is helpful to select objects for teaching that differ only in color (e.g., crayons, blocks of the same size and shape, squares of construction paper). Begin with the 3 primary colors: *red, blue,* and *yellow.* First, teach the child to sort the blocks, crayons, or paper by color (see item 2-1a.) to be sure that the child is able to discriminate one color from another. As you are teaching to sort, name the colors. After the child sorts accurately, mix the materials again and ask him or her to give you the "yellow" ones without providing an example of *yellow.* If he or she selects an incorrect one, say, "No, this one is yellow. Now find me another yellow one." After he or she can correctly select *yellow* without your providing an example, use the same procedure for *red* and *blue.*	1. During an art activity, mix *red, yellow,* and *blue* circles of construction paper and have children sort them and paste them on white pieces of paper that have a "model" ball in one corner. After children can sort correctly, begin asking them to select a crayon or other object by the color name. 2. Teach as in "Procedure" section to individual children who have difficulty. (Be sure to allow children to choose whatever colors they wish to use for most art work and talk about those colors. Use art work to teach something specific only once in awhile.)

Criterion: The child selects by name, *red, blue,* and *yellow* objects from groups that contain these 3 colors.

3   AREA: **2-I. Concepts: General**
BEHAVIOR: 2-Ie. Identifies *square* and *round*

Materials: A variety of objects that are *square* and *round* (e.g., blocks, balls, square and round pieces of construction paper)

Procedure	Group activities
Describe objects as *square* or *round* (e.g., point out signs when traveling or walking outdoors, point out characteristics of toys). Teach the child to sort *square* and *round* (e.g., "Put all the square blocks in this square box and all the round blocks in this round can"; if you have an assortment of plastic containers, "Put all the round lids in this box and the square lids in this box"). After the child can sort correctly, begin	1. Have the group work on sorting activities as in the "Procedure" section. Try to make it meaningful by building it into cleanup activities or art work (e.g., have different colored circles and squares and say, "Let's make one picture out of round circles, just round circles. Then make another out of just squares.").

(continued)

Procedure	Group activities
asking him or her to give you the shapes by name (e.g., "This is a round dish—can you find me a round lid?"; "I need a square block to go on this tower—can you find me a square one?")	2. Play a game in which you ask each child to find something *square* (or *round*) in the classroom. Work individually with children who have difficulty with the concepts.

Criterion: The child selects *square* and *round* objects upon request from a group containing both shapes, or the child labels objects correctly as *round* or *square*.

AREA: 2-I. Concepts: General
BEHAVIOR: 2-If. Understands *up*, *down*, *top*, and *bottom*

Materials: Normal home or classroom environment

Procedure	Group activities
Use these direction words when talking to the child about what you are doing, what he or she is doing, or what you both are seeing. Think about contrasts in your descriptions (e.g., "You are going up, now you're coming down."; "This is the top of the box and this is the bottom."). Check the child's understanding by giving instructions using these words or by saying, "This box is red on the top but it is white on the ____." (letting the child fill in the word "bottom").	1. Talk about activities and give instructions in the classroom as described in the "Procedure" section (e.g., "Put it up on the top shelf."). 2. Look for songs and finger plays that include these words (e.g., "Itsy, Bitsy Spider"). 3. Play a game where the object is for a child to follow an instruction as quickly as possible (e.g., "Susie, get on top of the table."; "Bill, touch the bottom of your foot.") The more the children can experience the meaning of the words, the better they will understand them.

Criterion: The child demonstrates an understanding of *up*, *down*, *top*, and *bottom*. Each must be demonstrated by following an appropriate instruction (e.g., "Bring me the box that is on the bottom shelf.") or by the child's using the word appropriately.

AREA: 2-I. Concepts: General
BEHAVIOR: 2-Ig. Understands *under*, *over*, *next to*, and *beside*

Materials: Normal home or classroom environment

Procedure	Group activities
As described in item 2-If., use these direction words when talking to the child about what you are doing, what he or she is doing, or what you both are seeing. Check the child's understanding by giving in-	1. Give instructions in the group where all of the children can learn from one example (e.g., "Come sit next to me."; "John, you sit beside Mary.").

(continued)

Procedure	Group activities
structions (e.g., "Bring me the ball that is under the chair.").	2. Set up obstacle courses for the children and describe their activities as they go through them using these and other concepts that relate to position. Also, use these words to describe activities as you watch the children on the playground. Ask the children questions that will facilitate their using these words also.

Criterion: The child demonstrates an understanding of *under, over, next to,* and *beside* by either following appropriate instructions or using the word appropriately.

AREA: **2-I. Concepts: General**
BEHAVIOR: 2-Ih. Understands *fast* and *slow*

Materials: Normal home or classroom environment

Procedure	Group activities
Proceed as in items 2-If. and 2-Ig. Think of ways throughout the day to integrate these words into activities that you are doing with the child or in the child's presence (e.g., "You're running too fast for me. Mommy is slow.").	Play a game outside in which children *run, stop, go fast,* and *go slow* on command.

Criterion: The child demonstrates an understanding of *fast* and *slow,* either through following two or more instructions including each of these words or by using the words appropriately in his or her own conversations.

AREA: **2-I. Concepts: General**
BEHAVIOR: 2-Ii. Understands *empty* and *full*

Materials: Normal home or classroom environment

Procedure	Group activities
Proceed as in items 2-If. and 2-Ih. Think of ways throughout the day to integrate these words into activities that you are doing with the child or in the child's presence.	Snack or lunch time is a good time to talk to the group about *empty* and *full* (e.g., empty or full: stomachs, glasses, plates).

Criterion: The child demonstrates an understanding of *empty* and *full* either through following two or more instructions including each of these words or by using the words appropriately in his or her own conversations.

AREA: 2-I. Concepts: General
BEHAVIOR: 2-Ij. Answers questions or makes statements indicating
an understanding that different activities occur at different times
of the day (e.g., breakfast in morning, sleep at night)

Materials: Normal home or classroom environment

Procedure	Group activities
Talk about the time of day and what you do during those times (e.g., "It's morning, time to wake up and have breakfast"; "You've had your lunch. Now it is time for your nap.") Ask the child during the course of the day what he or she thinks you are going to do next (e.g., "We've just had supper. What happens now?"). Read books to the child about daily activities and the times that they occur. Ask questions as you read to assess the child's understanding.	A preschool or day care situation lends itself well to learning about routines. Begin the day by describing what you will do (e.g., "First, we will play with the blocks and then with the wheel toys. Then we'll have art and go outside. Then it will be lunchtime. . . . "). Ask after each activity, "What comes next?" to see how well the children have learned the schedule. Also start some mornings by asking what they expect to do in the morning, or in the afternoon. Read books to the children about families and their activities during different times of the day.

Criterion: The child describes activities that occur in the morning and at night upon request, can tell you what time of the day an activity occurs when you describe it, or uses time-of-day statements correctly in conversation.

AREA: 2-I. Concepts: General
BEHAVIOR: 2-Ik. Selects "the one that is different" or "the one that is not the same"

Materials: Objects found in the normal home or classroom environment

Procedure	Group activities
Talk about how objects are alike (or the same) and different as you participate in activities with the child. Set up situations where you can focus on these concepts. For example, put 3 forks and 1 spoon on the table and say, "One of these objects is different from the others. Which one is it?" If the child does not respond or responds incorrectly, say, "These are all forks. This one is a spoon. It is different. Let's take it away and get one that is the same. We'll get another fork. Now they are all the same." If a child is slow to learn, use only 2 terms (e.g., same, different) until they are mastered. Then introduce "alike" and "not alike" so that the child comes	1. Read books during story time that introduce these concepts. 2. Gather together as many groups of 4 identical objects as there are children. Then exchange 1 object from each group with something from another group. Give each child a group of 4 objects and ask everyone to take the object that is different out of their sack and put it in the middle of the table. Correct any errors. Once they have done this, ask them to find 1 object on the table that is the same as in their group and put it in their pile. Children find this even more fun if

(continued)

Procedure	Group activities
to understand that they are interchangeable with same and different. For children who are learning more rapidly, the terms can be used interchangeably throughout teaching.	the objects are placed in a sack or other container for each child.

Criterion: The child selects the one that is different or not alike from a group of 3 or 4. The child must be able to make the choice 2 times with each description (e.g., different, not alike).

4

AREA: **2-I. Concepts: General**
BEHAVIOR: 2-Il. Understands *heavy* and *light*

Materials: Objects found in normal home or classroom environment

Procedure	Group activities
When you or the child picks up on object that is difficult to lift, describe it as "heavy." When 1 is easy to lift, describe it as "light." Do this especially when there is an opportunity to show big contrasts. For example, when walking outside you might find a bird feather. Talk about the feather and how "light" it is when you pick it up. Then look for something *heavy* such as a big rock. Pick it up and say, "Now this is heavy; see how heavy it is?" Then, when the child picks up something with effort ask him or her, "Is that heavy?" Also, get the child to guess by looking at something whether it is going to be *heavy* or *light;* then let the child test his or her idea. Collect big and small items that are both *heavy* and *light* so that you can teach the idea that size is not the only determinant of weight. For example, compare a large balloon and a medium-sized rock; talk about which one is big and which is little, and then ask, "Which one do you think is heavy?" Let the child compare different objects and talk about which object is heavy and which is light.	The same as in the "Procedure" section. When you collect materials to teach the concept, you can give each child a pair to pick up and have him or her tell the rest of the children about each object's heaviness and lightness. Then have the child pass the pair to another child to see if there is agreement (or pass them to you so that you can correct any errors in the concepts).

Criterion: The child uses the terms *heavy* and *light* correctly when picking up objects or can point to the correct item when asked, "Which one is heavy?" and "Which one is light?"

AREA: 2-I. Concepts: General

BEHAVIOR: 2-Im. Understands *around, in front of, in back of, between, high,* and *low*

Materials: Objects found in normal home or classroom environment

Procedure	Group activities
Teach these concepts as other position concepts (i.e., use the terms as you interact with the child). As you wrap a package talk about putting the ribbon *around* the box, describe the child's arms as being *around* your neck, tell the child to get *in front of* or *in back of* you when standing in line (help him or her get there if he or she does not understand at first), ask the child to sit *between* you and another person, or talk about reaching up *high* to get something or down *low* to get something else. Play games such as "Simon Says" using these terms (e.g., "Simon Says, put your hand in front of your face."). Use these terms as you describe pictures in books or magazines. Ask the child to find something in a picture by using one of these position terms (e.g., "Find the dog that is in back of the chair.").	The same as in the "Procedure" section. "Simon Says" is a particularly good group game for teaching these concepts. Lining up in the classroom, putting toys away, and finding objects are always good opportunities to teach these concepts and to determine which children know them.

Criterion: The child demonstrates an understanding of each of these concepts by using the words correctly, by following instructions including these words, or by being able to point to pictures (or parts of pictures) that show the concept.

AREA: 2-I. Concepts: General

BEHAVIOR: 2-In. Completes 2 analogies (i.e., sentences involving opposites)

Materials: Normal home or classroom environment

Procedure	Group activities
When riding in the car or in other situations where you are entertaining the child by talking to him or her, play a game of opposites. Think of the concepts that you are sure the child knows. Then, make up a sentence based on something you have just seen or that you are talking about to help the child think more about these concepts. For example, you might see a spider and say, "Look at that spider. A spider is little. An elephant is ____." (waiting for the child to fill in the word). If he or she does not supply the word, supply it and repeat the two sentences. Then try another comparison of the same sort (e.g., "The baby is little. Daddy is ____.").	The same as in the "Procedure" section. Build this into story time and other classroom activities where the group can finish the sentences together. Also check out each child's ability to do it on his or her own when you have a few minutes to spend with each child.

Criterion: The child completes 2 or more analogies involving different comparisons on several occasions.

AREA: **2-I. Concepts: General**
BEHAVIOR: 2-Io. Groups by 2 characteristics (e.g., size and color, shape and color)

Materials: Several collection of objects that vary on at least 3 dimensions: color, size, shape, or category (e.g., large and small, male and female dolls dressed in blue or red clothes; brown and white, large and small plastic [or paper] horses and dogs; blue and yellow, round and square, big and little blocks; lids to containers that are large and small, round and square, plastic [white] and metal [yellow])

Procedure	Group activities
First be sure that the child can sort materials by each characteristic included in the group. For example, if you had a group of large and small, male and female dolls dressed in red and blue clothes, you would first mix them up and aszk the child to "put all the big people here and all the little people here." After he or she did that, you would mix them again and say, "Now, let's see if you can put all of the girls here and the boys here." And then, "Now, let's see if you can put all of those in red clothes here and in blue clothes here." Always correct errors and let the child try it again. Make it fun by helping the child by picking one up and saying, "Let's see, where does this one go?" When the child can easily sort by each characteristic included in the group, mix the objects up and ask him or her to sort by 2 characteristics (e.g., "See if you can find all of the big girls."; "See if you can find all of the boys in blue clothes."). Help the child find ones that he or she has missed and correct any errors. Once he or she can sort one group of objects by 2 characteristics, try another group.	Make the "Procedure" section example into a group game. Give each child 1 of the objects from the group. For example, if you have plastic (or paper) horses and pigs that are brown and white, large and small, place 2 boxes on the table and say, "Look at your animal. If you have a horse, put it in this box. If you have a pig, put it in this box." Return all the animals to the children and say, "If you have a big animal, put it in this box. If you have a little animal, put it in this box." Repeat for brown and white. Once the children can sort correctly by 1 characteristic, say, "Now, let's see if I can trick you. Look at your animal. If it is a white horse, put it in this box (emphasize the words "white" and "horse")." If a child starts to make a mistake, ask him or her to look carefully. Explain again that you want only "white horses."

Criterion: The child sorts by 2 characteristics without help on at least 3 occasions.

4.5

AREA: **2-I. Concepts: General**
BEHAVIOR: 2-Ip. Understands *fat, skinny, thick,* and *thin*

Materials: A variety of objects from normal home or classroom environments that allow comparisons on these dimensions (e.g., fat versus skinny—magic marker and pencil, large dowel and small dowel; thick versus thin—paste and glue, magic marker and pencil)

Procedure	Group activities
Call the child's attention to these characteristics of the objects. Describe the *tall skinny* bottle and the *short fat* jar as you use them. Use *thick* and *thin* to	Playing guessing games about the descriptions of objects is a good way to teach these concepts. Put a group of objects that

(continued)

Procedure	Group activities
refer to objects that are "fat" and "skinny" as well as to fluids that are too *thick* to pour or quite runny. It is important for the child to learn that some of these words have different meanings in different contexts. Give the child instructions that involve these concepts (e.g., "Please bring me the fat marker."). Also, give the child opportunities to describe objects that he or she sees or feels. A good way to incorporate this concept into a game is to give one child an object that a second child cannot see. The first child is to describe the object without naming it so that the second person can guess what it is.	vary in size, texture, and shape into a sack. Pass it around and let each child reach in and find 1 object and try to describe it. Have the other children try to guess what it is. The adult should take a turn too, to model the use of the characteristics *fat, skinny, thick,* and *thin.*

Criterion: The child follows instructions that indicate an understanding of *fat, skinny, thick,* and *thin* or uses these words accurately in describing objects.

4.5

AREA: 2-I. Concepts: General
BEHAVIOR: 2-Iq. Understands *rough* and *smooth*

Materials: A variety of objects from normal home or classroom environments that allow comparisons on these dimensions (e.g., sandpaper and velvet, rough woven placemat and smooth table top)

Procedure	Group activities
Call the child's attention to these characteristics of the objects. When the child is touching something, ask him or her if it is *smooth* or *rough.*	Playing the game described in item 2-Ip., making sure to include different textured objects in the sack.

Criterion: The child follows instructions that indicate an understanding of *rough* and *smooth* or uses these words appropriately on at least 3 occasions.

4.5

AREA: 2-I. Concepts: General
BEHAVIOR: 2-Ir. Understands *backward* and *forward*

Materials: Normal home or classroom environment

Procedure	Group activities
Use these words when giving instructions to the child and when describing activities or events (e.g., "Your shirt is on backwards."; "You're walking backwards!"; "Move forward a little bit."). Check the child's understanding by giving specific instructions that include these words.	"Simon Says" or other movement games are excellent for teaching these concepts.

Criterion: The child follows several instructions that include *backward* and *forward* or uses these words in describing activities or events.

AREA: **2-I. Concepts: General**

BEHAVIOR: 2-Is. Understands materials and can tell of what material
common objects are made

Materials: Objects found in the normal home or classroom environment

Procedure	Group activities
Call the child's attention to the material from which common objects are made. Point out that objects are made of paper, rocks, concrete, cloth, rubber, and metal. Ask the child of what he or she thinks certain objects are made. It is especially easy to talk about materials when you are creating or repairing things or when you are observing someone else do them (e.g., flour is used to make bread, cloth is used and sewn to make a shirt, wood is used to fix a fence). Use stories in books to stimulate discussion of materials. One of the easiest to use is the story of "The Three Little Pigs" and their houses made of straw, sticks, and stone.	It is easy to prepare a lesson for a small or large group in which you bring objects made of different materials and ask the children of what they are made. You can also ask questions while reading stories to stimulate this kind of thinking.

Criterion: The child can give reasonable answers to 3 or more questions involving materials (The child may say rubber when something is actually made of plastic, but would not say the object is made of cloth or paper.).

4.5

AREA: **2-I. Concepts: General**

BEHAVIOR: 2-It. Sorts by categories (e.g., foods, clothes, toys, and mother's belongings)

Materials: Objects found in normal home or classroom environment

Procedure	Group activities
Look for opportunities to talk about categories of objects and have the child sort the objects (e.g., after the week's shopping, you can say, "We bought our food at the grocery store. Let's put the vegetables here, the meat here, the bread here, and the fruit here." and then hand the items one-by-one to the child to put in the appropriate place; when putting away toys you can ask him or her to put the animals in one place, and the cars in another).	1. Do group lessons on categories of food and get the children to identify parts of their lunch or snack by these categories. Cleanup time in the classroom almost always requires some kind of sorting by categories. Just make sure that you emphasize the category names. 2. Read books to the children on animals such as mammals, birds, and reptiles. When you do, talk about the characteristics that make the animals belong to each of these categories.

Criterion: The child sorts objects into 3 or more categories when given the names of the categories.

ᕼ

AREA: 2-I. Concepts: General
BEHAVIOR: 2-Iu. Labels all primary colors

Materials: Crayons, blocks, or other items that are primary colors (e.g., red, yellow, blue, green, black, white)

Procedure	Group activities
Most children will pick up color names from hearing them used and will begin to use them in describing objects. If this does not happen, first check to see if the child can match all primary colors. Give him or her a pile of blocks, select one and see if he or she can find one that is of the same color as yours. If the child cannot match, do not try to teach labeling. If he or she seems to be responding to lightness or darkness, rather than to color, or if he or she regularly confuses red and green, request that the child be tested for color blindness. If the child can match accurately, try to teach color names systematically by first presenting just 3 colors. Ask for 1 by name. If the child makes an error say, "No, this is ____ (show him or her the color), now give me ____." Mix the order of the colors and ask again for the same one. Once the child is reliable in selecting that color, use the same procedure for the second color. After he or she is reliable with that color, return to asking for the first to test his or her memory for that one. Only if the child is correct on those 2, do you go on to the third color. After the 3 are learned, introduce 1 more, and so on until all are mastered.	Art activities, as well as many other normal classroom activities, offer many opportunities to talk about colors. Work individually with children who have difficulty.

Criterion: The child names all primary colors either when asked, "What color is that?" or when describing objects on his or her own.

ᕼ

AREA: 2-I. Concepts: General
BEHAVIOR: 2-Iv. Labels *square, triangle,* and *circle*

Materials: Blocks, form board pieces, pieces of paper, or other objects in the shapes of *squares, triangles,* and *circles*

Procedure	Group activities
Label shapes you see in the environment (e.g., there is a circle around the picture in the book, the block is square, the "Yield" sign is a triangle). Label blocks by shape as the child plays with them. Ask the	In addition to labeling shapes as you see them in the classroom, plan a lesson in which you bring large shapes cut from paper or cardboard and talk about them (e.g., the

(continued)

Procedure	Group activities
child, "Is that a square or a triangle?" or "What shape is this?" Always reinforce correct answers (e.g., "You're right. That is a _____.") and incorrect answers (e.g., "I think you got fooled on that one. It is a _____.").	*round* circle, the *square* with 4 sides, the *triangle* with 3 sides). Ask a child to look around the room and find all of the *circles* that he or she can find. Ask another child to find all of the *squares* and another to find all of the *triangles* (be sure you have taped some up in unlikely places to add to those occurring naturally to make it a game).

Criterion: The child labels *circle, square,* and *triangle* when asked what shape it is or uses these words correctly when describing shapes.

5

AREA: **2-I. Concepts: General**

BEHAVIOR: 2-Iw. Names examples within a category (e.g., animals, objects in a kitchen, clothes)

Materials: Normal home or classroom environment

Procedure	Group activities
When doing household chores that keep you busy, entertain the child with conversations that encourage him or her to think about entities that go together for one reason or another. For example, say, "Let's pretend we're going to the zoo to see the animals. What animals would we see?"; "Let's shut our eyes and pretend we're in the kitchen. What would we see there?"; or "I'm thinking about furniture. Tell me all the things you can think of that are furniture." If the child gets stuck after naming 1 or 2 entities, name 1 yourself and give the child hints to help him or her come up with others (e.g., make an animal noise to help the child think of another animal, describe a table to help him or her identify that as a piece of furniture). Alternate between your naming the category and having the child name examples and letting the child name the category with you naming examples.	Letting children take turns picking a category and having the other group members name examples within the category is a good group game. Give hints to children who have difficulty so that they can experience success.

Criterion: The child names 3 examples within at least 3 categories.

AREA: **2-I. Concepts: General**

BEHAVIOR: 2-Ix. Compares sizes of familiar objects not in view

Materials: Normal home or classroom environment

Procedure	Group activities
When having a conversation with the child, ask him or her to think about 2 toys that he or she has or 2 other familiar objects. Then say, "Which one is bigger?" If the child is incorrect, get the objects for him or her to see, and ask again. Make this into a game, asking questions about objects one might see outside as well as familiar toys (e.g., "What is bigger, a turtle or a horse?") Always respond if the child asks you these kind of questions. Sometimes you may have to say you don't know or that "It all depends." The discussion will help the child think about the characteristics of objects and animals.	After you read a story that includes objects or people of different sizes, close the book and ask questions about which one was bigger (e.g., "Who was bigger—the fox or the chicken?"). Ask questions in group time like the ones described under "Procedure."

Criterion: The child correctly tells which of 2 familiar objects is bigger without being able to see them at the time the question is asked. He or she is able to do this with at least 3 pairs of objects.

AREA: **2-I. Concepts: General**

BEHAVIOR: 2-Iy. Completes sentences involving analogies (at least 5)

Materials: Normal home or classroom environment

Procedure	Group activities
See item 2-In.	See item 2-In.

Criterion: Child completes at least 5 different sentences involving analogies.

AREA: **2-I. Concepts: General**

BEHAVIOR: 2-Iz. Identifies an object that does not belong in a set and finds the one that does belong using up to 3 characteristics (e.g., size, shape, color, number, object class)

Materials: Blocks of different colors, sizes, and shapes; playing cards; a variety of small toys

Procedure	Group activities
Make a set of 4 pictures or objects in which 1 member does not belong. For example, 3 big square red blocks and 1 big red cylindrical block. Include as choices for the child both big and small red square blocks as well as big and small blocks of other shapes	Set up the example in the "Procedure" section in a group, letting different children choose which item should be deleted and which should be added, and discuss the reasons for doing so.

(continued)

Procedure	Group activities
and colors. Another set might include 3 jacks of spades and 1 jack of clubs. Choices would include black and red jacks, as well as other face cards. Still another might include 2 four-of-diamonds, 1 four-of-hearts, and 1 five-of-hearts. When a child makes choices about which item does or does not belong, ask why he or she made that choice. Talk about why you might make that choice or another.	

Criterion: On 5 different trials, using different materials, the child identifies an object that does not belong in a set and finds 1 that does belong using 2 or 3 characteristics (e.g., size, shape, color, number, object class). The child passes a trial if he or she gives a valid reason for the choice, even if it is different than yours, but he or she must demonstrate at least 2 characteristics for the reasoning.

2-II.

Concepts:
Size and number

Concepts related to size and number are best learned by having adults refer to these characteristics in the course of every day activities and by playing games that involve these concepts. Too often, children are taught to "count" before they have any basis for understanding what numbers mean. Of course, the child needs to be able to say numbers in sequence before he or she can count objects but *it is much more important for the child to learn to move his or her finger from one object to the next as he or she counts than to simply say the numbers.* It is also important for the child to be developing size and sequence concepts along with numbers since these concepts are closely related (e.g., a big pile of blocks has more blocks than a small one; a big number stands for more objects than a small number; our number system is based on repeating sequences of 10). While an adult takes these concepts for granted, a child must learn them through concrete experiences and through conversations with adults.

The child who cannot talk will not be able to do many of the items in this sequence as they are written. Such a child can learn and demonstrate mastery of size and number concepts through sorting and selecting activities (e.g., "Point to the big one"). If the child is also unable to manipulate objects or to point he or she can still learn these concepts through the use of pictures and demonstrations. The child can indicate his or her knowledge by using whatever response is available for him or her to select (e.g., pointing with eyes, leaning toward).

2. Concepts
II. Size and number

a. Uses or understands size words (e.g., big, little)
b. Selects *just one*
c. Answers number questions involving *one* and *two*
d. Gives/selects *two* and *three*
e. Follows instructions including *all* and *none* or *not any*
f. Matches a picture with 2 objects to the correct picture in a set that includes 1, 2, 3, and 4 objects
g. Understands: *tall, short, more,* and *less*

h. Matches pictures containing different configurations of objects up to 6
i. Gives *one more*
j. Counts up to 6 objects in a row
k. Answers addition questions involving +1 up to 5
l. Identifies (or correctly uses) *bigger* and *biggest, smaller* and *smallest,* and *larger* and *largest*
m. Counts 10 objects in a row
n. Understands *same number* and can sort a set into halves
o. Identifies *penny, nickel,* and *dime* when named

p. Counts correctly to 20
q. Matches 3-part sequences of pictures or objects depicting quantities up to 6
r. Gives the correct number of objects when asked—all numbers from 4 to 10
s. Tells current age, how old he or she was last year, and how old he or she will be next year
t. Answers addition questions involving +2 up to 10
u. Recognizes repeating pattern in a sequence and can continue it

2.5

AREA: **2-II. Concepts: Size and number**
BEHAVIOR: 2-IIa. Uses or understands size words (e.g., big, little)

Materials: A variety of toys and normal household and/or classroom objects of different sizes

Procedure	Classroom activities
When a child is using object labels or demonstrates an understanding of such labels, begin expanding on the labels by adding a size word. For example, if the child says "ball," say, "A ball, a big ball." If a small ball is near by, put it next to the large one and say, "This is a little ball; Big ball, little ball" (pointing). Look for opportunities throughout the day to comment on the size of objects, looking for obvious contrasts (e.g., a beach ball and a tennis ball; a dinner plate and a salad plate; a baby and a child who is walking). Work both on getting the child to select objects by size (e.g., "Give me the big one") and using *big* and *little* when labeling objects. If the child does not spontaneously begin to use size words, prompt the response by putting 2 objects of different sizes next to each other and saying, "this is a little bowl (pointing) and this is a ____". Wait for a response. If it is not forthcoming, finish the sentence yourself and repeat.	1. Read simple stories to the children that have size words in them; pause when you get to the word, point to the picture and see if they will fill it in (e.g., "When Goldilocks went to sit on Daddy Bear's chair, she found it was too ____."). 2. When the children clean up, have them put all the *big* blocks (or other objects) in one container and all the *little* ones in another. 3. Give instructions and ask questions that involve size concepts (e.g., "Please bring me the big book."; "Where is the big ball?).

Criterion: The child sorts at least 3 different kinds of objects by size, selects several *big* or *little* objects upon request, or uses size labels frequently and correctly in speech. The items used to test mastery of this item must be different than those used for training.

AREA: **2-II. Concepts: Size and number**
BEHAVIOR: 2-IIb. Selects *just one*

2.5

Materials: Any group of objects

Procedure	Classroom activities
Focus the child's attention on numbers by counting out loud at every opportunity (e.g., when getting the silverware to set the table, when getting mittens or socks for the child to put on). Hold up your fingers as you count. For example, hold up 2 fingers and say, "I need 2 socks." Then count the socks, *one* (hold it up), *two* (hold the second one up). Concentrate on the numbers up to 5 as these are the ones that will first become meaningful. Then begin giving instruc-	1. Play finger games or sing songs that involve counting and showing the quantity with fingers. 2. Pass around the container of scissors, hunks of clay, or markers with the instruction to take *just one*. Always correct errors in counting the objects one by one.

(continued)

Procedure	Group activities
tions that involve *just one* (e.g., "You can have just one cookie."; "Bring me just one spoon."). Always correct errors by counting (e.g., "Whoops, you took three cookies. See, one, two, three. I said just one. Here is just one cookie.").	

Criterion: The child selects *just one* on 3 or more occasions, without errors.

AREA: **2-II. Concepts: Size and number**
BEHAVIOR: 2-IIc. Answers number questions involving *one* and *two*

Materials: Normal home or classroom environment

Procedure	Group activities
Frequently ask the child number questions during the course of the day (e.g., "How many cookies do you have?": "Look at this bear; how many eyes does he have?"). If the child does not answer correctly, count aloud for him or her (e.g., "One, two. He has 2 eyes."). Then move on to another similar question (e.g., "Now, how many eyes does Momma have?").	Use snack time as well as other activity times to ask questions about numbers. Make sure that each child has a chance to respond before another child answers the question for him or her. Get the group to count together to check out an answer (e.g., "Let's see if John is right. Let's count the cookies. One, two, three."

Criterion: The child correctly answers 2 or more questions involving *one* and correctly answers 2 or more questions involving *two*.

AREA: **2-II. Concepts: Size and number**
BEHAVIOR: 2-IId. Gives/selects *two* and *three*

Materials: The usual objects of the environment

Procedure	Group activities
Follow the instructions for item 2-IIb. Look for opportunities throughout the day to have the child bring you *2* or *3* objects. Build this into daily routines such as setting the table (e.g., "Give me 2 forks."), cleaning up (e.g., "You pick up 2 toys and I'll pick up 2 toys."; "Bring 3 cookies.").	Let the children take turns handing out crayons or other objects (e.g., "Give everyone 2 crayons.") for classroom activities. When you pass out materials, count them out for each child; pass around a plate of cookies and ask each child to take a set number of cookies.

Criterion: Child selects 2 and 3 without error, on at least 5 occasions.

3

AREA: 2-II. Concepts: Size and number

BEHAVIOR: 2-IIe. Follows instructions including *all* and *none* or *not any*

Materials: Normal home and classroom environment

Procedure	Group activities
Use the words *all, none* and *not any* as you talk about what you are doing with the child (e.g., "Let's gather up all the toys. Whoops, we missed one, lets get all of them. Now there are not any toys"). Look for opportunities throughout the day to ask the child to bring you (or "pick up" or "give you") *all* of a groups of objects (e.g., "Put *all* the spoons in the dishwasher"). Also look for opportunities to say things like, "I don't have any. You see, there are none there." Also, pay attention to these words as you read stories or nursery rhymes (e.g., Old Mother Hubbard —"and then the poor dog had *none*").	Use the terms *all, none,* and *not any* as appropriate to describe activities in the classroom (e.g., "I want *all* of the girls over here and *all* of the boys over here."; "There are *not any* blocks on the shelves. Please put *all* the blocks on the shelves."). Also, look for stories to read that include these words. Use your finger on the picture to show that *all* includes every one. Make it clear that when objects are all gone there are *none*. Give instructions to individual children that involve giving you *all* of the crayons and putting *all* of the toys on the shelf.

Criterion: The child correctly follows instructions involving *all* on at least 3 different occasions and follows instructions involving *none* or *not any* on at least 3 different occasions.

3.5

AREA: 2-II. Concepts: Size and number

BEHAVIOR: 2-IIf. Matches a picture with 2 objects to the correct picture in a set that
includes 1, 2, 3, and 4 objects

Materials: A variety of matching sets of pictures containing 1, 2, 3, or 4 objects or people

Procedure	Group activities
Show 1 set of pictures and count aloud how many objects/people are in each picture. Give the child a picture that matches the picture of 2 objects and ask him or her to "put it on the one with the same number, the one just like it." If the child makes an error, help him or her count the number in the picture and then the number in each of the other pictures and give a second trial. If the child still has difficulty, try the following steps: 1. Present only 2 pictures (e.g., 1 and 4) and have the child match 1 to 1; then continue having him or her match 1 to 1 with only 2 choices (e.g., 1 and 3, 1 and 2). 2. Then try matching 1 to 1 with 3 and 4 choices.	All of the counting activities under item 2-IIb. are appropriate for these early number concepts.

(continued)

Procedure	Group activities
3. When the child is successful with matching 1 to 1 with 4 choices try getting him or her to match 2 to 2 again, first with 2 choices and then with 3 or 4 choices.	

Criterion: When given 4 choices, the child can match a picture of 2 objects to an identical picture of 2 objects on 3 consecutive occasions with different pictures each time.

3.5

AREA: **2-II. Concepts: Size and number**
BEHAVIOR: 2-IIg. Understands *tall, short, more,* and *less*

Materials: Books and objects found in the usual environment

Procedure	Group activities
Use these words as you talk to the child about the environment. Point out the contrasts (e.g., "That man is tall; that boy is short."; "You have more cookies than I do; I have less cookies than you."; "Now you have all the blocks; I have none."). Look for stories or nursery rhymes that use these words (e.g., "Old Mother Hubbard went to the cupboard to get her poor dog a bone. But when she got there, the cupboard was bare and the poor dog had none."). As you do this, begin to ask the child questions (e.g., "Which glass is tall?"; "Who has more spaghetti?"; "Were there any bones for the dog?") or give instructions (e.g., "Get your short pants.") that require the child to respond to these words. Think of as many ways to check on their understanding as possible. Always correct misunderstandings with good examples.	The same as in the "Procedure" section.

Criterion: The child must demonstrates an understanding of each concept on 3 or more occasions, either by following an instruction or correctly answering a question.

3.5

AREA: 2-II. Concepts: Size and number
BEHAVIOR: 2-IIh. Matches pictures containing different configurations of objects up to 6

Materials: Playing cards (e.g., Ace through 6), large dominoes or dice, or pictures with different configurations of objects (The configurations should be simple groupings of 1, 2, or 3 to facilitate matching.)

Procedure	Group activities
Place pictures of 2 dissimilar configurations on the table (e.g., **⁝** and a **⁙**) and give the child a picture to match. Use identical pictures (e.g., match 3 hearts to 3 hearts, in playing cards; a picture of 3 apples to another picture of 3 apples). Gradually work up to presenting 4 pictures at a time. You can make this into a "card game" by giving the child 4 cards face down and placing your cards face up. The child turns them up one at a time and tries to place them on your cards and "wins" if he or she gets all 4 on correctly.	Play a card game like the one described in the "Procedure" section only give each child 1 card to match to 1 of the 6 cards on the table or floor.

Criterion: When given at least 4 choices, the child matches pictures with 1, 2, 3, 4, 5, and 6 objects, making no errors, on 3 different days.

3.5

AREA: 2-II. Concepts: Size and number
BEHAVIOR: 2-IIi. Gives *one more*

Materials: Normal home or classroom environment

Procedure	Group activities
Use the terms *one* and *one more* when giving objects to the child (e.g., "You may have one cookie. Now you may have one more cookie.") or in other appropriate situations (e.g., "Let's put one more block on the tower."). Check the child's understanding by asking him or her to give you one block (or other object). When he or she has given you one, then ask for "one more." Then ask for "one more" when you have several. Always correct errors and immediately try the same instruction again to prompt a correct response.	There are many opportunities to use the term *one more* in a group setting (e.g., "I will give you one more"; "Let's sing one more song"). Check the child's understanding as described in the "Procedure" section.

Criterion: Child gives *one more* (and only one more) upon request on at least 5 occasions.

4

AREA: **2-II. Concepts: Size and number**
BEHAVIOR: 2-IIj. Counts up to 6 objects in a row

Materials: Those found in usual environments

Procedure	Group activities
Count objects frequently as you do activities with the child or as he or she accompanies you in your daily routines (e.g., "We need 6 forks. One, two, three, four, five, six. Count them with me: 1, 2, 3, 4, 5, 6."). Sing songs, read nursery rhymes or stories that involve counting (e.g., One little, two little, three little Indians . . .). Demonstrate counting objects 1 at a time in sequence. Help the child place his or her finger on the objects in sequence as he or she counts.	Do activities that are similar to the ones in the "Procedure" section. You may also look for art activities that involve counting (e.g., counting out 2 eyes to paste on a face, counting out 4 legs to paste on an oval to make a dog's body, counting out 6 legs to paste on an oval to make an insect). It is also useful to count the children at the table and then the number of cookies needed. Get the children to count together.

Criterion: The child can count 6 objects in a row when asked to do so on at least 5 different occasions.

4

AREA: **2-II. Concepts: Size and number**
BEHAVIOR: 2-IIk. Answers addition questions involving $+1$ up to 5

Materials: Any objects that can be manipulated and counted

Procedure	Group activities
Place out 2 objects and ask the child how many there are. Then place a third object and then say, "Now, how many are there?" Do this several times a day, with different numbers of objects (up to 5) as you are setting the table or doing other activities that involve counting out objects. Then begin asking questions without the objects present (e.g., "If you have 2 cookies and I give you 1 more, how many will you have?") If the child cannot answer the question, bring out concrete objects for him or her to count. Teach the child to use his or her fingers to help add one correctly.	Use the procedures described in the "Procedure" section asking different children in the group to respond. Use finger plays and songs that involve adding/subtracting 1 (e.g., One little blackbird sitting on a fence).

Criterion: The child correctly answers questions involving $2+1$, $3+1$, and $4+1$ on at least 5 different occasions.

4

AREA: **2-II. Concepts: Size and number**

BEHAVIOR: 2-III. Identifies (or correctly uses) *bigger* and *biggest, smaller* and *smallest, and larger* and *largest*

Materials: Objects or pictures that lend themselves to size comparisons

Procedure	Group activities
When you are playing with the child begin to use the terms *large* and *small* interchangeably with *big* and *little.* Make comments to emphasize the equivalence of the words. For example, "Look at that small mouse. He's really little!" Then begin to use instructions like, "There are 2 large blocks over there, bring me the bigger (or biggest) one." If you are unsure the child has a good grasp of the concepts, hold up 2 objects or pictures and say, "Which block is larger?" or "Which block is smaller?" If the child does not answer correctly, try using the terms *bigger* and *littler.* If he or she is correct with *bigger* and *littler,* say, "Yes, that one is bigger. It is the larger one." Again, emphasizing the equivalence of the terms.	1. Use instructions in construction or other activities that involve *bigger, larger, smaller,* and *littler.*
	2. Pass around a container of toys or pictures and ask each child to take out 2, 1 for each hand. Then go around the group having each child show the rest of the children his or her 2 toys and tell which one is *larger* and which is *smaller.* Correct errors. Then let the children compare their objects with those of the other children. Help them line them up from smallest to largest and you say, "See they get bigger, bigger, bigger, and this is the biggest" (touching each one as you talk). Have a child show how each one gets smaller; another show how they get larger, and so on.
Read stories to the child in which these terms are used. Stop in the story to point to the pictures or otherwise illustrate their meaning.	
Describe objects in the environment in these terms (e.g., "That is a big tree; that one is even bigger, and that one is the very biggest."; "That is a large house; this is a small house."). Help the child use the words by making comments like, "This is a small block, that one is even _____." (letting the child complete the sentence). Periodically test the child's understanding by asking him or her to give, show, or point to the larger (smaller, bigger) book (when there are 2), the largest (smallest, biggest) chair (when there are 3 or more).	

Criterion: The child correctly points to objects described by the adult as *bigger* and *biggest, smaller* and *smallest, larger* and *largest,* when asked on at least 3 occasions (for each word) or uses these terms correctly in conversation.

4

AREA: **2-II. Concepts: Size and number**
BEHAVIOR: 2-IIm. Counts 10 objects in a row

Materials: A normal household or classroom environment containing a variety of objects that can be easily manipulated and counted

Procedure	Group activities
Continue to count objects frequently as you do activities with the child or as he or she accompanies you in your daily routines (e.g., "We need 6 forks. One, two, three, four, five, six. Count them with me: 1, 2, 3, 4, 5, 6"; "How many fingers do you have? One, two, . . . ten."). Sing songs, read nursery rhymes or stories that involve counting (e.g., "One little, two little, three little Indians . . ."). If necessary, continue to prompt, counting objects one at a time in sequence.	Do activities that are similar to those described in the "Procedure" section. You may also look for art activities that involve counting (e.g., count out 8 colored circles to make balloons in a picture, count the children at the table and then the number of cookies needed). Get the children to count together.

Criterion: The child correctly counts 10 objects in a row without counting any object twice or skipping an object on at least 5 different occasions.

4.5

AREA: **2-II. Concepts: Size and number**
BEHAVIOR: 2-IIn. Understands *same number* and can sort a set into halves

Materials: Any objects that can be easily manipulated and counted

Procedure	Group activities
Use the idea of a fair division of materials to teach the child to sort a group of objects into halves and to understand *same number.* For example, bring out a plate of 4 cookies and say, "We are both going to have the same number of cookies." Count them out, "One for you and one for me, another one for you and another one for me. Now, how many cookies do you have? How many do I have? We both have 2, we have the same number." Then give the child 4 cookies (or blocks or other objects) and ask him or her to give the same number to him- or herself and to you. Help the child count them out loud. Once he or she is able to reliably divide 4, try it with 6 and then 8. Always correct errors and have the child repeat the activity when an error occurs.	With many children it works best to divide materials into pairs and let them practice as in the "Procedure" section after you have demonstrated the activity. You can also help generalize the skill by having a child pass out cookies or other snacks one at a time around the table until all are gone and then have each child count his or her own to see that all have the *same number* of cookies.

Criterion: The child correctly divides sets of 4, 6, and 8 objects into halves on at least 3 occasions.

4. 5

AREA: **2-II. Concepts: Size and number**
BEHAVIOR: 2-IIo. Identifies *penny, nickel,* and *dime* when named

Materials: Coins

Procedure	Group activities
Children are usually fascinated with money if they shop with their parents. When you go to the store, get out a church offering, or make other use of money, show the coins to the child and name them. Put loose change on the table and let him or her choose a *penny* for his or her bank or a *nickel* to take to the store. Let the child sort the *pennies, nickels,* and *dimes* into different containers. Correct errors and point out differences in size and color that help identify the coins.	Do a group lesson on money. Show the different coins and talk about the differences in size and color. Put a few coins on the table and let the children take turns identifying them and sorting them.

Criterion: The child can correctly select a penny, nickle, or dime when presented them on 3 or more occasions.

4.5   AREA: **2-II. Concepts: Size and number**
BEHAVIOR: 2-IIp. Counts correctly to 20

Materials: Normal home or classroom environment

Procedure	Group activities
Continue counting in daily activities and when reading books. After the child masters 10, work on 11 and 12; then 13, 14. Work up gradually and *always count objects as you count.* The child will have a difficult time understanding that each word stands for one more object unless this is reinforced regularly.	Count the children in the room and have them count along with you. They may have more fun (and a better understanding of numbers) if each child stands up when you point and say the number. You may also help counting by having the children count off the days of the month to the current date at the beginning of each day. You should be pointing to the spaces on the calendar as you count.

Criterion: The child counts correctly to 20 without help on 5 different occasions.

AREA:　**2-II. Concepts:　Size and number**
BEHAVIOR:　2-IIq. Matches 3-part sequences of pictures or objects depicting quantities up to 6

Materials:　Dice, playing cards, or other cards displaying different quantities with consistent configurations for each quantity

Procedure	Group activities
Place 3 cards or dice on the table. Give the child 6 items and ask him or her to take one just like yours. (Beside yours, *not* underneath it). If he or she chooses the correct cards but puts them in the wrong order, point out the order, correct it, give the child back the cards, and ask him or her to try again to make it just like yours. Then, let the child choose 2 cards to put together and you copy his or her pattern. Continue taking turns until you or the child is tired of the game. Try again later. If the child frequently reverses the order of the cards, it may help to create the sequences on sheets of paper with a colored heavy line on the lefthand side. Always place your first card next to the line and point out that it is next to the line. Help the child start by choosing "the card that goes next to the line, then the next one, and the next." The purpose of this item is to teach direction *and* sequence.	1.　It is hard for children this age to copy something held up in front of them. It is better to work with only a few children at a time, using the procedures in the section on the left. 2.　Prepare art projects where you have placed a sequence on the lefthand side of the paper and the child is given several cards and asked to reproduce the sequence on the righthand side, pasting it on when correctly done. 3.　It is also possible to divide the class into pairs and have them play a game where each of them attempts to match the sequence created by the other.

Criterion:　The child matches 4 or more sequences of 2 and 3 pictures or objects depicting quantity on 3 or more occasions.

5

AREA:　**2-II. Concepts:　Size and number**
BEHAVIOR:　2-IIr. Gives the correct number of objects when asked—all numbers from 4 to 10

Materials:　Any objects that can be easily manipulated and counted

Procedure	Group activities
As the child begins to count, ask him or her to give you particular quantities of the objects (e.g., "Please bring me 3 spoons."). If the child gives the wrong number help him or her count those that were brought and correct the error. Avoid saying, "That's wrong." or "I asked you for 3 and you brought me 4." Be sure that the child always ends up feeling successful.	Get the children to help count out materials for activities in the classroom. Count the number of children and then ask one child to bring you the same number of crayons and scissors. Correct errors.

Criterion:　The child gives 4, 5, 6, 7, 8, 9, and 10 objects when requested to do so. Must have success at least twice with each number.

AREA: **2-II. Concepts: Size and number**
BEHAVIOR: 2-IIs. Tells current age, how old he or she was last year, and
how old he or she will be next year

Materials: Normal home or classroom environment

Procedure	Group activities
Tell the child how old he or she is and encourage him or her to respond to the question, "How old are you?" both by saying the number and by holding up the correct number of fingers. Also, talk about how old the child's friends are. When birthdays come up, talk about being 1 year older, holding up another finger, and counting. Also, using the fingers, talk about how old he or she (or another child) was last year or before the birthday. Count birthday candles for siblings or friends, and emphasize the age last year, this year, and next year. Prompt friends to ask the child these questions about his or her age.	1. This concept is often easier to learn in a group where birthdays occur more frequently. Talk about age as in the "Procedure" section. Ask the children not only about their own ages and how old they will be next birthday, but ask them about their friends as well. Use birthday candles to help teach the concept when a child has a birthday. 2. On birthdays, the children may do art projects in which they glue on strips of paper indicating the correct number of candles now, last year, and next year.

Criterion: The child correctly tells current age, how old he or she was last year, and how old he or she will be next year on 3 different occasions.

5

AREA: **2-II. Concepts: Size and number**
BEHAVIOR: 2-IIt. Answers addition questions involving + 2 up to 10

Materials: Any objects that can be manipulated and counted

Procedure	Group activities
As you go about household routines or conduct special play/teaching sessions, place several objects out and ask the child to count them. Then, either place 2 more or ask the child to place 2 more. Then ask him or her how many there are. If the child does not know or answers incorrectly, ask him or her to count. Then begin asking questions without the objects present (e.g., "If you have 2 cookies and I give you 2 more, how many will you have?") Whenever the child cannot answer the question, bring out concrete objects for him or her to count. Also, show the child how to "count up" on his or her fingers (e.g., hold up 5 fingers and count them—1, 2, 3, 4, and 5), raise up 2 more, and continue the count (e.g., 6 and 7).	Use the procedures described to the left asking different children in the group to respond.

Criterion: The child correctly answers questions involving $2+2$, $3+2$, $4+2$, $5+2$, $6+2$, $7+2$, and $8+2$ on at least 5 different occasions.

5

AREA: **2-II. Concepts: Size and number**

BEHAVIOR: 2-IIu. Recognizes repeating pattern in a sequence and can continue it

Materials: Several decks of playing cards, different colored blocks, pictures of geometric forms, pictures that have the same form but in different colors—anything that will allow the building of repeating sequences

Procedure	Group activities
Talk about making patterns. Show the child a simple pattern (e.g., ace, jack, ace, jack). Then say aloud, "Ace, jack, ace, jack. What should come next?" If he or she does not know, say the sequence again and then say, "You see it is an ace. Every time there is a jack, an ace is next." Make another pattern involving just 2 choices. Then let the child make a pattern. Continue the activity by making a pattern based on 3 cards. The patterns can be just color (e.g., red, blue, green, red, blue, green) or both color and shape (e.g., red circle, blue square, blue triangle). Vary the materials you use (e.g., blocks, cards, silverware) to create greater interest for the child.	Follow the procedure to the left in a group, having the group guess which card, block, or other object comes next. Let the children take turns making patterns and having the other children guess what comes next.

Criterion: The child continues a pattern in a 3-part sequence, through all 3 parts, using at least 3 different materials.

3.

Symbolic Play

FROM VERY SIMPLE imitation of adult activities at age 2 to complex play involving other actors at age 5, this progression of pretend play activities is critical for the development of cognitive, language, and social skills. Such play helps a child develop ideas about objects and events that are not immediately present and allows for the exploration of possible consequences of actions.

Caregivers should encourage pretend play by engaging in such play with the child at an early age (e.g., by pretending to drink from an empty cup, saying, "Ooh, that was good milk"). Later, encouragement can be in the form of providing materials to encourage play, being willing to be one of the "actors" in the child's play, and, most important, being interested in the child's play. This sequence attempts to give somewhat more specific suggestions for helping the child move from one stage of pretend or symbolic play to the next. As in most other learning activities, one will be most successful when following the child's lead in the play.

Special attention should be given to the symbolic play of a youngster with severe physical limitations. He or she will often need adults to act out roles for him or her. Get the child involved by having him or her make decisions about the play. For example, get out the puppets and have the child tell you how the characters should behave. You move the puppet and let the child talk for it. If the child has limited speaking ability, ask questions such as, "Is this a nice wolf or a mean wolf?" or "Is he going to try to catch the bird?"

3. Symbolic Play

a. Engages in adult role-playing (e.g., cooks, hammers, talks on play telephone)

b. Pretends that objects are something other than what they are (e.g., blocks are food)

c. Assumes different roles in playing house or other activities

d. Represents more complex events in play (e.g., plays doctor with a doll or animal, goes shopping using a baby carriage or wagon as a shopping cart)

e. Pretend play includes a 3–4-part logical sequence that evolves as play proceeds

f. Uses materials to construct other objects

g. Uses dolls, stuffed animals, or puppets as participants in play—gives dialogue to them

h. Describes own activities during play

i. Builds large structures from blocks or chairs and centers play around them

j. Involves others in pretend play—discusses roles

k. Uses toy animals or dolls to act out "what would happen if"

l. Engages in complex adult role-playing (e.g., plays house with other children, solving problems as adults would solve them)

2. 5

AREA: **3. Symbolic Play**

BEHAVIOR: 3a. Engages in adult role-playing
(e.g., cooks, hammers, talks on play telephone)

Materials: Normal home or classroom environment

Procedure	Group activities
Allow the child to be with you and other members of the family when they are busy with activities. Let the child play with adult materials that are safe or small toy replicas of those materials (e.g., tools, pots, pans, dishes, play telephones). If he or she does not automatically imitate what others in the environment do with these materials, encourage him or her to do so by demonstrating an activity, and then handing him or her the materials to imitate you (e.g., pretend to pour something from a bottle into a pan, bang a toy hammer on a piece of wood, talk on the telephone).	Furnish classroom centers with materials that will encourage adult role-playing. Talk to parents about their activities so that materials can be included that will stimulate each child. For example, if some fathers carry briefcases to work and some carry lunch boxes, both should be included in the centers.

Criterion: The child is observed to play adult roles with toys on at least 3 occasions.

2. 5

AREA: **3. Symbolic Play**

BEHAVIOR: 3b. Pretends that objects are something other than what they are
(e.g., blocks are food)

Materials: Normal home or classroom environment

Procedure	Group activities
Play *pretend* with the child (e.g., pretend to feed a doll, to fight a fire with the toy fire truck, to eat Play Doh cakes). Respond to his or her pretend games as well. If the child presents you with a mud pie, pretend to eat it. If the child puts his or her legs over a broom or over a push toy with a long handle, ask the child if he or she is riding a horse.	Provide simple materials that will encourage pretend play. When the children are playing with Play Doh, engage them in making "hamburgers" and "eating" them. Build block structures yourself and label them as houses, animals, and so forth.

Criterion: The child demonstrates pretending that an object is something else on at least three occasions.

AREA: **3. Symbolic Play**

BEHAVIOR: 3c. Assumes different roles in playing house or other activities

Materials: Normal home or classroom environment

Procedure	Group activities
When you play with the child, model taking different roles. For example, you can pretend to be the baby and have the child "feed you" or otherwise take care of you. You can also suggest a different role for the child (e.g., "Let's pretend you're Daddy and you're going off to work. What do you need?").	Provide a variety of materials in the center of the classroom arranged for dramatic play or housekeeping. Model role-playing if necessary, but the children will probably model it for one another. Place the child who is doing little role-playing with other children who are doing a lot of it.

Criterion: Child assumes at least 3 different roles in play. This may be done spontaneously or in response to a suggestion from someone else, but the child must indicate some understanding of the 3 roles by the use of different props or by different behaviors (e.g., sucking a bottle or crying for baby, putting on a hat for daddy, using a stethoscope for doctor).

3

AREA: **3. Symbolic Play**

BEHAVIOR: 3d. Represents more complex events in play (e.g., plays doctor with a doll or animal, goes shopping using a baby carriage or wagon as a shopping cart)

Materials: Dolls, stuffed animals, wagons or other wheel toys, empty or full cans or boxes of food, or pots and pans

Procedure	Group activities
Encourage complex fantasy play by modeling this kind of play for the child and by participating with the child if he or she tries to involve you (e.g., take the role of the storekeeper if the child comes and says he or she is shopping). Occasionally make suggestions without actually structuring the play for the child (e.g., "This bear has hurt its leg. It needs a doctor."; "I see you have your wagon. Are you going shopping today?").	1. Provide a center for fantasy play that is equipped with various dress-up clothes, food containers, pots and pans, wheel toys, or play money. Encourage a mixture of children with different levels of fantasy to play in the center. Observe the play to determine how different children are progressing.
	2. Use circle time occasionally to tell (not read) a story that you can *act out* for the children and *model* fantasy play. For example, you could tell the story of *The Three Bears* using different voices and pantomiming the actions for the different characters.

Criterion: The child spontaneously represents complex events in fantasy play on three occasions.

3.5

AREA: **3. Symbolic Play**
BEHAVIOR: 3e. Pretend play includes a 3–4-part logical sequence that evolves as play
proceeds

Materials: Dolls, stuffed animals, wagons or other wheel toys, empty or full cans or boxes of food,
pots and pans, real or play tools

Procedure	Group activities
Proceed as in item 3d. Also, make a point of talking about sequence in your daily activities when the child is watching (e.g., "First we get the pan hot and then we put in the egg. We turn it over when is done on that side and then we put it on the plate.").	Proceed as in item 3d.

Criterion: The child demonstrates a 3–4-part logical sequence in fantasy play on at least 3 occasions.

3.5

AREA: **3. Symbolic Play**
BEHAVIOR: 3f. Uses materials to construct other objects

Materials: Blocks, scraps of cloth, boxes, lids, plastic containers, empty spools

Procedure	Group activities
Give the child time to play with materials that lend themselves to construction activity. Do not interfere with the way he or she uses these materials, but observe and talk to the child about what he or she is doing (e.g., "What are you making? You're stacking them up high. Is that a tower?"). Occasionally play along side the child and create *simple* objects yourself (e.g., a snake from pop beads, a house of blocks or boxes, a car of spools and a box).	Have a center that includes construction materials. Proceed as in the "Procedure" section. Occasionally ask children to tell you or the other children about what they have constructed.

Criterion: The child uses materials to construct other objects and communicates what the object is. Communication may be verbal or through actions (e.g., hooking 2 boxes together and pushing them saying, "Choo, choo").

AREA: **3. Symbolic Play**

BEHAVIOR: 3g. Uses dolls, stuffed animals, or puppets as participants in play—gives dialogue to them

Materials: Dolls, stuffed animals, or puppets

Procedure	Group activities
Model these behaviors for the child by playing with him or her using puppets or dolls. Talk for the characters. This is a good way to prepare a child for an activity. For example, if the child is going to the doctor, you might have one puppet or doll be a doctor and another a little girl. The little girl is scared but the doctor is nice and she lets the doctor listen to her heart and look in her ears. The doctor tells her what a good girl she is and her mommy is proud of her. Observe and listen to the child as he or she plays. If the child continues to play without dialogue or uses only one character (e.g., doll, animal) in play, occasionally join the play with another toy and introduce dialogue and a different role.	1. Maintain a dramatic play area and mix the fantasy play ability levels of the children who are in it together. Observe each child to determine their progress. 2. Do circle activities as in item 3d.

Criterion: The child gives dialogue and/or different roles to stuffed dolls, animals, or puppets in play on at least 3 occasions.

AREA: **3. Symbolic Play**

BEHAVIOR: 3h. Describes own activities during play

Materials: Normal home or classroom environment

Procedure	Group activities
Listen to the child. If the child does not describe his or her own activities either to himself or to you, encourage this by commenting on them yourself (e.g., "It looks like that truck is carrying a big load."), by asking questions about what he or she is doing (e.g., "Where is the truck going with such a big load?"), and by modeling this behavior during your own activities (e.g., "Let's see, I think I'll dig all the holes before I put the flowers in.").	Describe activities for groups of children as in the "Procedure" section.

Criterion: The child spontaneously describes his or her own activities during play on at least 3 occasions (not in response to questions).

AREA: **3. Symbolic Play**

BEHAVIOR: 3i. Builds large structures from blocks or chairs and centers play around them

Materials: Normal home or classroom environment

Procedure	Group activities
Demonstrate to the child how you can build a "play house" or a "private place." Make a room or a garage from a few old towels or sheets draped over chairs or a table, or simply arrange chairs to separate spaces. Let the child play with what you have created and change it as he or she wishes. If limited space is available, set aside special times (e.g., rainy days) when you bring out materials that will encourage this kind of activity. If the child does not readily respond, you may suggest some play activities (e.g., "This is the doll's house and this is your house. Maybe you can go and visit and have some cookies.").	Plan a group activity where the children use furniture or blocks to construct a road, a train, or separate rooms. Allow and encourage this kind of activity during free play.

Criterion: The child builds large structures and centers play around them without adult suggestion.

4.5

AREA: **3. Symbolic Play**

BEHAVIOR: 3j. Involves others in pretend play—discusses roles

Materials: Normal home or classroom environment

Procedure	Group activities
Model this behavior in your play with the child. For example, suggest that you will be the baby and the child will be the parent and then say, "Am I going to be a crying baby or a happy baby?" Respond to any efforts of the child to involve you in his or her pretend play. Sometimes play a role in an unexpected way to see if he or she will correct you and tell you the way you should play the role.	Observe the children as they play together in the housekeeping or dramatic play areas of the classroom. Encourage them to discuss roles if they do not do it spontaneously by asking questions.

Criterion: The child involves others in pretend play and discusses roles with them on at least 3 occasions (The child may initiate the involvement or just respond to others' requests to join him or her.).

AREA: **3. Symbolic Play**

BEHAVIOR: 3k. Uses toy animals or dolls to act out "what would happen if"

Materials: Toy animals, dolls, and/or puppets

Procedure	Group activities
Encourage this behavior for the child by playing with 2 dolls, puppets, or animals and having an event occur that requires some action (e.g., one doll falls and scrapes its knee). Ask the child what will happen next (e.g., "Oh dear, the doll scraped its knee. What is it going to do?"). Act out what the child tells you or give him or her the doll to act it out. If the child does not tell you or act out the part, suggest what might happen and act it out.	Encourage this behavior as in the "Procedure" section.
Observe the child carefully while playing alone or with other children to determine if he or she is beginning to use fantasy play to act out solutions to problems or to consider different outcomes for a situation.	

Criterion: The child uses dolls or toys to act out "what would happen if" on at least 3 occasions.

AREA: **3. Symbolic Play**

BEHAVIOR: 3l. Engages in complex adult role-playing (e.g., plays house with other children, solving problems as adults would solve them)

Materials: Normal home or classroom environment

Procedure	Group activities
Model this behavior for the child as you engage in fantasy play with him or her. That is, assume different roles, suggest problems, and try to get the child to act out solutions to the problems. Be sure the child has opportunities to play and practice these behaviors with other children.	Provide many opportunities for fantasy play in the classroom.

Criterion: The child engages in complex adult role-playing with adults or other children on at least 3 occasions.

Reasoning

4.

THE ABILITY TO REASON depends on a person's ability to make observations about the world, draw conclusions based on those observations, and then predict future events based on his or her experiences and knowledge. The foundations of adult reasoning skills are laid in early childhood, primarily in the child's attempt to make sense out of the world in which he or she lives. It is important that the adult encourage the child to think about the world, to notice when events follow a particular pattern, and to predict what will happen next. It is also important for the adult to recognize the limitations in the child's understanding. The preschool child is influenced far more by what he or she sees, hears, and feels than by adult logic. If a snake made from Play-Doh looks bigger than a Play-Doh ball, it *is* bigger, regardless of how many times an adult shows that it is the same piece of Play-Doh, just in a different shape. The role of the adult is not to convince, but to help the child explore, experiment, draw his or her own conclusions, and change those conclusions as he or she is confronted with new experiences.

The purpose of this sequence is to help the child become aware of his or her world, to be curious, to be able to discuss perceptions and conclusions with adults, and to develop both confidence and pleasure in his or her efforts to understand.

Children with special handicapping conditions may have to be taught to demonstrate their reasoning skills in different ways than those included in the items of this sequence. The teacher may have to be creative in modifying items to accommodate the child's disabilities. For example, it may be necessary to use identifying responses (e.g., pointing, eye gaze) instead of verbal responses and object manipulation for a child who cannot talk or pick up and manipulate objects.

4. Reasoning

a. Experiments with cause and effect in play

b. Answers at least 1 "why do" question correctly (e.g., "Why do we have [or use] stoves?"; "Why do we use umbrellas?")

c. Identifies *silly* or *wrong* pictures or events

d. Answers 2 or more "what do you do when" questions (e.g., hungry, tired, thirsty)

e. Describes simple absurdities seen in

pictures or in real life (e.g., an adult sucking his or her thumb, going to bed with clothes on)

f. Responds appropriately to "tell me how" or "how do you" questions (e.g., "Tell me how [how do] you make a sandwich?")

g. Describes what "will happen next"

h. Finds "one to go with this" (e.g., nail with hammer, thread with needle, shoe with sock)

i. Reasons about experiences and asks and answers questions (e.g., "Why can't I . . . ?"; "What will happen if . . . ?"; "Why doesn't it . . . ?"; "Why did ____ do ____?")

j. Reasons about future events (e.g., "If ____ happens, I will . . . ")

AREA: **4. Reasoning**

3

BEHAVIOR: 4a. Experiments with cause and effect in play

Materials: Normal home or classroom environment

Procedure	Group activities
Make it clear to the child that you are interested in how everything works (e.g., when giving the child a bath, show him or her how heavy toys sink to the bottom of the tub and how light ones float; show him or her how cars and trucks stay still on a level surface but go down when the surface is tilted). Then observe the child when he or she is playing alone or with other children. Watch for activities that indicate that he or she is experimenting with the ideas that you have shared with him or her or is experimenting on his or her own (e.g., The child may put a car in a paper tube, pick up the tube and the car rolls out. Then, the child does it several times again, watching for the car to come out or, perhaps, blocking the end to prevent it from coming out.).	1. Have the children collect rocks, sticks, or leaves when out walking. Put them, one-by-one, in a tub of water to see what floats and what sinks. 2. Bring household gadgets to school to show how they work (e.g., an old-fashioned egg beater that will make bubbles in the water if a little soap is added). 3. Provide a lot of materials for free play that will lend themselves to experimentation (e.g., blocks, cars, paper tubes, containers of different sizes).

Criterion: On at least 3 occasions, the child is observed to experiment with some materials or objects, apparently trying to understand how they work.

3

AREA: **4. Reasoning**

BEHAVIOR: 4b. Answers at least 1 "why do" question correctly (e.g., "Why do we have [or use] stoves?"; "Why do we use umbrellas?")

Materials: Normal home or classroom environment

Procedure	Group activities
Talk about why you do different chores in your daily routine and why it is important for the child to do chores or to wash his or her hands. Provide reasons for many of the requests you make of the child (e.g.,"You need to put on your boots to keep your feet dry. It is cold and wet out there."). When the child begins to ask "why?" provide an answer. Occasionally ask questions that you will answer in order to model appropriate responses (e.g., "Why do we drink our milk? Because we want to get big and strong."). Then, gradually begin to ask the child "why" and "why do" questions. *Do not* focus on a child's motives when asking these questions. That is, don't ask the child, "Why do you hit your sister?" or	1. A discussion of classroom safety rules provides a good opportunity to practice "why" and "why do" questions. Always give a reason for a rule and then ask the group questions such as, "Now, who can tell me why we wash our hands before lunch?" 2. When reading stories to the group, stop and ask "why" and "why do" or "why did" questions.

(continued)

Procedure	Group activities
"Why do you color on the walls?" Children of this age have little understanding of their motives. In this item, trying to assess their understanding of the world around them is more important.	

Criterion: The child correctly answers 3 or more "why" or "why do" questions.

3.5

AREA: **4. Reasoning**

BEHAVIOR: 4c. Identifies *silly* or *wrong* pictures or events

Materials: A collection of toys, books with pictures of funny or unusual events (e.g., Dr. Suess books), normal household or classroom objects

Procedure	Group activities
Laugh often with the child. When you make mistakes that create spills or have other obvious consequences, point them out to the child, saying something like, "Mommy was silly. She wasn't watching what she was doing and made a big mess!" At other times deliberately do something *wrong* or *silly* (e.g., give the child his or her plate upside down and act as if you are going to put food on it; start to put the child's coat, bib, or other clothing on yourself). If the child notices and either fixes the error or laughs, say something like, "Oops, Mommy was silly. She . . . ." (identifying the silly act). Talk about pictures in books as you read them, trying to identify unexpected or *silly* occurrences (The Dr. Suess books give many opportunities for this). Also, describe the child's mistakes as silly (e.g., "You're being silly to try to put that great big block in that little hole."). If you have made it clear to the child that you also make mistakes and can laugh about them, he or she will be able to accept his or her own errors and laugh about them, too. The child will also be more aware of what he or she is seeing and doing and will be able to think better about the way in which activities should be done.	1. Bring humor into the classroom so that the children can laugh about their own and others' mistakes. 2. Play a game with a small group of children in which you ask them to "fix what is *wrong* or *silly*." Collect a group of toys and present 2 or 3 at a time, doing something unusual with each toy. Ask who can fix it or make it right. For example, you might hold a baby doll in your arm as if to feed but then suck on the bottle yourself; or you might put a toy cow in the front seat of a truck and a man in the back. 3. When you are reading books, talk about *silly* or unusual events that you see.

Criterion: The child identifies *silly* or *wrong* pictures or events on at least 5 occasions. Identification may be in the form of pointing and laughing, fixing what is wrong, or talking about it (if good descriptions are offered, pass the child on item 4e).

AREA: **4. Reasoning**

BEHAVIOR: 4d. Answers 2 or more "what do you do when" questions
(e.g., hungry, tired, thirsty)

Materials: None

Procedure	Group activities
Talk frequently to the child about how you feel and why you do the actions that you do (e.g., you're tired, so you rest; you're hungry, so you eat). Use the same terms when talking about the child's needs and actions (e.g., instead of asking the child, "Do you want some water?" ask, "Are you thirsty?"). Ask the child "what do you do" questions within the context of daily activities. For example, ask the child, "Are you hungry?" and when he or she replies, "Yes," say, "Well, now, what do we do when we're hungry?" If you get no response, say, "I think we eat something. Would you like a cracker?"	1. Several times a week have a short period during circle time in which you talk about a feeling or experience and what one does about it. For example, one day talk about being hungry—what it feels like, what everyone in the group likes to eat. You might also bring some different foods in for the children to taste or bring in various foods that animals eat (e.g., oats, grass, sunflower seeds) and let the children feel and/or taste them. 2. At the next circle time, you can say, "Yesterday we talked about being hungry. Who can tell me what we do when we are hungry?" After several children answer say, "Today we're going to talk about being thirsty. What does it feel like to be thirsty?"

Criterion: The child answers 2 or more "what do you do when" questions. Each question should be answered 2 times, on different days.

AREA: **4. Reasoning**

BEHAVIOR: 4e. Describes simple absurdities seen in pictures or in real life
(e.g., an adult sucking his or her thumb, going to bed with clothes on)

Materials: A collection of toys, books with pictures of funny or unusual events (e.g., Dr. Suess books), normal household or classroom objects

Procedure	Group activities
Proceed as in item 4c. However, for this item, have the child verbalize what is *wrong* or *silly*.	Play a "Guess what's silly" game. Collect a few toys and sit with the children in a circle. Do something unusual with the toys and ask the children to guess what is *silly* (e.g., stand a doll on its head in a doll chair, turn a wagon upside down and load toys on it to pull, build a "Mr. Potato Head" with feet on the top of his head). After a child tells you what is wrong, let him or her fix it.

Criterion: The child tells what is *silly* or *wrong* in 3 or more pictures or events.

AREA: **4. Reasoning**

BEHAVIOR: 4f. Responds appropriately to "tell me how" or "how do you" questions
(e.g., "Tell me how [How do] you make a sandwich?")

Materials: Normal home or classroom environment

Procedure	Group activities
Show the child how you do certain activities and talk to him or her about those activities (e.g., "I'll make you a sandwich. First we'll get the bread. Then we'll spread the mayonnaise on, like this. Then we'll put on some cheese. Put this piece of bread on top of that one, and there it is!") Allow the child to help and participate whenever possible. Another time say, "I'm going to make you a sandwich. Now, you tell me what to do. What do I do first?" Do it exactly as the child tells you so that he or she will know when something was left out.	There will be many opportunities in a group setting to demonstrate and talk about "how to do" art projects or other activities. Occasionally give the instruction to one child, let him or her complete the project, and then tell another child how to do it as you listen and clarify if necessary.

Criterion: The child responds appropriately to 3 or more "tell me how to" requests. It is not necessary that the child be able to describe every step correctly, but that the general idea is clear.

4.5   AREA: **4. Reasoning**

BEHAVIOR: 4g. Describes what "will happen next"

Materials: Story books or pictures

Procedure	Group activities
When reading to the child, stop midway in the story and ask, "What do you think will happen next?" If he or she cannot respond, you suggest a couple options and see which the child thinks might happen. Try to choose some very outlandish possibility and one more in keeping with the story to see if the child is really understanding the story. Look for pictures in magazines or books where something is happening that lends itself to asking, "What will happen next?" (e.g., a child falling down in a mud puddle, people walking in the rain, a man getting into a car). If the child does not answer you tell what you think might happen next.	Do the activities in the "Procedure" section in a small group.

Criterion: The child responds appropriately to "What will happen next?" at least 5 times. The answers should be logically related to the pictures or to the story, although they may not be accurate for the story or what you would propose for the pictures.

4.5

AREA: 4. Reasoning
BEHAVIOR: 4h. Finds "one to go with this" (e.g., nail with hammer,
thread with needle, shoe with sock)

Materials: Normal home or classroom environment

Procedure	Group activities
Talk about your activities as you do them with the child. Make a point of showing the child how certain actions are used together. Ask the child to bring you the thread when you are sewing or a nail when you are hammering. Occasionally place 3 or 4 objects out and say to the child, "I'm going to use this (e.g., the hammer). What else do I need?"	Bring a collection of tools and other objects from home if they are not available in the classroom. Pass one out to each child and see if they can tell what it is. If not, see if the other children can identify it. Then, put out a pile of objects that would logically go with those items you distributed and ask the children to find the ones that go with what they are holding (e.g., screwdriver and screw, hammer and nail, jar and lid, shoe and sock, canned food and can opener, needle and thread, pin and pincushion, paperclip and paper, fork and plate).

Criterion: The child can find "the one that goes with this" out of a group of 4 choices. He or she must be able to do this with 5 different objects.

4.5

AREA: 4. Reasoning
BEHAVIOR: 4i. Reasons about experiences and asks and answers questions
(e.g., "Why can't I . . . ?", "What will happen if . . . ?",
"Why doesn't it . . . ?", "Why did ____ do ____?")

Materials: None

Procedure	Group activities
The best way to teach a child to reason about their experiences is to talk about your experiences and those of the child. Ask yourself questions out loud (e.g., "What will happen if I put this banana in the freezer?"), answer the question (e.g., "I think it might get really hard, but taste good."), and then, if appropriate, test out your answer, showing the child. Give the child reasons for the decisions you make (e.g., "You can't do that because. . . . ") and explain why events happen in a particular way (e.g., "The sack broke because it was too full and heavy."). Listen to and answer the child's questions!	1. Always give reasons for rules and decisions within the classroom. 2. Encourage the children to bring objects of interest to class to share with the other children. Collect materials yourself to bring, looking particularly for ones that will promote a discussion about how items work or the ways in which animals behave. For example, a bird nest could lead to a discussion of how the eggs are protected and kept warm so they can hatch, why the nest needs to be up high away from predators, and so forth.

(continued)

Procedure	Group activities
	As items are brought to the group to share, ask a lot of questions to try to get the children to give their perceptions and reasons before you share with them what you know.

Criterion: The child demonstrates reasoning about his or her experiences by either asking or answering questions on at least 5 different occasions.

5

AREA: **4. Reasoning**

BEHAVIOR: 4j. Reasons about future events (e.g., "If ____ happens, I will . . . ")

Materials: Normal home or classroom environment

Procedure	Group activities
This is an extension of item 4i. The difference is that the child is able to reason not only about what has happened, but what might happen in the future. Promote this as in item 4i. Give the child opportunities to experiment with the environment. Let him or her mix colors of water paint to see what new colors are made, let him or her help in household chores, talk about these experiences, and, on the basis of what happened in one situation, ask him or her to guess what will happen in another (e.g., "If you fill that sack too full, what might happen when we try to carry it?").	Prepare a science center in the room with objects you collect. Help the children do simple experiments (e.g., Fill a glass with water and then try placing different objects in it to see what will make it overflow. Ask the children to anticipate what will happen before each object is tried. Also, ask them to give reasons for their answers.).

Criterion: The child demonstrates reasoning about future events on at least 5 occasions by appropriately answering questions such as, "What will happen if . . . ?" or "What will you do if . . . ?"

5-I.

Visual Perception: Block designs

Thesе visual perception activities require children to interpret and organize information about form and space. The development of these skills provides a foundation for the later development of academic skills such as math, reading, and writing. The visual perception section in divided into two components: block designs and puzzles and matching skills.

Due to the heavy emphasis on visual information, these activities are generally not appropriate for children with significant visual impairments. Some of the activities can be modified to depend on tactile cues rather than visual ones. For instance, the blocks of a block design can be glued together for a child with a visual impairment to feel and then replicate.

Children with poor motor coordination may have difficulty with the motor aspects of some of these tasks. Sometimes tasks can be modified to accommodate poor motor control (e.g., use larger blocks, Velcro, or bristle blocks for block design activities).

5. Visual Perception
I. Block designs

a. Imitates block train
b. Imitates block building
c. Imitates block bridge
d. Copies horizontal bridge
e. Imitates 5-block gate

f. Copies horizontal block patterns (Group 1)
g. Copies horizontal block patterns (Group 2)

AREA: **5-I. Visual Perception: Block designs**
BEHAVIOR: 5-Ia. Imitates block train

3

Materials: 1-inch blocks

Procedure	Group activities
Place 10 blocks on table in front of a child. Tell the child that you are going to make a train. Align 4 of the blocks and place a fifth block on top of the first block. Push your *train* along the table while making a train sound. Then ask the child to use the rest of the blocks to make a train like yours. Leave your train in sight, but out of reach. Demonstrate this activity several times and give physical assistance if necessary.	1. Read a story about trains. Then place some blocks on a table and encourage the children to make a train. Note that trains can be made of different lengths. Ask the children to make either a big or small one. 2. Encourage the children to use large wooden or cardboard blocks to make trains, as well as other vehicles.

Criterion: The child imitates a block train.

AREA: **5-I. Visual Perception: Block designs**
BEHAVIOR: 5-Ib. Imitates block building

3

Materials: 1-inch blocks

Procedure	Group activities
Place 10 blocks on a table in front of a child. Tell the child that you are going to make a building. Align 4 of the blocks and place a fifth block on top of the second block. Then ask the child to use the rest of the blocks to make a building like yours. Leave your *building* in sight, but out of reach. Demonstrate the activity several times and give physical assistance if necessary.	Encourage the children to use blocks of various shapes and sizes to make buildings that include both horizontal and vertical parts.

Criterion: The child imitates a block building.

3

AREA: **5-I. Visual Perception: Block designs**
BEHAVIOR: 5-Ic. Imitates block bridge

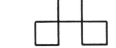

Materials: 1-inch blocks

Procedure	Group activities
Place blocks on the table in front of the child. Tell the child that you are going to make a bridge. Place 2 blocks on the table with a small space between them. Place a third block on top of the 2 blocks, forming a bridge. With a pencil, demonstrate going *under the bridge* to draw the child's attention to the open gap. Then ask the child to make a bridge like yours. Leave your bridge in sight, but out of reach. Remind the child that a car needs to be able to pass under the bridge, so he or she should leave a space between the bottom 2 blocks. Demonstrate this activity several times and give physical assistance if necessary.	Help the children build a network of roads and bridges with large wooden blocks for small cars to drive on, over, and under.

Criterion: The child imitates a 3-block bridge.

AREA: **5-I. Visual Perception: Block designs**
BEHAVIOR: 5-Id. Copies horizontal bridge

3.5

Materials: 1-inch blocks

Procedure	Group activities
Place blocks on a table in front of a child. Out of the child's view, build a bridge design horizontally (e.g., flat) on the table. Then show the design to the child and ask him or her to make one like yours. If the child is not successful, demonstrate how to make the design. If needed, draw the design on paper, and ask the child to make the design by placing the blocks directly on the paper. Then, see if he or she can build the design off the paper. On a different occasion, again present a completed design and see if he or she can copy the design without further assistance.	Do the same activity as in the "Procedure" section.

Criterion: The child correctly copies a horizontal bridge.

AREA: 5-I. Visual Perception: Block designs
BEHAVIOR: 5-Ie. Imitates 5-block gate

4.5

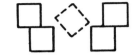

Materials: Ten 1-inch blocks

Procedure	Group activities
Place blocks on a table in front of a child. Tell the child that you are going to make a gate. Place 2 blocks on the table with a small space between them. Place a single block on top of each of these blocks, setting the blocks off to each side, leaving a wider gap at the top. Turn the fifth block on edge and balance it in the gap, resting on the initial 2 blocks. This can be a difficult design to achieve since blocks often slide when attempting to balance one on an angle, or since children accidentally knock over parts with their hand while building. Use wooden blocks and a building surface that is not slick to offer the best opportunity for success. Ask the child to build a gate like yours. If the child still has difficulty, try stabilizing the first 2 blocks for him or her, while he or she completes the design.	Do the same activity as in the "Procedure" section with a group.

Criterion: The child imitates a 5-block gate.

AREA: 5-I. Visual Perception: Block designs
BEHAVIOR: 5-If. Copies horizontal block patterns (Group 1)

4.5

Materials: 1-inch blocks

Procedure	Group activities
Place blocks on a table in front of a child. Out of the child's view, build your first design horizontally (e.g., flat) on the table. Then show the design to the child and ask him or her to make one like yours. If the child is not successful, then demonstrate how to make the design. If needed, draw the design on paper, and ask him or her to make it by placing blocks directly on the paper. Then, see if he or she can build the design off the paper. On a different occasion,	Do the same activity as in the "Procedure" section with a group.

(continued)

Procedure	Group activities
again present the completed design and see if the child can copy it without further assistance. Repeat this procedure with a second design.	

Criterion: The child correctly copies horizontal block patterns (Group 1).

5

AREA: **5-I. Visual Perception: Block designs**
BEHAVIOR: 5-Ig. Copies horizontal block patterns (Group 2)

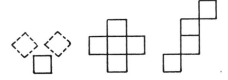

Materials: 1-inch blocks

Procedure	Group activities
Place blocks on a table in front of a child. Out of child's view, build your first design horizontally (e.g., flat) on the table. Then show the design to the child and ask him or her to make one like yours. If the child is not successful, demonstrate how to make the design. If needed, draw the design on the paper, and ask him or her to make it by placing the blocks directly on the paper. Then, see if the child can build the design off the paper. On a different occasion, again present your completed design and see if he or she can copy it without further assistance. Repeat this procedure with a second and third design.	Do the same activity as in the "Procedure" section with a group.

Criterion: The child correctly copies horizontal block patterns.

5-II.

Visual Perception:
Puzzles and matching

5. Visual Perception
II. Puzzles and matching

a. Places *round*, *square*, and *triangular* forms in form board (same orientation)
b. Places *round*, *square*, and *triangular* forms in reversed form board
c. Puts together two kinds of 2-piece puzzles
d. Puts together a puzzle with 4 or 5 interconnected pieces
e. Matches geometric forms (orientation irrelevant)

f. Matches at least 8 geometric shapes
g. Completes 8–10-piece interconnected puzzles
h. Imitates construction of a simple visual pattern using parquetry blocks
i. Completes a 12–20+ piece interconnected puzzle
j. Matches letters and numbers
k. Matches name and short words

2.5   AREA: **5-II. Visual Perception: Puzzles and matching**
       BEHAVIOR: 5-IIa. Places *round*, *square*, and *triangular* forms
                   in form board (same orientation)

Materials: A form board that has *round*, *square*, and *triangular* cutouts, along with shapes that fit
into these spaces

Procedure	Group activities
Present form board to a child with various shapes in place. Remove the shapes one at a time and place them on a table directly below the matching opening in the form board. Ask the child to put the shapes back into the puzzle (i.e., form board). If the child has difficulty in doing this, demonstrate it for him or her. If the child is still not successful, cover all openings except the circle and give the child only that shape to put in place. Give the child physical assistance if necessary, then gradually fade your help. When the child is successful, give him or her both the circle and the square to place. When the child can consistently place 2 shapes into the puzzle, add the triangle.	Do the same activity as in the "Procedure" section with a group.

Criterion: The child places *round*, *square*, and *triangular* forms in their correct hole.

2.5   AREA: **5-II. Visual Perception: Puzzles and matching**
       BEHAVIOR: 5-IIb. Places *round*, *square*, and *triangular* forms in reversed form board

Materials: A form board that has *round*, *square*, and *triangular* cutouts, along with shapes that fit
into these spaces

Procedure	Group activities
Present a child a form board with various shapes in place. Remove the shapes one at a time and place them on a table below the matching opening in the form board. Rotate board 180° and place it in front of the child (i.e., above shapes). Ask the child to put the shapes back into the puzzle (i.e., form board). If the child has difficulty in doing this, demonstrate it for him or her. Encourage the child to look carefully. Use appropriate word labels. For instance, when the child is holding the *round* shape, say, "You have a circle. Put it in the circle (round) hole. Where does the circle go?"	Do the activity described in the "Procedure" section with a group.

Criterion: The child places *round*, *square*, and *triangular* forms in correct holes when the form board is reversed.

AREA: **5-II. Visual Perception: Puzzles and matching**

3

BEHAVIOR: 5-IIc. Puts together two kinds of 2-piece puzzles

Materials: Simple pictures on cardboard: some cut in half diagonally, others cut in half vertically

Procedure	Group activities
Make several puzzles by gluing clear, simple pictures on square pieces of cardboard, about 6″ × 6″ and then cutting it in half, either vertically or diagonally. Place one of the pictures in front of the child, correctly put together. Then take the picture apart, partially rotating pieces. Ask the child to put the puzzle back together. Encourage him or her to focus on the picture to be completed (i.e., "Can you fix the car? Try to put it back together."). If the child has difficulty, show him or her how to put the puzzle together, then take it apart for him or her to do again. If he or she is unsuccessful, try putting one half in correct orientation and asking the child to finish the puzzle. Physically assist him or her if needed.	1. Have the children select a magazine picture and help them glue it on a square of cardboard. Cut it into a puzzle as described to the left. Encourage the children to put it back together. 2. Have the children select a magazine picture. Let them cut it in half. Help them glue it on a piece of paper in the correct orientation so that they have a complete picture again.

Criterion: The child is able to correctly put together two kinds of 2-piece puzzles.

3

AREA: **5-II. Visual Perception: Puzzles and matching**

BEHAVIOR: 5-IId. Puts together a puzzle with 4 or 5 interconnected pieces

Materials: Several puzzles with 4 or 5 pieces that interconnect

Procedure	Group activities
Give the child an assembled puzzle. Encourage him or her to look at the picture and tell you what it is. Ask the child to remove the pieces. Then ask him or her to put the puzzle back together. If he or she has difficulty, put in some of the pieces and ask him or her to put in the last 1 or 2. Remind the child to turn or rotate puzzle pieces, if needed, in order to make them fit. When the child learns to complete 1 puzzle, try a different one. Allow the child to have success with a number of 4- and 5-piece puzzles before moving to more complex ones.	Do the activity described in the "Procedure" section with a group.

Criterion: The child is able to put together several different puzzles with 4 or 5 interconnected pieces.

AREA: **5-II. Visual Perception: Puzzles and matching**
BEHAVIOR: 5-IIe. Matches geometric forms (orientation irrelevant)

Materials: Two sets of cards with the designs: a square, a square with an "X" stretching from its corners, a square with a diagonal line through it, a square with the bottom half darkened

Procedure	Group activities
Make 2 sets of 4 cards, using the designs described under "Materials." Place 1 set of cards in a line in front of the child. Shuffle the remaining cards. One at a time, hand the cards to the child. Ask him or her to place each card on the one that is the same. If the child has difficulty, demonstrate matching all the cards. Then ask the child to try again. If he or she still has difficulty, present only 2 design cards at a time. When the child can successfully match the designs with a choice of 2, try 3, and then 4 different designs.	Give each child a card with one of the designs, described under "Materials," on it. Hold up a large card showing 1 of the designs. Ask the children to stand up if their design matches.

Criterion: The child is able to match 4 geometric forms.

4

AREA: **5-II. Visual Perception: Puzzles and matching**
BEHAVIOR: 5-IIf. Matches at least 8 geometric shapes

Materials: Shape puzzle with at least 8 shapes or 2 sets of matching cards with at least 8 different shapes drawn on them

Procedure	Group activities
Place a puzzle before a child. Remove all the shapes and place them above the puzzle. Ask the child to put the shapes back into the puzzle. If the child has difficulty, demonstrate how to put the shapes into the puzzle. Then remove the shapes again and ask the child to complete the puzzle. If the child is still unsuccessful, start with 4 common shapes such as the circle, square, triangle, and star. When the child is successful, add one shape at a time until he or she is able to do 8 different ones. When adding each new shape, point out to the child how it is different from similar shapes (i.e., circle and oval). When the child is successful with a flat puzzle, try a shape ball (made by Tupperware) to offer the child a greater challenge.	1. Use a large vertical flannel board with shapes on it. One at a time ask each child to come forward. Hand each one a shape and ask him or her to put it in the matching shape. 2. Using Play-Doh or cookie dough, make various shapes using cookie cutters. Talk about the different shapes.

Criterion: The child is able to match at least 8 geometric shapes.

4

AREA: 5-II. Visual Perception: Puzzles and matching
BEHAVIOR: 5-IIg. Completes 8–10-piece interconnected puzzles

Materials: Several wooden puzzles with 8–10 pieces that interconnect

Procedure	Group activities
Give the child an assembled puzzle. Encourage him or her to look at the picture and to tell you what it is. Ask the child to remove the pieces. Then ask him or her to put the puzzle back together. If the child has difficulty doing this, put in some of the pieces and ask him or her to put in the last 1 or 2. Remind the child to turn or rotate the puzzle pieces, if needed, in order to make them fit. When the child learns to complete 1 puzzle, try a different one. Allow the child to have success with a number of 8–10-piece puzzles before moving on to more complex ones. Select puzzles that have been cut logically, so that they are relatively easy to put together. Try the puzzles yourself, particularly if the child is having difficulty. Some wooden puzzles are surprisingly difficult due to the way the pieces have been cut.	Do activity as in the "Procedure" section in a group.

Criterion: The child is able to put together several different puzzles with 8–10 interconnected pieces.

4.5

AREA: 5-II. Visual Perception: Puzzles and matching
BEHAVIOR: 5-IIh. Imitates construction of a simple visual pattern using parquetry blocks

Materials: Set of parquetry blocks (e.g., squares, triangles, diamonds)

Procedure	Group activities
In child's view, place together 4–5 parquetry blocks forming a simple pattern or design. Ask the child to copy your pattern, making his or hers look just like yours. If the child has difficulty, begin with a simple pattern of 2 blocks, using squares first. Gradually expand the number of blocks and type of blocks used. After you have used squares, try triangles, then diamonds. If difficulty still persists, try having the child duplicate your design by building his or her directly on top of yours.	Do activity as described in the "Procedure" section in a group.

Criterion: The child is able to imitate construction of several simple visual patterns of 4–5 parquetry blocks.

AREA: **5-II. Visual Perception: Puzzles and matching**
BEHAVIOR: 5-IIi. Completes a 12–20 + piece interconnected puzzle

Materials: Several puzzles with 12–20 + pieces that interconnect

Procedure	Group activities
Give the child an assembled puzzle. Encourage him or her to look at the picture and tell you what it is. Ask the child to remove the pieces. Then ask him or her to put the puzzle back together. If the child has difficulty in doing this, put in some of the pieces and then ask him or her to complete it. If the puzzle has definite sides and corners, show the child how to find those pieces and to put them in first. Remind him or her to turn or rotate puzzle pieces, if needed, in order to make them fit. When the child learns to complete 1 puzzle, try a different one . Try the puzzles yourself, particularly if the child is having difficulty. Some wooden puzzles are surprisingly difficult due to the way the pieces have been cut.	Children may work in small groups to put together a large floor puzzle.

Criterion: The child is able to put together several different puzzles with 12 or more interconnected pieces.

5

AREA: **5-II. Visual Perception: Puzzles and matching**
BEHAVIOR: 5-IIj. Matches letters and numbers

Materials: Two sets of cards with alphabet and numbers from 1–9

Procedure	Group activities
Place 4 cards in front of a child. Initially select letters that are very different in appearance (e.g., A, O, L, S). Then hand the child a second card with 1 of these 4 letters on it. Ask the child to place it on the letter that is the same or that matches. If the child has difficulty in doing this, demonstrate matching the 4 cards and then repeat the procedure. If necessary, begin with matching only 2 cards at a time, then 3, and then 4. When the child can readily match 4 dissimilar letters, try matching with letters that are similar (e.g., P, B, R, D). Repeat the procedure with number cards.	1. Hang a chart on the wall at circle time that shows all of the letters of the alphabet, with pockets beneath each letter. Shuffle alphabet cards and distribute them to the children (each child may have several cards). Point to the first letter and ask the person who has the card that matches to bring it up and place it in the pocket below the correct letter. Continue this activity until the alphabet is completed. 2. A commercial alphabet or number puzzle can be assembled by the children alone or in small groups.

Criterion: The child is able to correctly match letters and numbers.

AREA: **5-II. Visual Perception: Puzzles and matching**
BEHAVIOR: 5-IIk. Matches name and short words

Materials: Two sets of cards with a name and a variety of short words

Procedure	Group activities
Place 4 word cards in front of a child. Show the child his or her name card, telling him or her what it says. Initially select words that are very different in appearance (e.g., John, cat, go, fish). Then hand the child a second card with 1 of these 4 words on it. Ask the child to place it on the word that is the same or that matches. If the child has difficulty doing this, demonstrate matching the 4 cards and then repeat the procedure. If necessary, begin with matching only 2 cards at a time, then 3, and then 4. When the child can readily match 4 dissimilar words, try matching with words that are similar (e.g., cat, car, hat, sat). If this is too difficult, the child may need more experience with a variety of visual-perceptual tasks (e.g., puzzles, building with blocks, copying simple block designs) before he or she is ready to discriminate subtle differences.	During circle time, hold up each child's name on a card, one at a time. Ask each child to take their name card and to put it in the pocket on the wall that also bears their name.

Criterion: The child is able to match his or her name and several other short words.

6.

Expressive Vocabulary

T HIS SEQUENCE INCLUDES items related to a child's ability to name objects and pictures and to define words. Items related to the child's larger vocabulary (i.e., the words he or she can understand but may not use or be able to define) are included in the Receptive Skills sequence in the communication domain and in the Concepts sequences of the cognitive domain.

Because this sequence requires intelligible speech, it is inappropriate for many children who have handicaps that significantly interfere with speech production. The focus of attention in their cases should be on receptive vocabulary that can be targeted through the other sequences mentioned above. A few children who are using manual signs, communication boards, or other forms of augmentative communication can appropriately work through this sequence, using that system instead of the spoken words. One should be very cautious in interpreting the rough age levels provided for this sequence when alternatives to speech are used. For the most part, these alternatives require greater cognitive sophistication than speech (e.g., pointing to a written word rather than to say a word), making the age estimates too low. However, there are some instances where an alternative mode might require less sophistication (e.g., pointing at an object that was heard while it was hidden rather than naming the object heard while it is still hidden).

If a child is unable to speak well enough to be understood, alternative modes of communication may be used to demonstrate his or her expressive vocabulary (e.g., a picture, a word board, an electronic communication device, manual signs).

6. Expressive Vocabulary

a. Names most common objects when seen
b. Names objects that are heard
c. Names objects touched or handled
d. Names 2 or more pictures of common objects

e. Names 6 or more pictures of common objects
f. Uses at least 50 different words
g. Names 8 or more line drawings of common objects
h. Names most pictures of familiar objects

i. Names pictures of objects seen primarily in books (e.g., farm animals or tractors for city children)

j. Defines 2 or more simple words (e.g., "What do we mean by _____?", "What is a _____?")

k. Defines 5 simple words

l. Defines 10 simple words

2.5

AREA: **6. Expressive Vocabulary**
BEHAVIOR: 6a. Names most common objects when seen

Materials: Whatever objects are found in the normal environment

Procedure	Group activities
Name objects in the child's environment as he or she plays with them, looks at them, or otherwise indicates an interest in them. Comment on the object's characteristics (e.g., "See this ball. It is round and can roll"; "Let's use this sponge to clean up your juice. Feel how soft and squishy it is."). Listen for the child's attempts to imitate the names of the objects and then begin asking, "What is this?" or, simply hold the object up to see if the child will name it as he or she sees or reaches for it.	Talk about the various objects in the classroom and name them. Use circle time to bring in new objects to talk about and name. Have the children also bring in objects to be discussed. As the children are playing, stop by each one and ask occasionally, "What is that?" or "What are you playing with?"

Criterion: The child names most of the objects seen in his or her environment (at least 20).

2.5

AREA: **6. Expressive Vocabulary**
BEHAVIOR: 6b. Names objects that are heard

Materials: A variety of toys and normal household objects that make distinctive noises (e.g., rattle, bell, telephone, doorbell)

Procedure	Group activities
Name objects as the child handles them. Also name environmental noises (e.g., "That's the telephone"; "That's the doorbell") when they occur. Listen for the child's attempts to imitate these words after you have said them or to use them spontaneously. Once you know he or she can say one or more of the words, ask, "What was that?" or "What did you hear?" when the noise occurs. You can also play a game where you show the child 3 or 4 objects and demonstrate the noise that each one makes. Then hide the toys under the table or behind your back and use one to make a noise. Ask, "What was that?" or "What did you hear?"	1. Play the listening game with the children. Show them toys or objects, one at a time, and demonstrate the noise that each one makes. As you show each object, name it. Then put it out of view and make the noise again. Ask, "What was that?" After going through 3–5 objects, put them all in a box with tall sides. Put your hand in and make a noise with 1 object. Ask what object made the noise. Let the children take turns reaching into the box and making a noise with something the other children cannot see while the other children guess which toy made the noise. A day or two later, try the listening game without first showing the children the objects and naming them. 2. For circle time, hide a common household object or a familiar toy from the classroom in a box or sack. Reach in and manipulate it so that it makes a noise. Ask,

(continued)

Procedure	Group activities
	"Who knows what is in my box?" At other times, introduce something you suspect they will not know. Their guesses will create a lot of interest in whatever you intend to show to them (e.g., the rustle of autumn leaves; the sound of a tambourine or other musical instrument that you will use during a music activity).

Criterion: The child names at least 3 different objects that are out of sight by the sounds they make at least 1 day after a teaching session in which they were taught; or names at least 3 different objects by their sounds spontaneously (e.g., says "telephone" when the telephone rings in another room).

2.5

AREA: **6. Expressive Vocabulary**
BEHAVIOR: 6c. Names objects touched or handled

Materials: A variety of toys and normal household or classroom objects that have different textures or consistencies (e.g., sponge, washcloth or towel, block, cookie, stuffed animal)

Procedure	Group activities
Proceed as in item 6a., allowing the children to feel the objects as you name them (you may rub the objects over the skin of the children who are too physically handicapped to manipulate them on their own). Hide an object in a sack and let the child put in his or her hand and tell you what he or she feels. (This is a great activity to keep children occupied during long car trips.)	Play the "feely game" like you did the listening game, using both objects you have taught them to identify and new objects as a way of arousing their interest in them.

Criterion: The child names 3 or more objects that he or she cannot see but can feel.

2.5

AREA: **6. Expressive Vocabulary**
BEHAVIOR: 6d. Names 2 or more pictures of common objects
BEHAVIOR: 6e. Names 6 or more pictures of common objects

Materials: Books, magazines, pictures

Procedure	Group activities
Spend time with the child "reading" books and magazines. To begin with, select books with simple pictures that include only 1 or 2 objects per page. Name the objects and talk about them (e.g., "See the ball. It is round and red."). Help the child point to the	Spend time each day showing and reading books to the children. Do not be concerned with reading a whole story. Rather, tell a story as you point to the pictures. Select books with large pictures and always read

(continued)

Procedure	Group activities
objects that you name. Then begin turning the pages, waiting for the child to name the objects, or asking, "What is this?" Always indicate your pleasure when the child points to the objects or names them.	with the book facing the children. Talk about the pictures and ask them to point to different objects in the pictures. Then begin asking, "What is this?" Or, read a story and let the children fill in parts of it by naming pictures that you point to (e.g., "Little Boy Blue come blow your ____."; "And then Mickey gave Minnie a great big ____.").

Criterion: The child names 2 (for item 6d.) or 6 (for item 6e.) pictures of objects spontaneously or when asked "What is that?" This must occur several hours or a day after a session in which the names of the objects were taught.

2.5

AREA: **6. Expressive Vocabulary**

BEHAVIOR: 6f. Uses at least 50 different words

Materials: Normal home or classroom environment

Procedure	Group activities
Talk to the child a lot and listen to what he or she says. Keep a record of different words. It may help to have several notebooks in different parts of the house. Count as a word any sound that the child makes consistently to mean a particular object, even if it is a poor approximation of your pronunciation of the word (e.g., "bawa" for water). Say the word correctly after the child, both to let the child correct you if you have misinterpreted the word and to give him or her a better model to imitate. *However, do not force the child to correct the pronunciation.* Talking needs to be fun, not work!	In circle and other group activities, make sure that each child has a chance to talk. Listen carefully and repeat back your understanding of each child's words. Be excited about the new words that each child learns. Introduce new and interesting materials in a circle activity, talk about them and then pass them around. Listen to the words that the children use as they see, feel, smell, or manipulate them. Try to keep track of the new words they say.

Criterion: The child uses at least 50 different words in his or her spontaneous speech (i.e., when asking for objects, telling you about something, looking at books).

AREA: **6. Expressive Vocabulary**
BEHAVIOR: 6g. Names 8 or more line drawings of common objects

Materials: Books with line drawings (i.e., black and white drawings with relatively few details rather than colored pictures; coloring books are good for this purpose)

Procedure	Group activities
Introduce books with line drawings in them for story time. Tell stories about the pictures, and have the child point to objects in the pictures, as in item 6d.	1. Same as item 6d. but using line-drawings. 2. Give children a page to color that is a line drawing. Ask them what it is they are going to color (do not try to get them to "stay within the lines," just let them color).

Criterion: The child names 8 or more line drawings of common objects at least several hours after a session in which those names were taught.

AREA: **6. Expressive Vocabulary**
BEHAVIOR: 6h. Names most pictures of familiar objects

Materials: Books, magazines, pictures

Procedure	Group activities
Proceed as in item 6d.	Proceed as in item 6d.

Criterion: The child names most pictures when asked, "What is that?" or names them spontaneously while looking at a book.

3.5

AREA: **6. Expressive Vocabulary**
BEHAVIOR: 6i. Names pictures of objects seen primarily in books
(e.g., farm animals or tractors for city children)

Materials: Story books, nursery rhyme books

Procedure	Group activities
Read books with pictures that are about objects or events that are unfamiliar to the child's daily experiences (e.g., you might choose a book about animals seen only in a zoo or on TV for a child who has little opportunity to visit zoos). Point to the pictures as you read and talk about the special characteristics that make something what it is (e.g., "This is a zebra. Look at its stripes").	Same as in the "Procedure" section. Remember, *always read with the book facing the children.*

Criterion: The child names 10 or more objects seen primarily in books. This must occur several hours or a day after a lesson in which the names of the objects were taught.

4

AREA: **6. Expressive Vocabulary**
BEHAVIOR: 6j. Defines 2 or more simple words (e.g., "What do we mean by _____?",
"What is a _____?")
4.5   BEHAVIOR: 6k. Defines 5 simple words
5   BEHAVIOR: 6l. Defines 10 simple words

Materials: Normal home or classroom environment

Procedure	Group activities
Look for opportunities to ask the child what a word means. For example, when the child hears you use an unfamiliar word and he or she asks you what it means, tell the child and then say, "Now, I want to ask you one. What is a ball?" Or, play a game so that when the child asks you for a shoe, you give him or her a shirt. When he or she says, "No, I want my shoes." say, "Oh, what is a shoe?" If the child has trouble getting started, say, "A shoe is something that. . . ."	Plan lessons where you introduce several simple objects (e.g., shoe, hat, telephone). Introduce one at a time and ask, "What is this?" Once it is named, put it out of sight and, say, "Now, let's think, what is a _____ anyway? Can anyone tell me what a _____ is?" Help the children give more and more complex answers. For instance, if one says, "A hat is something you wear," you can say, "Yes, it is something to wear, but where do you wear it? Do you wear it on your big toe?"

Criterion: The child defines 2 (for item 6j.), 5 (for item 6k.), or 10 (for item 6l.) words without adult prompting (a simple answer like "you wear it" is acceptable at this level).

7.

Interest in Sounds and Language Functions

IN ORDER FOR A CHILD to learn to talk, it is essential that he or she be interested in sounds. In most children, their early interest in environmental sounds progresses to an interest in the sounds and meanings of words. It is important for caregivers to reinforce this interest at every phase of the child's development by repeating sounds for the child, sharing his or her pleasure in new words and sounds, and calling attention to sounds through reading and making rhymes. This is a short sequence of items but it is important for all other aspects of language development.

7. Interest in Sounds and Language Functions

a. Identifies objects, people, and events by their sounds
b. Listens carefully to new words, may ask for repetition
c. Repeats new words to self
d. In play, uses different voices for different people
e. In play or conversation, uses statements such as, "He said . . . "

f. Asks word meanings or otherwise indicates awareness that words mean something
g. Makes rhymes to simple words
h. Soon after hearing the meaning of a new word, uses it in his or her own speech

3   AREA: **7. Interest in Sounds and Language Functions**
          BEHAVIOR: 7a. Identifies objects, people, and events by their sounds

Materials: Normal home or classroom environment that includes a variety of objects that make
             different sounds

Procedure	Classroom activities
Make it clear that you think listening is interesting and fun. Do the following activities. Play games with the child in which you make a sound with a toy behind your back and say, "Listen, what's that?" If the child doesn't tell you, bring it out and show it to him or her, name it, and then try it again. Once the child gets it right, try another toy. As you hear environmental sounds (e.g., a car in the driveway, the telephone ringing, the vacuum running in the next room), stop what you are doing, look interested, and say, "Listen, what's that?" Take the child to see the source of the sound and talk about it. When another member of the family or another familiar person is approaching, ask them to speak to the child before they can be seen. When you hear the voice say, "Listen, who is that?" or "Who is here?" Name the voice for the child if he or she does not name it. Play a game in which you place 2 or 3 toys in front of the child. Cover them with a cloth and then make a sound with one of them under the cloth. Remove the cloth and have the child point to the one that produced the noise.	In a noisy classroom, it is more difficult to isolate sounds. Be sure to use the activities described in the "Procedure" section during circle time when it is relatively quiet. Also make a point of reading stories to children with different voices for the different characters. Ask at the end, "Who talks like this?" (e.g., making the big deep voice of the Daddy bear).

Criterion: The child identifies a variety of sounds (at least 10 different ones) either by naming them, pointing to the objects or people that produced them, or otherwise making a clear indication.

3   AREA: **7. Interest in Sounds and Language Functions**
          BEHAVIOR: 7b. Listens carefully to new words, may ask for repetition
               BEHAVIOR: 7c. Repeats new words to self
3
Materials: Normal home or classroom environment

Procedure	Classroom activities
Observe the child as you read stories or talk to him or her. Deliberately use words that he or she is unlikely to have heard before and watch for a reaction. If there is no response say the word several times and show the child what it means (e.g., point to the ob-	1. Bring relatively unusual objects to the class to show during circle time, snack time, or another relatively quiet period. Introduce the word first. For example, "I have a pomegranate in my pocket. Does anyone

(continued)

Procedure	Group activities
ject, do the activity). Make it clear that you think words are fun!	know what a pomegranate is?" Show them the fruit and then let them practice saying "pomegranate." Show them what it looks like on the inside and let them taste it. 2. Read books with unusual sounding words in them (e.g., Dr. Suess books), and talk about the words and identify them with the characters or events in the stories.

Criterion (for item 7b.):   The child asks you to repeat a word, asks what a word means, or otherwise indicates an interest in a new word on at least 5 occasions.

Criterion (for item 7c.):   The child repeats a new word to him- or herself shortly after hearing it and without being prompted to repeat it by an adult, on at least 5 occasions.

_3.5_

AREA: **7. Interest in Sounds and Language Functions**
BEHAVIOR: 7d. In play, uses different voices for different people

Materials: Dolls, puppets, stuffed animals or other toys that facilitate role-playing

Procedure	Classroom activities
When you read to the child, always use different voices for the different characters. When the child becomes familiar with a story, let the child tell it to you as he or she looks at the pictures. Listen to see if the child also uses different voices for the different characters. Model using different voices for different characters when playing with the child using puppets, stuffed animals, or dolls.	1. Read to the children using different voices for the different characters. After a story is familiar, read along and stop when it comes time for one of the characters to speak and say to a child, "What did the big bad wolf say?" Listen to see if the child adopts the big bad wolf's voice even if he or she does not get the words right. 2. Introduce puppet play in small group activities, playing the role of one puppet with an appropriate voice and encouraging the children to play the roles of other puppets. Listen for the use of different voices for different puppets.

Criterion: The child is observed to alter his or her voice to portray the role of a puppet, doll, or story character on at least 5 occasions.

AREA: **7. Interest in Sounds and Language Functions**

4 BEHAVIOR: 7e. In play or conversation, uses statements such as, "He said . . . "

Materials: Normal home or classroom environment

Procedure	Classroom activities
Model the use of "He said . . . " and "She said . . . through reading books to the child, through talking to him or her about experiences, and through engaging him or her in imaginative play. Let the child talk on the telephone to relatives or friends and ask, "What did he (or she) say?" Listen to the child as he or she talks to you and as he or she plays imaginative games by him- or herself or with other children.	Do activities as in the "Procedure" section with a group.

Criterion: The child uses "He said . . . " or "She said . . . " (or an equivalent that indicates that he or she understands different parts of a conversation) on at least 5 different occasions. Some children will use terms like "he goes . . . " instead of "he said . . . " when playing or reporting a conversation; this is acceptable if it is clear that the child is using this term with the same meaning as "he said . . . ."

AREA: **7. Interest in Sounds and Language Functions**

4.5 BEHAVIOR: 7f. Asks word meanings or otherwise indicates awareness that words mean
                          something

Materials: Normal home or classroom environment

Procedure	Classroom activities
Indicate an interest in words. Try to introduce new and interesting sounding words to the child through reading or conversations. If the child does not ask what a word means, ask him or her if he or she knows what it means and then tell the meaning. Always answer the child when he or she asks the meaning of a word. If you do not know the meaning, show him or her how you can look it up in a dictionary. Make it clear that you appreciate his or her interest in words.	Try to introduce a new word every day at circle time, lunch, snack, or whenever the children are together. Have a picture to go with the word that is hung on the wall for the day and look for a story or an activity that relates to the word. Invite the children to bring in a word they want the other children to know.

Criterion: The child asks the meaning of a word, questions you when you use a new word, tells you the meaning of a word, or otherwise indicates an understanding that words mean something on at least 5 occasions.

4.5

AREA: **7. Interest in Sounds and Language Functions**
BEHAVIOR: 7g. Makes rhymes to simple words

Materials: Normal home or classroom environment

Procedure	Classroom activities
Read rhymes to the child. Play rhyming games with the child when trying to distract him or her in the car, while doing household chores, while sitting down and reading, or playing with him or her. Say, "How many things can we find that rhyme with (or sound like) red? There's a bed. What else can we find?" If the child can't do it, help him or her by giving hints. For example, touch the child's head and say, "What's this?" When the child says, "Head," say, "Good, head rhymes with red. Now let's see what else we can find."	During a circle activity, say a word and see if each child can name something that rhymes with it. To begin with, it helps to give each child a picture of something that will rhyme with the word you have chosen. If they name the wrong object in the picture, help them find the right name to make the rhyme.

Criterion: The child can name 1 or more rhyming words for at least 3 different words.

AREA: **7. Interest in Sounds and Language Functions**
5 BEHAVIOR: 7h. Soon after hearing the meaning of a new word, uses it in his or her own
speech

Materials: A normal home or classroom environment

Procedure	Classroom activities
You really cannot teach this item except by setting an example of an interest in words and by letting the child know that you appreciate his or her efforts to communicate. Listen and indicate interest!	Listen to each child's efforts to communicate. Ask other children to be quiet and then to listen to what one child has to say. Reward talking by listening!

Criterion: The child is observed to use a new word in his or her speech shortly after hearing it or having its meaning explained.

8.

Receptive Skills

MANY OF THE ITEMS NORMALLY included under *receptive language* skills in other curricula are included in the cognitive domain under the Concept sequences of the CCPSN. This Receptive Skills sequence is made up of a mixture of receptive language items including: concept items that did not neatly fit into the other sequences, some items assessing receptive vocabulary, and items involving following instructions and responding appropriately to questions. This mixture probably makes the items less ordinal than would be desirable, but the alternative is too many short sequences. Therefore, it is important to assess a child through 2 levels of failure to accommodate varying skills in the different kinds of items that are included.

The criteria for mastery on many of these items specifies that the child must "respond appropriately to. . . . " An appropriate response may be different for a normally developing child and a child who has a handicapping condition. For example, for those children who cannot talk, an appropriate response may be a gesture, pointing to a picture, or some other way of indicating an understanding of a question or request.

8. Receptive Skills

a. Understands *look*
b. Identifies pictures of familiar objects
c. Follows 1-step commands related to 2 objects or an object and a place (e.g., "Put the ___ on/in the ___"; "Take the ___ to the ___")
d. Identifies 6 body parts
e. Identifies 10 or more line drawings of objects when the objects are named
f. Identifies 5 or more objects by usage (e.g., "Show me what we drink out of")
g. Responds appropriately to "where" questions
h. Responds appropriately to "why" questions
i. Responds to "yes/no" questions with appropriate words or gestures (e.g., Do you want ___?"; "Is that your ___?")
j. Responds appropriately to "who" and "whose" questions
k. Identifies pictures of objects by function (e.g., "Show me the one that ___")

l. Follows 2-step commands involving sequence (e.g., "Put the doll on the shelf and then bring me the ball")

m. Responds appropriately to "which" and "how many" questions

n. Names objects by function (e.g., What cuts the grass?")

o. Follows 3-step instructions in sequence involving 2–3 different objects (e.g., "Put the doll on the shelf, put your shirt in the hamper, and bring me the ball.")

p. Responds appropriately to statements or questions involving regular plurals

q. Understands statements or instructions involving negations (e.g., "The dog is not big"; "Do not take the red one")

r. Responds appropriately to "how far" questions

s. Responds appropriately to questions involving time concepts (e.g., before, after, today, tomorrow, tonight)

AREA: **8. Receptive Skills**

2·5 BEHAVIOR: 8a. Understands *look*

Materials: Normal home or classroom environment

Procedure	Group activities
Call the child's attention to objects and occurrences in the environment by saying, "Look," and pointing. Gradually stop pointing and say, "Look at the ____." (if he or she does not look with that instruction, prompt by pointing). When you are showing the child how to do something, say, "Look at Daddy. See how I ____." When you are looking at books together, say, "Look at the ____."	Show a picture book to a small group of children. Say, "Look at the ____," as you point to it. Ask children to look at special objects or to look at you when you are giving some instruction.

Criterion: The child looks when told to look for something. For this item it is less critical that he or she look at the correct object (that is more vocabulary) than that the child do something to indicate that he or she is looking (e.g., turn his or her head, move his or her eyes as if to search).

AREA: **8. Receptive Skills**

2·5 BEHAVIOR: 8b. Identifies pictures of familiar objects

Materials: Picture, books, magazines, catalogs, picture cards

Procedure	Group activities
Sit with the child to look at books and pictures. Point to objects as you name them. Then ask the child to point to them. If he or she does not do this, help the child by saying the name of the object and then placing his or her hand or finger on it. Then say, "That's right, that is the ____!"	Sit with a small group to look at books and pictures. Always face the pictures toward the children. Point to objects as you name them. Put the picture close to each child in turn and ask him or her to, "Point to the ____" or "Show me the ____." Help if necessary.

Criterion: The child points to 10 or more pictures of familiar objects without prompts.

Note: Some children react very negatively to someone holding their hand or finger to help them point. If the child does respond with resistance or fussiness, just continue to point yourself and explore other possible responses for the child. For example, some children will not point to objects but will kiss them.

2. 5

AREA: 8. Receptive Skills
BEHAVIOR: 8c. Follows 1-step commands related to 2 objects or an object and a place
(e.g., "Put the ____on/in the ____"; "Take the ____ to the ____")

Materials: Normal home or classroom environment

Procedure	Group activities
Give the child instructions throughout the day and give as much help as necessary to be sure that he or she has success in following them. Be sure to make instructions appropriate to the physical capabilities of the child.	Guide children in small groups to make a game of giving instructions to one another.

Criterion: The child follows 5 different 1-step commands related to 2 objects or 1 object and a place.

AREA: 8. Receptive Skills
2.5   BEHAVIOR: 8d. Identifies 6 body parts

Materials: Dolls, animals, pictures of people and animals

Procedure	Group activities
Play games with the child where you name and touch parts of his or her body (e.g., "Here comes a little bug, walking up your arm and tickles your ear"). When the child is touching your face, name the part that he or she is touching (e.g., "That's Mommy's nose."). Name another part of your face or body (e.g., "Where's Mommy's eye?") and help the child touch it if he or she does not do it without a prompt. Then ask the child where his or her eyes, nose, hair, or ears are located. When he or she is correct say, "That's right, that's your ____." When the child is wrong say, "That's your ____. Here is your ____." When looking at pictures together, point to body parts and ask the child to do so, prompting as necessary.	Sing songs that involve touching body parts. For example, "If you're happy and you know it . . . (clap your hands, touch your nose, stomp your feet, touch your hair)."

Criterion: The child identifies 6 body parts. Each part must be identified in 5 different trials, without errors.

3   AREA: **8. Receptive Skills**

BEHAVIOR: 8e. Identifies 10 or more line drawings of objects when the objects are named

Materials: Cards or books with line drawings of familiar objects

Procedure	Group activities
Proceed as in item 8b.	Proceed as in item 8b.

Criterion: The child points to 10 or more line drawings of objects without prompts.

AREA: **8. Receptive Skills**

3   BEHAVIOR: 8f. Identifies 5 or more objects by usage
(e.g., "Show me what we drink out of")

Materials: Normal home or classroom environment

Procedure	Group activities
Talk about objects as you use them (e.g., "Let's drink out of the blue cup today."; "I'm going to cut the paper with these scissors."). Occasionally place 3 or 4 objects in front of the child and say, "Show me the one that we _____." (e.g., drink out of, cut with, use to wash our face, carry money in).	Bring a collection of interesting objects to circle time and ask the children to tell you for what they are used. Repeat the children's correct answers for the children who may not know. Tell them the uses of those objects that they do not recognize. Let them use or pretend to use the objects. On the next day, bring out the objects again and take turns asking the children to identify them by use (e.g., "Show me the one we use to pound in the nails."; "Show me the one we throw."). Try to include some very easy items for the slower children in the group to assure that everyone will have success.

Criterion: The child identifies 5 objects by usage, each on 3 or more occasions. (It is important to use varying instructions so that the child can accomplish this task when asked to "show me," "point to," "give me," "find the.")

3   AREA: **8. Receptive Skills**

BEHAVIOR: 8g. Responds appropriately to "where" questions

Materials: Normal home or classroom environment

Procedure	Group activities
As you do activities with the child, talk about the places that objects/people are or the places where ob-	Sing the finger song ([to the tune of "Frére Jacque"] "Where is thumbkin, Where is

(continued)

Procedure	Group activities
jects belong, introducing the topic with a "where" question (e.g., "Where's Daddy? He's in the kitchen."; "Where did we leave your ball? It must be outside."; "Where are the crayons? They're in the drawer. Let's get them."). Frequently use "where" when talking about the child's belongings (e.g., "Where is your coat?"; "Where is your cup") Also, use "where" as you teach other concepts. For example, in teaching body parts you can say, "Where is your nose?"	thumbkin, Here I am [hold up one thumb]. Here I am [Hold up second thumb]. How are you today sir [one thumb bows several times to the other]? Very well, I thank you [the other bows]. Run away [one hand behind the back]. Run away" [the other hand behind the back]—continue with "pointer," "tall man," "ring man," and "pinkie.").

Criterion: The child points to indicate where, retrieves an object, or tells a location in response to 5 different "where" questions. It is not critical that the child be correct about the location; only that he or she understands that a "where" question requires a location response.

3

AREA: 8. Receptive Skills
BEHAVIOR: 8h. Responds appropriately to "why" questions

Materials: Normal home or classroom environment

Procedure	Group activities
Use the term "why" as you discuss how various objects work in the environment (e.g., Why is this chair so hard to move? I guess it is because it is so heavy."; "Why are you crying? Did you fall down and cut your knee?"). Give reasons for decisions or instructions (e.g., "You can't do that because . . . ."; "I can't lift it because it is too heavy."). Ask the child "why" questions after you have read him or her a story (e.g., "Why did the third little pig build his house out of stones?") or as events occur during the day. If the child does not respond, give him or her some choices for a response (e.g., "Was it because he wanted a strong house to keep out the wolf?"; "Why can't you bring it to me? Is it too big to carry?").	1. Discuss classroom rules with the group. Give the children reasons for each rule. Then review by asking, "Why don't we run in the hall?" or "Why do we hold hands when we cross the parking lot?" 2. After you read a story, ask "why" questions about the events in the story. Provide answers if the children cannot.

Criterion: The child responds appropriately (gives reasons) to 5 or more "why" questions. It is not necessary that his or her reasons be good ones, but it is necessary that the child understands that a "why" question requires some kind of reason.

Note: Once young children learn to say "Because . . . " in response to "why" questions, adults have a tendency to expect them to know why they do certain actions and ask, "Why did you hit Johnny?"; "Why did you write on the wall?"; or "Why did you wet your pants?" Children at this age often do not understand their own motives. They act on impulse. Do not get angry with the child who does not answer.

3.5

AREA: **8. Receptive Skills**

BEHAVIOR: 8i. Responds to "yes/no" questions with appropriate words or gestures (e.g., "Do you want _____?"; "Is that your _____?")

Materials: Normal home or classroom environment

Procedure	Group activities
Frequently ask the child questions that can be answered by "yes" or "no." Since some children get in the habit of saying (or shaking the head) "no" to any question, it is important to make the child "responsible" for his or her responses. Therefore, you must act on the basis of the child's response, not on the basis of what you think. For example, if you say, "Would you like some juice?" and the child looks like she wants it but says, "No," put it away. If he or she then says, "Juice" (or the equivalent), say, "Oh, you do want some. Say 'yes' (or 'uh-huh')," wait for a response, and pour it.	In play activities or art activities, give the children *many* opportunities to make choices (e.g., "Do you want this puzzle?"; "Do you want juice?"; "Do you want to play with the _____?"); If you give them the opportunity to make choices, abide by their decisions (Don't ask, "Do you want me to leave you here?" when you know you cannot do that).

Criterion: The child responds to 10 or more different "yes/no" questions with the appropriate words or gestures.

3.5

AREA: **8. Receptive Skills**

BEHAVIOR: 8j. Responds appropriately to "who" and "whose" questions

Materials: Normal home or classroom environment

Procedure	Group activities
Use the terms "who" and "whose" when talking about people and objects in the environment (e.g., "Do you know who is coming to dinner? Grandma is coming."; "Whose sock is this? I think it is Mary's."). Particularly ask questions and make statements that are related to the child (e.g., "I found somebody's toe in the water. Whose toe is it? Is it yours?"; "Whose jacket is here on the floor? I think it is Johnny's. Please come pick it up.").	Ask "who" and "whose" questions in the group to work on other concepts (e.g., "Who has on a red shirt today?"; "Whose birthday is today?", "Whose mother brought cupcakes for snacks?", "Who can find a big yellow block for me?").

Criterion: The child responds to "who" and "whose" questions by indicating a person, at least 5 responses to each kind of question. The response may be in the form of pointing or a statement (It is not necessary that the child be correct, only that he or she knows that "who" or "whose" questions require a response indicating a person).

3·5

AREA: **8. Receptive Skills**

BEHAVIOR: 8k. Identifies pictures of objects by function
(e.g., "Show me the one that ____")

Materials: Pictures of familiar objects

Procedure	Group activities
Proceed as in item 8f., except talk about pictures as well as objects when describing function and ask the child to identify objects by function. Try to do this in a natural way—(e.g., when looking at books or catalogs, when seeing signs along the highway).	1. Bring pictures of objects to the group and talk about their functions as in item 8f. 2. Plan a field trip to the fire station or doctor's office. Collect pictures of objects that were demonstrated to the children during the field trip. Ask if they remember "which of these was used to . . . ?"

Criterion: The child identifies at least 10 different pictures of objects by function. He or she must be able to choose correctly from at least 3 alternatives each time.

AREA: **8. Receptive Skills**

4

BEHAVIOR: 8l. Follows 2-step commands involving sequence
(e.g., "Put the doll on the shelf and then bring me the ball)

Materials: Normal home or classroom environment

Procedure	Group activities
Gradually increase the complexity of the instructions you give to the child and decrease the amount of help you provide. When you move to 2-step commands begin by using a lot of gestures to help the child focus attention. Gradually withdraw these gestures so that the child must rely on the words alone. Assure success by adding gestures whenever the child gets confused. When you begin to add sequence to the command, stress the words that indicate the sequence (e.g., "Do this *and then* that.").	Proceed as in the "Procedure" section but with the children in a group.

Criterion: The child follows 5 different 2-step commands involving sequence, getting the sequence correct without gestural prompts.

4

AREA: 8. Receptive Skills
BEHAVIOR: 8m. Responds appropriately to "which" and "how many" questions

Materials: Normal home or classroom environment

Procedure	Group activities
The terms "which" and "how many" will be used frequently in teaching concepts (see sequences 2-I. and 2-II.) The issue for this item is that the child understands the kind of response that is to be given. Unlike the Concepts sequences, it is not necessary that the child's response be correct. For example, when asked, "Which one is bigger?" the child may point to the wrong object, but if he or she points at all, he or she indicates an understanding of the term "which" or "which one." Likewise, when asked, "How many balls are there?" the child gets credit on this item for answering with any number, whether correct or incorrect.	Do activity as in the "Procedure" section but with a group of children.

Criterion: The child responds appropriately to at least 5 "which" and 5 "how many" questions. That is, he or she points or otherwise indicates an object or person when asked "which" and responds with a number when asked "how many."

AREA: 8. Receptive Skills
4

BEHAVIOR: 8n. Names objects by function (e.g., "What cuts the grass?")

Materials: Normal home or classroom environment

Procedure	Group activities
Try asking the child questions of this nature when riding in the car, doing housework, or at other times when you are busy but are talking to the child. Make it a game by thinking of funny incidents related to something the child has recently observed or experienced (e.g., "What chews up Daddy's shoes?"; "What makes the car go?").	Play a guessing game in the group where you ask funny questions. Devise easy or hard questions to accommodate the abilities of different children and to assure success for all.

Criterion: The child names at least 10 different objects by function.

AREA: 8. Receptive Skills

BEHAVIOR: 8o. Follows 3-step instructions in sequence involving 2–3 different objects (e.g., "Put the doll on the shelf, put your shirt in the hamper, and bring me the ball.")

Materials: Normal home or classroom environment

Procedure	Group activities
Continue to increase the complexity of the instructions you give to the child and decrease the amount of help you provide. As you move from 2-step to 3-step instructions, always repeat them twice, using clear gestures. If the child has difficulty with the sequence, gently remind him or her (e.g., "Do you remember what I asked you to do next? It was to _____."). Assure success by giving as much help as necessary and reward the end result with praise regardless of how much you had to help. Gradually decrease the amount of help you provide as the child becomes better at the task. *Never belittle the child's efforts to comply*—comment on the part he or she does right and help him or her with the rest.	This is basically an individual activity, although you can make a group game by having the children take turns giving and trying to follow silly instructions (e.g., "Put your hands on your head, then touch your knees, and stomp your feet.").

Criterion: The child follows 5 different 3-step instructions, involving a specified sequence and different objects, getting them correct without gestural prompts.

AREA: 8. Receptive Skills

BEHAVIOR: 8p. Responds appropriately to statements or questions involving regular plurals

Materials: Normal home or classroom environment

Procedure	Group activities
Ask the child questions or give instructions that will help you know whether he or she understands plurals (e.g., "Bring me the balls."; "Are your dolls in there?"). If the child brings only one ball when you have asked for balls, say, "Thank you. That is one ball. Can you bring me some more balls?" Emphasize the "s" as you say "balls." As you go about daily activities, talk about objects, emphasizing the plural forms (e.g., "You found a rock. Let's find more rocks.").	Work on plurals as you work on number concepts. Talk about "one truck" and "two trucks," or "one block" and "six blocks."

Criterion: The child indicates an understanding of regular plurals by correctly following instructions or answering questions on 5 different occasions.

4. 5

AREA: **8. Receptive Skills**

BEHAVIOR: 8q. Understands statements or instructions involving negations
(e.g., "The dog is not big"; "Do not take the red one")

Materials: Normal home or classroom environment

Procedure	Group activities
When you are reading stories to the child or talking about events or objects in the environment, use "not" as appropriate. To check on the child's understanding, give instructions that will allow him or her to demonstrate that understanding. For example, you might say when looking at a picture of 2 dogs, "Which dog is not big?" or as the child is getting dressed you might say, "Go get a shirt, but do not get the red one." If the child makes an error, try to determine why he or she is having difficulty as you correct him or her. For example, if the child points to the larger of the 2 dogs when you asked him or her to show you the one that is not big, say, "Well, which dog *is* big?" If the child then indicates some dog that is not even in the picture, he or she may understand the concept but just believe that both the dogs are small. Then, you can say, "Yes, but if I say this dog *is* big, then which one is *not* big?" Or, if the child is clearly confused by the concept of "not," help by saying, "This dog is big. This dog is little. The little dog is *not* big."	Play a game where you put a group of items on the table and give instructions to the children (e.g., "Everyone take a box. Now put something in the box that is red. Now put something in the box that is not red."). You can use this kind of game for teaching a variety of concepts at one time and the children will correct each other.

Criterion: The child demonstrates an understanding of negations by following instructions or answering questions on at least 5 different occasions.

5

AREA: **8. Receptive Skills**

BEHAVIOR: 8r. Responds appropriately to "how far" questions

Materials: Normal home or classroom environment

Procedure	Group activities
Talk about distances to the child. For example, talk about the sun, moon, and stars being far, far away; that it is not far to the store; that the other car stopped "just this far" (holding up your hands) from mine; or that it is 1 mile to school and 10 miles to the next town. Answer the child's questions when he or she begins to ask "how far" (a child usually asks this kind of question several times before he or she is able	Talk about distance concepts in a group as in the "Procedure" section. This is readily done when demonstrating many art projects, when talking about where children live, and when introducing visitors to the classroom and telling where they live. Ask questions in the group of individual children as described in the "Procedure" section.

(continued)

Procedure	Group activities
to answer one). Then, check the child's understanding by asking questions. It is not critical that the child have a clear understanding of distance for this item, but that he or she knows that a "how far" question requires an answer that includes distance concepts (e.g., close, not far, long ways away) or time concepts (e.g., a long time away, hours away, a few minutes away).	

Criterion: The child responds appropriately to different "how far" questions.

5

AREA: **8. Receptive Skills**

BEHAVIOR: 8s. Responds appropriately to questions involving time concepts (e.g., before, after, today, tomorrow, tonight)

Materials: Normal home or classroom environment

Procedure	Group activities
Use time concepts frequently throughout the day (e.g., "Wash your hands before lunch."; "After you pick up the toys, you can have a snack."; "Today we are going to the store."; "Tonight we're going to have spaghetti for dinner."). Begin to ask questions or give instructions to check the child's understanding of these concepts (e.g., "What happened before that?"; "Do you go to school tomorrow?"; "After you get your coat, please bring me my gloves.").	Use group time to talk about what the children are going to do at different times during the day, did at home yesterday or last night, and plan to do tomorrow. The sharing of experiences and time perceptions in the group will help individual children master the concepts.

Criterion: The child responds appropriately to questions involving time concepts (e.g., before, after, today, tomorrow, tonight) at least 2 times for each concept.

9.

Conversation Skills

WHEN WORKING ON LANGUAGE skills with youngsters who are handicapped, it is easy to become so engrossed with teaching vocabulary and concepts, that the give and take of conversation is neglected. Conversations should always be the basis of language instruction. A child's motivation to learn language will be strongly influenced by how responsive people are to his or her efforts to communicate. This sequence includes items that indicate a child's involvement in the communication process: communicating to get needs met, establishing and maintaining contacts with others, and giving and getting information.

If a child cannot talk or is unintelligible, it is important to maintain communication through other means (e.g., gestures, manual signs, a communication board). Above all, the adult must be responsive to the child's attempts to communicate!

9. Conversation Skills

a. Requests objects or activities with words or signs
b. Greets familiar people with word or sign
c. Asks simple questions (e.g., "What doing?"; "Where going?")
d. Asks "yes/no" questions with appropriate inflection
e. Comments on appearance or disappearance of objects or people
f. Requests assistance (e.g., "Help!"; "You do it.")
g. Requests permission (e.g., "Johnny go out?"; "I turn it?")
h. Sustains conversation for several turns
i. Changes speech depending on listener (e.g., talks differently to babies and adults)
j. Talks on telephone and waits for his or her turn to respond
k. Uses words to describe attributes of toys or foods (e.g., shape, size, color, texture, spatial relationships)
l. Completes incomplete sentences begun by an adult (e.g., analogies, words in familiar stories)
m. Describes what is happening or what he or she is seeing
n. When asked to "tell all about" a picture, names 3 or more elements or describes what is happening
o. Responds correctly to "what do you do" and "why do we" questions
p. Tells a story by looking at pictures
q. Describes functions of objects

r. Answers "what is," "whose," "who," and "how many" questions appropriately (if not correctly)

s. Communicates cause-and-effect relationships (e.g., "It is broken and doesn't work any more.")

t. Uses contingent queries to maintain a conversation (e.g., "Why did he do that?"; "Then what happened?")

u. Creates interest in a listener by indirect references (e.g., "I have a new toy in my room.")

v. Communicates knowledge about the world to peers and adults

w. Makes statements about cause and effect (e.g., uses such words as "because" and "since"—"I can play because I am not sick any more.")

x. Tells 2 familiar stories without pictures for help—includes all important parts

2.5

AREA: 9. Conversation Skills
BEHAVIOR: 9a. Requests objects or activities with words or signs

Materials: Normal home or classroom environment

Procedure	Group activities
Before beginning to try to teach this item, be sure that the child has 2 prerequisite skills: 1) he or she is already able to make choices between objects (e.g., he or she points to objects to indicate his or her wants or selects 1 object from a group to play with), and 2) he or she is able to imitate simple words *or* is able to imitate simple signs. Hold up objects and as he chooses one say, "Oh, you want the ____. Say ____?" Continue to hold the object until he or she makes a sound other than crying or makes an appropriate sign. Then give the child the object, naming it again as you give it to him or her. Gradually require the sound or sign to be a more correct production of the word before giving the object. Do not anticipate the child's needs so that he or she will have a reason to ask for objects. Respond quickly the first few times that the child asks you for the object in order to teach him that asking is an effective way of getting needs and wants met.	Set up the day in the classroom so that all of the children have many opportunities to make choices (e.g., "Do you want to play with this doll or with this truck?"; "Do you want milk or juice?"). Listen for requests that come without your offering the choice. Try to respond to them as quickly as possible. If the child cannot have what he or she is asking for say something like, "I know you want the ____, but you will have to wait until Johnny's through with it." Communicate that you understand and appreciate the request even if you cannot grant it.

Criterion: The child makes at least 3 requests a day (through words or signs) on 3 different days.

2.5

AREA: 9. Conversation Skills
BEHAVIOR: 9b. Greets familiar people with word or sign

Materials: Normal home or classroom environment

Procedure	Group activities
Model saying (or signing), "Hello," "Good Morning," or whatever is appropriate to the child, to members of the family who enter the room, or to visitors who come to the house. Ask the child to say, "Hello" or some other greeting to people as they come. Don't try to force the shy child to talk, but continue providing experiences that will facilitate talking. Give the child a hug or other indication of pleasure when he or she does greet you or others with a word or sign.	Model greeting others by showing your welcome to the children or visitors as they come into the room. When visitors come, introduce them and say, "Can you all say 'Good Morning' to Mrs. Jones?" When you hear a child give a proper greeting, say something to him or her to indicate that you heard and are pleased.

Criterion: The child greets 3 different people appropriately *without being asked to do so*.

2.5

AREA: **9. Conversation Skills**

BEHAVIOR: 9c. Asks simple questions (e.g., "What doing?"; "Where going?")

Materials: Normal home or classroom environment

Procedure	Group activities
Ask the child questions frequently. If he or she does not answer, model appropriate answers for him or her. For example, if you ask the child, "What are you doing?" and he or she does not reply, you might say, "It looks like you're taking your dog for a ride in the truck. Is that what you're doing?" Respond quickly when the child asks questions of you.	1. Ask questions about a story as you read it to the children. Also ask individual children questions throughout the course of the day. 2. Sometimes begin a circle activity without talking to see if it will prompt the children to ask questions. For example, begin to take some interesting objects out of a paper sack, or begin to make something out of scraps of paper. Answer questions as they are asked and try to prompt children who are silent to ask questions by asking them what they think is going on.

Criterion: The child asks at least 3 different questions a day on 3 different days.

2.5

AREA: **9. Conversation Skills**

BEHAVIOR: 9d. Asks "yes/no" questions with appropriate inflection

Materials: Normal home or classroom environment

Procedure	Group activities
Proceed as in item 9c (i.e., model asking questions and respond to whatever questions the child asks).	Proceed as in item 9c.

Criterion: The child asks 3 different "yes/no" questions per day on 3 days (It is not necessary for the child to have the correct word order as long as the inflection indicates a question—"Mommy's going to the store?" is all right if the inflection for a question is heard.).

3

AREA: **9. Conversation Skills**

BEHAVIOR: 9e. Comments on appearance or disappearance of objects or people

Materials: Normal home or classroom environment

Procedure	Group activities
Help the child become aware of his or her world by commenting on what you see and do not see. As the child empties his or her cup, look in it and say, "All gone." or "No more milk." If the child asks for a parent who has gone to work say, "Mama's gone to work." Ask the child "where" questions (e.g., "Where's Daddy?"; "Where's your potatoes?") Listen for the child to ask you "where" questions or to comment on objects, or people who are coming or leaving, appearing or disappearing.	1. Put away something that has been a standard part of the classroom for some period of time. Notice who comments on the disappearance or asks questions about it. Then talk to the group about it. 2. Whenever a child is missing from the class, ask the children if they know who is missing. 3. Put something new in the classroom without saying anything about it. Notice who comments about it. Then talk about the object to the group.

Criterion: On several occasions, the child comments on the appearance or disappearance of objects or people without being prompted or asked questions.

3

AREA: **9. Conversation Skills**

BEHAVIOR: 9f. Requests assistance (e.g., "Help!"; "You do it.")

Materials: Toys or other objects that will challenge the child (e.g., puzzles, wind-up toys)

Procedure	Group activities
Model asking for help within the family (e.g., "Please help me pick up the toys."; "Please hold this box so I can open the door."). Give the child challenging toys to work with (e.g., puzzles, wind-up toys). Offer help to the child if he or she has trouble (e.g., "Do you want me to help you?"; "Let me help you"). Whenever possible give the child a choice as to whether you help him or her —don't just do activities for the child. Some children have a strong need to do activities on their own. Respond positively to requests for help. Indicate an appreciation for how hard the task is, do only as much as necessary to help the child, and praise the child for trying hard.	Ask the children to help you and to help each other in play activities throughout the day.

Criterion: The child requests help from an adult or another child when a task is difficult on 3 different occasions.

3

AREA: **9. Conversation Skills**

BEHAVIOR: 9g. Requests permission (e.g., "Johnny go out?"; "I turn it?")

Materials: Normal home or classroom environment

Procedure	Group activities
Model respect for family rules and personal property by requesting permission within the family setting. Ask the child if you can have a piece of his or her cookie or play with his or her toy. Likewise, ask other family members these kinds of questions. Listen for the child to begin asking permission to do activities. Respond positively to these requests. If the requests cannot be granted, tell the child why not and, if appropriate, when they can be granted (e.g., "You can't go outside now. It's too rainy. We'll go out when the rain stops.").	Model respect for the rules of the classroom and for the rights of individual children by asking permission of them when appropriate. For example, when a child is coloring ask him or her if you can use the red crayon to make a sign for the classroom or ask one child if he or she will let another play with him or her in the block corner.

Criterion: The child requests permission from an adult or child at least 5 times.

3

AREA: **9. Conversation Skills**

BEHAVIOR: 9h. Sustains conversation for several turns

Materials: Normal home or classroom environment

Procedure	Group activities
Talk to the child about activities that he or she is doing, ones that you are doing, or plans for such activities. Take time to listen to the child's responses and let him or her direct the conversation.	Arrange the classroom so that small groups of children play together in a center with materials. Listen to their efforts to converse with each other. At times, stop at a center and talk to the children, trying to allow them to lead the conversation.

Criterion: The child sustains a conversation for several (e.g., 3 or 4) turns, on at least 5 occasions.

3·5

AREA: **9. Conversation Skills**

BEHAVIOR: 9i. Changes speech depending on listener
(e.g., talks differently to babies and adults)

Materials: Normal home or classroom environment

Procedure	Group activities
The primary ways of teaching this skill are to give the child opportunities to observe you interacting with various people and to model talking differently to people of different ages when engaging in pretend play with the child, with puppets, or with dolls. Give the child as many opportunities to interact with people of different ages and backgrounds as possible. Observe and listen to these interactions to see how the child adjusts his or her speech or other behaviors to accommodate the person with whom he or she is interacting.	1. Model talking differently to different people through the voices you assume and the language you use when reading stories or engaging in pretend play with the children. If you are in a day care center where infants and/or toddlers are also kept, take the class to visit the younger class and "help" with the babies. Observe the ways in which the children communicate with these youngsters. 2. If the group setting is one where children with various handicaps are integrated into the group, you may be able to see children changing their manner of speech to accommodate the understandings of different children.

Criterion: The child is observed to change voice tone and/or language when talking to different people on at least 3 occasions.

3·5

AREA: **9. Conversation Skills**

BEHAVIOR: 9j. Talks on telephone and waits for his or her turn to respond

Materials: Real telephone, play telephone

Procedure	Group activities
Give the child opportunities to talk to people who call on the telephone. Also, have pretend conversations with the child using a play telephone. Model talking and waiting for a response before talking any more.	None

Criterion: The child talks on the telephone, listens to the response, and talks again; taking at least 3 turns, on 3 different days.

3.5

AREA: **9. Conversation Skills**

BEHAVIOR: 9k. Uses words to describe attributes of toys or foods (e.g., shape, size, color, texture, spatial relationships)

Materials: Normal home or classroom environment

Procedure	Group activities
Talk to the child about objects that he or she is looking at, holding, or playing with—anything engaging his or her interest. Describe the objects in terms of their size, color, or texture. Give the child choices that involve using descriptive terms. For example, ask, "Do you want the red ball or the green ball?" or "Do you want the long socks or the short socks?" Or ask, "Which one do you want?" when the child makes a general request. When you show the child something new or different, encourage him or her to describe it (e.g., "What color is it?"; "How does it feel?"; "How does it smell?").	Bring something interesting to show to the children at circle time and encourage them to talk about it. Ask questions to encourage them to use concepts that they have learned to describe the object.

Criterion: The child uses words to describe at least 2 attributes for 5 different toys, foods, or other objects.

3.5

AREA: **9. Conversation Skills**

BEHAVIOR: 9l. Completes incomplete sentences begun by an adult (e.g., analogies, words in familiar stories)

Materials: Normal home or classroom environment

Procedure	Group activities
When you are reading one of the child's favorite stories, stop in the middle of a sentence to see if the child will fill in the rest (e.g., "First, Goldilocks tasted the porridge in the ____."). Say, "That's right," if he or she fills it in correctly. Go on to fill it in yourself if the child does not. When you are showing the child something, describe part of it and leave the sentence unfinished so that the child can complete it for you. For example, you might show him or her how a wind-up toy works and then say, "Now I'm going to wind it up and then it's going to ____." Help the child to practice concepts that he or she has learned by starting sentences and letting him or her finish them (e.g., "This apple is red, this lemon is ____.").	Do the activities in the "Procedure" section during circle time with the whole group. Have the children take turns completing the sentences.

Criterion: The child completes 3 or more sentences per day on different 3 days.

3.5

AREA: **9. Conversation Skills**

BEHAVIOR: 9m. Describes what is happening or what he or she is seeing

Materials: Normal home or classroom environment

Procedure	Group activities
Talk a lot to the child so that he or she has a model for talking about his or her own experiences. Several times a day, ask the child what he or she is doing, what he or she is seeing, or what is happening. Listen carefully to the child's answers and fill in words as necessary to help him or her express him- or herself. Make it clear that you are interested in what the child has to say.	Encourage the children to describe events to one another as they play. Put children who have difficulty expressing themselves in centers with children who are outgoing so that there will be good models for talking about experiences.

Criterion: The child describes what is happening or what he or she is seeing at least 2 times a day on 3 different days either spontaneously or in response to questions.

4   AREA: **9. Conversation Skills**

BEHAVIOR: 9n. When asked to "tell all about" a picture, names 3 or more elements or describes what is happening

Materials: Pictures in which something interesting is happening (e.g., picture of: a child who has fallen in a mud puddle, a child who is in the bathtub, a mother who is unloading groceries from a car; advertisements in magazines)

Procedure	Group activities
Show a picture to the child and say, "Look at this. Tell me what you see."; "What can you tell me about this picture?"; or "Tell me all about this picture". If the child makes no response, point to different parts of the picture and say, "What is that?" Then say, "And what do you think is happening?" If the child does not reply, tell him or her what you think is happening. Do this frequently as you look through books or magazines.	Follow the procedure to the left with a group of children. Ask different children to answer the questions so that they can learn from each other's answers.

Criterion: When asked to tell about a picture, the child spontaneously names 3 or more elements in a picture or describes what is happening.

4

AREA: 9. Conversation Skills
BEHAVIOR: 9o. Responds correctly to "what do you do" and "why do we" questions.

Materials: Normal home or classroom environment

Procedure	Group activities
Ask the child questions that relate to his or her own experiences. (e.g., "What do you do if you're hungry?"; "What do you do if you hurt your knee?"; "What do you do if you want to play with Johnny's truck?"; "Why do we have to take a nap?"; "Why do we cook the spaghetti?"). If the child does not answer, tell him or her the answer. The issue is not just having the information, but knowing how to form an answer to questions of this sort.	During circle time or when you are with 2 or 3 children playing together, ask "what do you do" and "why do we" questions that relate to the current activity. Try to give different children opportunities to answer so that they can learn from one another.

Criterion: The child responds appropriately to at least 2 "what do you do" and 2 "why do we" questions.

4

AREA: 9. Conversation Skills
BEHAVIOR: 9p. Tells a story by looking at pictures

Materials: Books with a lot of pictures

Procedure	Group activities
Read a book to the child one or more times while showing him or her the pictures. Then ask him or her to "read" the story to you. Then have him or her try to tell a story from the pictures in a new book *before* you have read the story.	Proceed as in the "Procedure" section with the group in circle time or with a small group of children in a center.

Criterion: The child tells a story by looking at the pictures on at least 3 occasions (3 different sets of pictures).

4

AREA: 9. Conversation Skills
BEHAVIOR: 9q. Describes functions of objects

Materials: Normal home or classroom environment

Procedure	Group activities
Talk about objects and what they are used for as you go through daily routines. Then, begin asking the child, "What do we do with that?" or "What is	Bring a sack of objects to look at during a group time. As you bring out each one, ask one of the children what it is used for. If he or

(continued)

Procedure	Group activities
this for?" When you introduce the child to a new object, ask him or her what he or she thinks it might be used for. Let the child try it and find out and then describe it.	she cannot answer, move on to the next child, and so on.

Criterion: The child describes the functions of 5 or more objects either spontaneously or when asked "What do we use this for?"; "Why do we have these?"; or "What do we do with this?"

4

AREA: **9. Conversation Skills**

BEHAVIOR: 9r. Answers "what is," "whose," "who," and "how many" questions appropriately (if not correctly)

Materials: Normal home or classroom environment

Procedure	Group activities
Always answer the child's questions. Ask him or her a lot of questions during the course of the day using "what," "whose," "who," and "how many". If the child answers incorrectly, reward him or her for trying by saying something like, "That's a good guess, but I think . . . ."(giving the correct answer).	When reading stories or engaging in activities at circle time or in small groups ask questions in the form described to the left, giving different children opportunities to answer. Encourage discussion of answers in the group.

Criterion: The child answers at least 2 questions appropriately in each form (e.g., what, whose, who, how many). For the purposes of this item, the issue is *not* the correctness of the answer; rather, it is the child's ability to put together the right kind of sentence to answer the question. That is, a "what is" question should be answered with the name of an object, a "who" or "whose" question should be answered with the name of someone, and a "how many" question should be answered with a number.

4.5 AREA: **9. Conversation Skills**

BEHAVIOR: 9s. Communicates cause-and-effect relationships (e.g., "It is broken and doesn't work any more.")

Materials: Normal home or classroom environment

Procedure	Group activities
Talk to the child frequently, explaining why events happen, using cause and effect statements. Also, build this kind of explanation into stories that you read to the child. Ask the child questions that will facilitate his or her using cause and effect statements (e.g., "How did this happen?"; "What did you do?").	A group setting provides many opportunities to talk about cause and effect (e.g., the effects of objects on each other, the effects of children on objects, the effects of children on each other). Use these opportunities to model talking about cause and effect. Also, ask questions to facilitate the children's use of cause and effect statements.

Criterion: The child communicates at least 5 different cause and effect relationships over a week's time.

4.5

AREA: 9. Conversation Skills
BEHAVIOR: 9t. Uses contingent queries to maintain a conversation
(e.g., "Why did he do that?"; "Then what happened?")

Materials: Normal home or classroom environment

Procedure	Group activities
Model conversational skills for the child when you talk to him or her. When the child makes a statement and then stops, ask questions that relate to what she has just said to encourage the child to tell you more. Some good examples are: "Then what did he do?"; "Why did you do that?"; and "What happened next?" The best questions cannot be answered with "yes" or "no," and really encourage the continuation of a conversation. Then, when you are telling the child something, stop after a sentence or so to see if the child will try to get you to continue by asking appropriate questions. If the child does not, say something like, "Do you want to know what happened next?" and wait for an indication of "yes" before continuing.	One of the best ways to encourage this skill in groups is to tell stories including long pauses as exciting points so that the children will try to get you to continue. Those who are already using questions to maintain a conversation will serve as good models to those who are not.

Criterion: The child uses at least 2 contingent queries to maintain a conversation on 3 different occasions.

4.5

AREA: 9. Conversation Skills
BEHAVIOR: 9u. Creates interest in a listener by indirect references
(e.g., "I have a new toy in my room.")

Materials: Normal home or classroom environment

Procedure	Group activities
Model this skill for the child throughout the day (e.g., "Guess what nummy thing we're having for lunch."; "I have something new for us to play with."; "I found something you lost under the couch."). Respond enthusiastically to the child's attempts to imitate this behavior. For example, if he or she says, "I found something outside," act very interested, spend some time looking at what was found, and talk about it.	Use indirect references to create interest when introducing new activities or new toys to the children in the classroom. Respond to the children's attempts to interest you through similar behaviors.

Criterion: The child uses indirect references to create interest in a listener on at least 3 different occasions.

5

AREA: **9. Conversation Skills**

BEHAVIOR: 9v. Communicates knowledge about the world to peers and adults

Materials: Normal home or classroom environment

Procedure	Group activities
Make it a common practice to talk to the child about the objects or activities that you are seeing and doing together and about those you know about. Use this talking to both entertain and to teach the child when you are busy with chores around the house, are riding in the car, or taking walks outdoors. Tell the child what you know about nature (e.g., what is happening when the bee lands on the flower, how the bird is building her nest). Listen carefully to the child's questions and answer them. Also listen to the child's attempts to communicate his or her understandings to you. Respond with interest. Also, listen to what he or she says to other children.	1. Plan field trips for the children to the fire station, zoo, or other places of interest and talk about the experience when you return. Encourage the children to tell their parents about what they saw and did. Alert parents to the activity so that they will ask questions if the child does not tell about the experience spontaneously. 2. Plan science activities in the classroom (e.g., planting seeds, capturing a caterpillar and observing its development into a moth or butterfly). Talk about this information and encourage the children to talk to their parents about it.

Criterion: The child attempts to communicate his or her knowledge about some event or experience to others at least 5 times. The communications should be taking place with both adults and peers unless circumstances are such that peers are not available who can understand the child.

5   AREA: **9. Conversation Skills**

BEHAVIOR: 9w. Makes statement about cause and effect (e.g., uses such words as "because" and "since"—"I can play because I am not sick any more.")

Materials: Normal home or classroom environment

Procedure	Group activities
When you tell the child "no," tell him or her a rule, or explain events, and give reasons (e.g., "You mustn't run into the street because you'll get hurt."; "You have to stay in because it is raining outside."; "Since Daddy has to work late, we'll eat supper alone."; "Because you've been such a good boy, I'm going to take you to the mall."). This will help the child feel that the world is a somewhat predictable place, that there are reasons that events occur. Listen, particularly when the child is arguing with you about a rule or decision, to see if he or she also gives reasons for his or her point of view. Listen to the reasons that the child gives to siblings or playmates for household rules or his decisions.	Set aside a group time now and then to talk about rules of behavior in the classroom. Ask the children why they think a particular rule is enforced (e.g., "Why don't we run in the hallway?"; "Why do we ask before we take something from someone else?"). Discuss the answers they give.

Criterion: The child makes statements about cause and effect related to rules of conduct or events that have occurred in at least 5 such statements.

AREA: **9. Conversation Skills**
BEHAVIOR: 9x. Tells 2 familiar stories without pictures for help
—includes all important parts

Materials: Normal home or classroom environment

Procedure	Group activities
Ask the child to tell you a story. Chose one that you have read to him or her several times or one that you have just finished reading to the child. Do not let the child use pictures for help. Prompt as necessary with questions such as, "And then what happened?"	Go over a story after you have read it to the group. Ask who can tell you the whole story. Try to give each child an opportunity to tell a story over a period of time. Prompt with questions as necessary.

Criterion: The child tells at least 2 familiar stories without pictures for help, including all of the important parts of the story, *without* prompts.

10.

Sentence Construction

HUMAN BEINGS APPEAR to be "wired" to learn language with its complex grammatical structures. It is unclear how much caregivers can influence the rate at which these structures are learned. However, it is apparent that children must hear the structures and have the opportunity to practice them. Most caregivers naturally adapt their speech so that they are always just one step ahead of the child in the complexity of the speech they use, thereby giving the child models for the next structures to be learned. For normally developing children, this is enough. For children with special needs, more repetition and greater emphasis may be needed to encourage development. However, *do not nag* children about grammar. It is important that caregivers and parents not interfere with the communication process in a child who is having specific difficulty with grammar.

This sequence includes the grammatical forms as they are generally mastered by normal children and suggestions for emphasizing the structures to be learned in the general activities of daily living. Some children may need time to work individually in speech/language therapy, concentrating on sentence construction. However, the rest of the time, learning should be encouraged by listening to the child, reinforcing correct structures by responding to them in a normal communicative fashion, and simply repeating incorrect structures in a correct form to provide a model. Avoid paying too much attention to errors.

It is important to provide opportunities for children to learn these grammatical forms, even if the children cannot talk. This can be done through reading and talking to the children so that they hear the forms repeatedly. A speech/language therapist will be able to make specific suggestions to promote the mastery of grammatical structures through the various forms of augmentative communication.

10. Sentence Construction

a. Uses 2-word utterances to indicate: possession (e.g., "Mommy's sock."; "My doll.") and action (e.g., "Eat cookie."; "Find shoes.")

b. Uses 2-word utterances to indicate: non-existence (e.g., "No juice."; "Daddy bye-bye.") and recurrence (e.g., "More juice.")

c. Uses 2-word utterances to indicate: specificity (e.g., "This toy."; "That box.")

and characteristics (e.g., "Hot stove."; "Pretty bunny.")

d. Uses "s" on the ends of some words to form plurals

e. Uses auxiliary verbs, usually shortened (e.g., gonna, wanna, hafta)

f. Uses "ing" on verbs (e.g., "I helping.")

g. Uses negative terms (e.g., can't, don't)

h. Uses personal pronouns (e.g., me, you, mine, your)

i. Uses prepositional phrases (e.g., in house, on table)

j. Uses 3-word phrases to specify (e.g., "That big one."; "This finger hurt."), to indicate rejection (e.g., "No scary book."; "No want that."), and/or to describe (e.g., "The big dog.")

k. Uses 3–4-word complete sentences that include subject-verb-object (e.g., "Mommy open that."; "Mommy make big mess.")

l. Asks "wh" questions (e.g., why, what, where)

m. Uses "I" instead of given name

n. Uses "s" or "es" on ends of words to indicate possession

o. Uses prepositional phrases in sentences (e.g., "Put it *on my lap*.")

p. Uses most irregular past tense verb forms correctly

q. Uses quantity terms (e.g., some, many, most, few, all)

r. Uses "and," "but," "or", and "because" to connect 2 sentences into one (e.g., "It hit me but it didn't hurt.")

s. Uses "ing" words other than as verbs (e.g, "Hitting is not nice."; "He got hurt running fast.")

t. Correctly differentiates past, present and future verbs; regular and irregular verbs

u. Correct word order in "wh" questions (e.g., "Why is John here?")

v. Uses endings on verbs or nouns to indicate the activity of a person or thing (e.g., driver, painter, guitarist)

w. Uses comparatives (e.g., big, bigger, biggest; small, smaller, smallest; sad, sadder, saddest)

2.5   AREA: **10. Sentence Construction**

BEHAVIOR: 10a. Uses 2-word utterances to indicate: possession (e.g., "Mommy's sock.";
            "My doll.") and action (e.g., "Eat cookie."; "Find shoes.")

2.5 BEHAVIOR: 10b. Uses 2-word utterances to indicate: nonexistence (e.g., "No juice.";
            "Daddy bye-bye.") and recurrence (e.g., "More juice.")

2.5 BEHAVIOR: 10c. Uses 2-word utterances to indicate: specificity (e.g., "This toy."; "That
            box.") and characteristics (e.g., "Hot stove."; "Pretty bunny.")

Materials: Normal home or classroom environment

Procedure	Group activities
When the child is using 1-word utterances to communicate, respond to him or her by repeating what was said and expanding on it. For example, when the child says, "Hot," you say, "Yes, *hot*. Hot *stove*."; when the child holds out his or her glass and says, "Juice," you say, "Do you want *more juice*? Here's *more* juice." (give a special emphasis to the word you are using to expand the child's statement). Talk to the child frequently during the course of the day. Do not talk "baby talk" but do place extra emphasis on short phrases that the child will be more likely to imitate.	None

Criterion: The child uses at least one 2-word utterance in each of the categories listed.

AREA: **10. Sentence Construction**

2.5   BEHAVIOR: 10d. Uses "s" on the ends of some words to form plurals

Materials: Normal home or classroom environment

Procedure	Group activities
Make a special effort to pronounce the "s" on the end of words indicating a plural. Use numbers and other quantity words when talking about objects that you are seeing or playing with (e.g., "I have just 1 block. You have a lot of blocks."; "Here, you can have 2 cookies."; "Look at this picture. There is only 1 puppy. See here, there are 3 puppies—1, 2, 3.") Listen for the child to begin using "s" on the ends of words to indicate plurals.	Sing songs, read nursery rhymes, and do finger plays that involve both singular and plural nouns. Emphasize the "s" on the plurals so that the child will hear it.

Criterion: The child uses plurals for at least 5 different words. At this stage, it is counted as correct if the child incorrectly forms plurals for irregular words (e.g., says "mans" instead of "men").

2.5

AREA: **10. Sentence Construction**
BEHAVIOR: 10e. Uses auxilliary verbs, usually shortened (e.g., gonna, wanna, hafta)

Materials: Normal home or classroom environment

Procedure	Group activities
Make sure that you are using auxilliary verbs in your conversations with the child. They will come very naturally if you describe your activities to the child as you do them (e.g., "Now I'm going to wash the dishes."; "I have to change your diaper before we go out."; "I want to go outside.").	None

Criterion: The child uses at least 2 auxilliary verb forms, 2 or more times.

AREA: **10. Sentence Construction**
BEHAVIOR: 10f. Uses "ing" on verbs (e.g., "I helping.")

3

Materials: Normal home or classroom environment

Procedure	Group activities
Talk to the child frequently about what you are doing and about what he or she is doing. You will naturally include a lot of verbs with the "ing" ending (e.g., "We are going . . . "; "I am doing . . . "; "Grandma is coming."). Listen for the child to begin using "ing" on the end of verbs. Repeat the "ing" verbs back to the child when he or she does use them (e.g., "Yes, we are *going* home.").	None

Criterion: The child using "ing" on the end of at least 5 different verbs.

AREA: **10. Sentence Construction**
3   BEHAVIOR: 10g. Uses negative terms (e.g., can't, don't)

Materials: Normal home or classroom environment

Procedure	Group activities
You will use these terms naturally with the child as you talk to him or her about your daily activities. Listen to the child so that you will hear when he or she begins to use them. Let the child know you have heard and understand by repeating his or her sen-	None

(continued)

Procedure	Group activities
tence in some natural way (e.g., the child says, "Can't go," and you say, "The car can't go. The car must be broken. Let's see if I can fix it.").	

Criterion: The child uses at least 2 different negative terms on 3 different days (e.g., cannot, can't, don't, won't, hasn't).

3

AREA: **10. Sentence Construction**
BEHAVIOR: 10h. Uses personal pronouns (e.g., me, you, mine, your)

Materials: A normal home or classroom environment

Procedure	Group activities
Be sure that you use personal pronouns when talking to the child rather than always referring to yourself as "mommy" or "daddy" or to the child by his or her name. For example, say, "You are my big boy," rather than "Johnny is my big boy."; and say, "I'm going to the store," rather than "Daddy is going to the store." Listen to the child so that you will hear when he or she begins to use these pronouns. Do not correct the child if he or she gets them wrong (e.g., "Me going to the store."), but continue to model the correct usage.	Read stories to the children with many conversations in them. These will include the usage of numerous personal pronouns.

Criterion: The child uses at least 3 personal pronouns each on 2 or more occasions.

AREA: **10. Sentence Construction**
3   BEHAVIOR: 10i. Uses prepositional phrases (e.g., in house, on table)

Materials: Normal home or classroom environment

Procedure	Group activities
Emphasize prepositions as you talk to the child about activities that you are doing or about what is happening (e.g., Your ball is *under* the table."; "Let's put the sheets *on* the bed."; "Put your toys *in* the toy box."). Listen for the child's first attempts to use these words. Encourage the use of prepositions by asking the child where objects are (e.g., "Where's your book?"). If the child does not reply or just points, say, "I see it. It is *on* the table."	Plan a circle activity to teach contrasting prepositions (e.g., "in" and "on"; "on" and "under"). Place as object in a position (e.g., a block under a cup) and ask where it is. You can also hide objects in or under containers and have the children guess where they are.

Criterion: The child uses at least 2 different prepositions in phrases each used 2 or more times.

3

AREA: **10. Sentence Construction**

BEHAVIOR: 10j. Uses 3-word phrases to specify (e.g., "That big one."; "This finger hurt."), to indicate rejection (e.g., "No scary book."; "No want that."), and/or to describe (e.g., "The big dog.")

Materials: Normal home or classroom environment

Procedure	Group activities
As the child uses 2-word phrases, expand on them to encourage the production of longer phrases. For example, if the child says, "That one," say, "Oh, you want *that big one.*" Read very simple picture books to the child. Talk about the pictures. Encourage the child to talk about them. Listen for 3-word phrases.	Read very short and simple books to the children. Be sure there are a lot of pictures and relatively few words. Talk about the pictures. Encourage the children to talk about them and to point to parts of the pictures.

Criterion: The child uses at least five 3-word phrases on several days.

3.5

AREA: **10. Sentence Construction**

BEHAVIOR: 10k. Uses 3–4-word complete sentences that include subject-verb-object (e.g., "Mommy make big mess.")

Materials: Normal home or classroom environment

Procedure	Group activities
Continue to expand the child's phrases, saying complete sentences that contain the words from his or her phrases. Continue to talk to the child about what you are doing and what you are seeing. Read simple stories to the child.	Read simple stories that have a lot of pictures to the children. Talk about the stories. Ask questions or make comments as you read.

Criterion: The child uses at least 3 complete 3–4-word sentences a day for 3 days. The sentences must have a subject, a verb, and an object.

3.5

AREA: **10. Sentence Construction**

BEHAVIOR: 10l. Asks "wh" questions (e.g., why, what, where)

Materials: Normal home or classroom environment

Procedure	Group activities
Ask the child questions frequently and provide answers for him or her if he or she is unable to produce them. When the child begins to ask you questions,	Bring objects from nature to circle time. Ask the children questions (e.g., "Why does this leaf have a big hole in it?"; "What eats

(continued)

Procedure	Group activities
always try to answer. Many children this age use "wh" questions as a way of maintaining a conversation. They are less interested in the answers than in keeping the adult talking. It is important not to be frustrated if the child continues to say "why" after you have given the reason several times. Go on to talk about something else.	acorns?"). Respond to the children's questions.

Criterion: The child asks 5 or more "wh" questions.

3. 5

AREA: **10. Sentence Construction**
BEHAVIOR: 10m. Uses "I" instead of given name

Materials: Normal home or classroom environment

Procedure	Group activities
When talking to the child, use pronouns as you would if talking to an adult. That is, say, "He did it," "You are going . . . ," "I want some juice now," or "You are funny," rather than using people's names as one often does when talking to a baby. Listen to the child so that you will notice when he or she begins to use pronouns, particularly when the child begins to say "I."	None

Criterion: The child uses "I" instead of his or her given name at least half the time.

3. 5

AREA: **10. Sentence Construction**
BEHAVIOR: 10n. Uses "s" or "es" on ends of words to indicate possession

Materials: Normal home or classroom environment

Procedure	Group activities
When you are talking to the child, make sure you are clearly saying the "s" on the end of names when you are indicating that something belongs to someone (e.g., "That's Daddy's comb."; "That's John's book.").	None

Criterion: The child uses "s" or "es" on the ends of words to indicate possession on at least 5 occasions.

Ұ

AREA: 10. Sentence Construction
BEHAVIOR: 10o. Uses prepositional phrases in sentences (e.g., "Put it *on my lap.*")

Materials: Normal home or classroom environment

Procedure	Group activities
As you are teaching the concepts "in," "on," "around," and "under" to the child, emphasize the whole phrase (e.g., "I am putting the blocks *in the box.*"; "Bring me the toy that is *under the table.*"). Make a point of asking the child questions that are likely to elicit prepositional phrases (e.g., "Where is the pencil?"; "Where shall I put this?"). Listen to what the child says.	Periodically, play a hiding game: hide something in the classroom and have the children guess where it is hidden. After a guess, the child can go look to see if he or she is correct. Model complete sentences for the children (e.g., "It is under John's coat.") so that they do not use the prepositional phrase alone (e.g., "Under John's coat.").

Criterion: The child uses preposition phrases in sentences (must include a verb) at least 5 times.

4

AREA: 10. Sentence Construction
BEHAVIOR: 10p. Uses most irregular past tense verb forms correctly

Materials: Normal home or classroom environment

Procedure	Group activities
Talk to the child and listen to what he or she says. When the child uses a verb form incorrectly (e.g., "he goed" instead of "he went") do not be critical, but simply repeat what the child said, using the correct verb form).	None

Criterion: The child uses most irregular past tense verb forms correctly (does not make errors more than 1 or 2 times a day).

Note: Some dialects include different verb forms than standard English. It is useful for the child to hear the standard English forms because these are what he or she will be taught to read. However, the child should not fail this item if he or she is consistently using the verb forms of his or her culture.

4

AREA: 10. Sentence Construction
BEHAVIOR: 10q. Uses quantity terms (e.g., some, many, most, few, all)

Materials: Normal home or classroom environment

Procedure	Group activities
Use quantity terms when you talk to the child. Ask him or her questions and give instructions that use these terms (e.g., "You may have some jelly beans. Woops, that's too many! You can only have a few this close to dinner. How about 3—1, 2, 3."). Ask the child questions that are likely to elicit the use of quantity terms as you read books and look at pictures. Combine counting objects with the use of these words (e.g., "He took *most* of the apples. He left just a *few*. Let's count how many he left. 1, 2, 3.").	Collect pictures that have various numbers of objects in them. Show 2 of them to the children and ask questions related to quantity (e.g., "Which picture has the most ____?" "Which picture has just a few ____?"). Combine this with counting activities.

Criterion: The child uses at least 3 different quantity words, each on 3 or more occasions.

4-5

AREA: 10. Sentence Construction
BEHAVIOR: 10r. Uses "and," "but," "or," and "because" to connect 2 sentences into one
(e.g., "It hit me but it didn't hurt.")

Materials: Normal home or classroom environment

Procedure	Group activities
Talk to the child, read to the child, and listen to the child talk. Occasionally expand his or her sentences with "and, "but," "or," and "because." For example, if the child says, "I fell down," you might say, "You fell down but you didn't cry," or "You hurt yourself but I'll kiss it and make it better."	Encourage show and tell activities. These tend to give you good opportunities to hear children express their ideas and to model more complex language for them.

Criterion: The child makes 2 sentences into 1 with "and," "or," "but," or "because" at least 5 times.

4.5

AREA: 10. Sentence Construction

BEHAVIOR: 10s. Uses "ing" words other than as verbs (e.g, "Hitting is not nice."; "He got hurt running fast.")

Materials: Normal home or classroom environment

Procedure	Group activities
Notice when you are using "ing" words when talking to the child and listen to see if he or she begins to use them as well.	None

Criterion: The child uses at least 3 "ing" words other than as verbs.

4.5

AREA: 10. Sentence Construction

BEHAVIOR: 10t. Correctly differentiates past, present, and future verbs; regular and irregular verbs

Materials: Normal home or classroom environment

Procedure	Group activities
Talk to the child, read to him or her and ask questions in which you use the correct forms of verbs. Listen to the child as he or she talks. When the child makes errors, repeat his or her sentence with the correct verb in it. For example, if the child says, "I go tomorrow," you say, "Yes, you *will go* tomorrow."	None

Criterion: The child correctly differentiates past, present, and future verbs, regular and irregular—no more than 1 error in an extended conversation.

Note: Some dialects include different verb forms than standard English. It is useful for the child to hear the standard English forms because these are what he or she will be taught to read. However, the child should not fail this item if he or she is consistently using the verb forms of his or her culture.

5

AREA: 10. Sentence Construction

BEHAVIOR: 10u. Correct word order in "wh" questions (e.g., "Why is John here?")

Materials: Normal home or classroom environment

Procedure	Group activities
Talk to the child frequently and model correct speech. When the child uses the wrong order in the sentence, repeat it back to him or her with the correct order.	Ask a lot of questions after you read stories to the children. In these questions, you will be modeling the correct word order for questions.

Criterion: The child uses correct word order in "wh" questions. He or she rarely makes errors.

5

AREA: 10. Sentence Construction

BEHAVIOR: 10v. Uses endings on verbs or nouns to indicate the activity of a person or thing: (e.g., driver, painter, guitarist)

Materials: Normal home or classroom environment

Procedure	Group activities
Talk to the child about objects or events that you see or read about. Refer to the child as a painter when she is painting a picture or to yourself as a driver when you drive the car. Listen for the child's attempts to use these words. Listen also for words that he or she may make up using the "er" ending (e.g., a stick may become a "poker" when it is used to poke something into a hole).	Cut out pictures of people doing different activities and talk about them in the group. Let the children share their experiences with people doing similar activities (e.g., tell about when the painter came to their house).

Criterion: The child uses endings on verbs or nouns to indicate the activity of a person or object in at least 5 different words.

AREA: 10. Sentence Construction

BEHAVIOR: 10w. Uses comparatives: big, bigger, biggest; small, smaller, smallest; sad, sadder, saddest)

Materials: Normal home or classroom environment

Procedure	Group activities
Talk to the child about objects or events that you see or experience. Make a point of using comparative terms. Ask the child questions (e.g., "Which one is bigger?"; "Which one is heavier?"; "Which one is fatter?"; "Which one is the fattest?"). Ask the child to describe pictures or objects to you. This will facilitate his or her use of these terms.	Collect pictures and objects to show the children at group time. Have several groups that include 3 objects so that you can talk about: small, smaller, and smallest; and heavy, heavier, and heaviest. Let the children touch, lift, smell, and otherwise experience the objects and have them describe them.

Criterion: The child uses all 3 forms (e.g., big, bigger, biggest) on at least 5 different words.

11.

Responsibility

ASSUMING RESPONSIBILITY for one's own behavior is an important part of the growing-up process. When children are developing normally, they often seem to demand the right to take responsibility (e.g., "I want to do it myself!"). They are also more likely to explore actively and get themselves into situations where adults have to teach them about dangers and taking care of belongings. Children who are handicapped frequently have fewer of these experiences and their caregivers may feel more protective of them. They may grow up rather passive and unable to assume any responsibility for themselves or others unless a conscious effort is made to teach them. It is important that caregivers make this effort. Although the child who is physically handicapped may not be able to run out into the street, for example, it is still important for him or her to know that streets are dangerous and that there are precautions that must be taken when crossing.

This sequence suggests ways to teach responsibility not only through direct control of one's behavior but through knowing the rules of safety, caring for property, and functioning in the community.

The amount of responsibility a child can assume may be limited by his or her handicapping conditions. However, it is very important to avoid limiting the child additionally by overprotecting him or her. Self-esteem is higher in children who are given responsibilities within a family and in other settings. Thus, caregivers should encourage as much responsibility as a child is physically and cognitively able to assume. As you work through this sequence, modify items as necessary to reach that goal for each child.

11. Responsibility

a. Avoids common dangers (e.g., broken glass, high places, busy streets, big animals)

b. Knows what toys can and cannot do and uses them appropriately

c. Puts toys away neatly when asked (may have to be reminded)

d. Follows rules given by adults for new activities or simple games

e. Answers questions related to self-care

(e.g., "Why shouldn't you play with knives?"; "Why should you look before crossing the street?")

f. Shows care in handling small animals or potentially breakable objects.

g. Responds appropriately to instructions given in a small group

h. Plays in own neighborhood without constant adult supervision

i. Buys simple objects in store without help (i.e., gets object or tells clerk what he or she wants, provides money, and waits for change)

j. Answers telephone appropriately and delivers message

2·5

AREA: **11. Responsibility**

BEHAVIOR: 11a. Avoids common dangers (e.g., broken glass, high places, busy streets, big animals)

Materials: Normal home or classroom environment

Procedures	Group activities
Talk to the child about being careful as you do activities together. For example, as you approach the street say, "We have to be careful that no cars are coming. Look both ways. Do you see a car coming? O.K., now we can cross the street."	A group setting will give you many opportunities to talk about rules of safety. You may want to devote a few minutes every week to a quick review of safety rules at school (e.g., "What do we do in the hall? Do we run? No, we walk. Johnny, why don't we run? Because we might fall and get hurt.").
Always give reasons for prohibitions (e.g., "I don't want you to do that because you might fall and get hurt."; "Some dogs are friendly, some are not. We don't know that dog so we won't try to pet him.").	
If the child starts to do something dangerous, calmly but firmly stop him or her and explain why he or she must not do that. If the child persists, a punishment (e.g., time out) is in order.	
It is important that you communicate to the child that you expect him or her to be responsible and that you notice and comment when he or she is responsible. Don't always stop the child before he or she has a chance to decide an appropriate action. For example, if you (or the child) breaks something made of glass, don't immediately pick up the child. Wait to see if he or she starts to approach it. If the child moves away, says "uh oh" or takes other appropriate action, say, "That's a good boy. Leave it there and I will clean it up so you won't get hurt."	

Criterion: The child avoids common dangers most of the time; that is, you do not have to stop the child and retrieve him or her from a bad situation more than once a week.

Note: Some children are, by nature, highly active and impulsive. They are much more likely to do dangerous things without thinking about them. It is especially important to be vigilant to keep these children safe. It is also important to remain calm, to continue telling them the reasons for rules, and to be very attentive to them when they do manage to obey the rules.

3

AREA: **11. Responsibility**

BEHAVIOR: 11b. Knows what toys can and cannot do and uses them appropriately

Materials: A general assortment of appropriate playthings

Procedures	Group activities
When the child gets a new toy or visits another child who has different toys than the ones at home, take time to show the child what the toy is used for and how it works. Talk about it as you show the child. The child may be curious and experiment with other ways to use the toy. Or, he or she may be unable to use the toy in the way intended and will try to do something inappropriate with it. Do not interfere unless the experimentation is clearly inappropriate or dangerous (e.g., throwing something breakable, trying to pull the toy apart). At those times, say something like, "That toy is not for throwing. It will break. You see, it works like this." Help the child use it appropriately. If the toy is clearly "too old" for the child, remove it and get him or her interested in another toy.	Introduce new toys or materials to the group with demonstrations on how they are to be used.

Criterion: The child almost always knows what toys can and cannot do and uses them appropriately. The child may experiment with new toys but will be careful. He or she does not break the toy or do something highly inappropriate with it in his or her experimentation.

3 . 5

AREA: **11. Responsibility**

BEHAVIOR: 11c. Puts toys away neatly when asked (may have to be reminded)

Materials: Normal home or classroom environment

Procedures	Group activities
Have a routine of having the child help put toys away when he or she is through playing with them. Often, children are overwhelmed if there are too many objects to pick up at once. If a child has a hard time getting started, ask him to help you pick up. Praise the child for his or her help. By staying with the child or nearby, offering encouragement and praise the child will learn to complete the task.	In a group setting, it is very helpful to teach the children to always put something away when they are through with it, unless another child has asked to play with it. When it is time to clean up, everyone should be involved. Give a lot of praise to children as they clean up. Pay special attention to those who are cleaning up rather than nagging those who are not helping (e.g., "Boy, I like the way Johnny and Susan are cleaning up."). You may want to put stars on a chart for "good citizens"—those who help keep the room neat. (If you make such a chart, comment only on those who get stars. *Do not* say anything about those who do not.)

Criterion: The child usually puts toys away neatly when asked (may be reminded 1 or 2 times).

3-5

AREA: **11. Responsibility**

BEHAVIOR: 11d. Follows rules given by adults for new activities or simple games

Materials: Normal home or classroom environment

Procedures	Group activities
When you are going someplace new that requires some rules, always tell the child the rules ahead of time. Repeat several times to be sure he or she understands (e.g., "We're going into a store with a lot of pretty things. You may look, but you must not touch."; "When we go into the mall there will be a lot of people. You must keep hold of my hand so we can stay together.").	Try very simple games with the children in a group. For example, Drop the Handkerchief, Animal Lotto (or other simple matching games), and games that require the group to imitate the leader.
Play simple games with the child (e.g., Slap Jack —give equal numbers of cards to players who turn over a card onto a central stack. Whenever a jack is turned up, everyone tries to slap it. The person who slaps the most jacks wins; Candyland or other very simple board games—where the adult can help count if the child has difficulty).	

Criterion: The child follows rules given by adults for new activities or simple games. The child must regularly attempt to follow the rules. If he or she does not, it is important to determine if the child is deliberately uncooperative or if he or she does not understand the rules.

4

AREA: **11. Responsibility**

BEHAVIOR: 11e. Answers questions related to self-care (e.g., "Why shouldn't you play with knives?"; "Why should you look before crossing the street?")

Materials: Normal home or classroom environment

Procedures	Group activities
Always explain the reasons for a safety rule or for rules for self-care (e.g., washing hands, combing hair). Occasionally check out the child's understanding of the rules by asking him or her questions about them (e.g., "Why don't you . . . ?"; "Why do you . . . ?").	Discuss rules for safety and self-care during small group times. Check the children's understandings by asking questions about these activities.

Criterion: The child answers 5 or more questions related to safety and self-care.

4

AREA: **11. Responsibility**

BEHAVIOR: 11f. Shows care in handling small animals or potentially breakable objects

Materials: Normal classroom or home environment

Procedure	Group activities
Give the child opportunities to handle objects that might break or to pet baby animals. Talk about being careful. Show how to be gentle and careful.	1. Bring objects like birds' nests, old hornets' nests, or other relatively fragile objects to the class for nature study. Show them to the children and talk about how they are made. Let the children take turns handling them after telling them they must be careful or the objects will break. 2. It is also good to have some live animals in the classroom if circumstances allow. Learning to treat a hamster or guinea pig gently is a good lesson for the children.

Criterion: The child usually shows care in handling small animals or potentially breakable objects and the caregiver feels comfortable allowing the child to touch and handle them.

4-5

AREA: **11. Responsibility**

BEHAVIOR: 11g. Responds appropriately to instructions given in a small group

Materials: Normal home or classroom environment

Procedure	Group activities
Invite other children to your home or to go with you on outings; or, take your child to Sunday School or other group settings where you or another adult will be giving instructions to several children at once. Always provide simple instructions and check the children's understanding by asking questions.	Give instructions clearly to the group when introducing new activities or planning for an excursion.

Criterion: The child responds appropriately to instructions given in a small group most of the time (i.e., listens, answers questions related to the instructions, and follows the instructions).

AREA: **11. Responsibility**

BEHAVIOR: 11h. Plays in own neighborhood without constant adult supervision

Materials: Normal home or classroom environment

Procedure	Group activities
Gradually give the child increasing responsibility for his or her own behavior. Require that the child let you know if he or she is going outside and that he or she ask permission to go play at another child's house. Praise the child for following the rules and for being responsible.	None

Criterion: The child plays in his or her own neighborhood without constant adult supervision.

Note: This may not be an appropriate item for some neighborhoods where children are not safe going unaccompanied by an adult.

5

AREA: **11. Responsibility**

BEHAVIOR: 11i. Buys simple objects in store without help (i.e., gets object or tells clerk what he or she wants, provides money, and waits for change)

Materials: Money

Procedure	Group activities
When you go shopping, take the child. Let him or her observe how you pay for objects, and get change. Give the child a small amount of money (e.g. 50¢ or $1.00) and let him or her precede or follow you through the checkout line with his or her money and something that he or she wishes to purchase (e.g., gum, fruit, candy, crackers, a small toy). If the child does not know how to give the money and the item to the clerk, and wait for change, instruct him or her. Gradually give less help. Eventually try taking the child to the store and letting him or her go through the line alone while you watch from the other side.	Set up a play store for the children with play money and cans or boxes to be bought. Have one child act as the storekeeper and others as shoppers.

Criterion: On 3 occasions, the child buys something in the store without help (i.e., gets object or tells clerk what he or she wants, provides money, and waits for change).

5

AREA: **11. Responsibility**
BEHAVIOR: 11j. Answers telephone appropriately and delivers message

Materials: Telephone

Procedure	Group activities
Let the child talk to people who call you on the telephone. Have him or her practice "answering the telephone" with a play telephone. Then allow him or her to answer your telephone. Prompt the child as to what to say (e.g., "Hello. This is Johnny. Do you want to talk to my mother?").	Have the children call each other on toy telephones in the group. Listen to their conversations.

Criterion: The child answers the telephone appropriately (as taught) and delivers the message, on 5 different occasions.

12.

Self-Concept

A PERSON'S SENSE OF SELF, or self-concept, includes a sense of identity (e.g., who I am, how I look and feel, where I fit in the family and community) and feelings or value judgments about that identity. The preschool years lay the foundations for the experience of the self for the rest of an individual's life. It is especially important that young children feel valued by their caregivers and their peers in order for them to value themselves. Good feelings about themselves give them enthusiasm for trying and the ability to cope with failure.

This sequence includes the components of a healthy self-concept. However, it will be up to caregivers to provide the affect that will make it work. In all activities, the child should experience more positive than negative feedback from his or her caregivers and peers. Children are quick to pick up on adult attitudes and feelings. If the adult values and accepts the child with special needs, the other children will be likely to do so as well.

12. Self-Concept

a. Expresses feelings of *interest, pleasure, surprise, excitement, warning,* and *complaint* (4 or more)
b. Knows age (e.g., tells or holds up fingers)
c. Makes positive statements about self
d. Tells own first name
e. Shows pride in achievements
f. Answers correctly when asked if he or she is boy or girl
g. Tells own first and last name
h. Calls attention to own performance

i. Expresses enthusiasm for work or play
j. Identifies own feelings
k. Can tell what eyes, ears, and nose are used for
l. Talks about own feelings in relation to events
m. Shows interest in own body—asks questions about its functions
n. Answers questions about grooming or self-care (e.g., "Why comb hair?")
o. Seeks activities that challenge skills

AREA: **12. Self-Concept**

BEHAVIOR: 12a. Expresses feelings of *interest, pleasure, surprise, excitement, warning,* and *complaint* (4 or more)

Materials: Normal home or classroom environment

Procedure	Group activities
One cannot teach a child to feel. The issue for this item is that the child *expresses* his or her feelings. In order to encourage this expression, the caretaker should make an effort to understand what the child is feeling and then respond appropriately to that feeling. It is important for children to learn that their feelings are valid and that they are acceptable people, regardless of how they feel. Some ways to help children express their feelings are:	1. During the day's activities respond to children's feelings, share your feelings, and talk to the children about each other's feelings.
1. Look for indications of feelings in the child's behavior and then respond by labeling the feeling that you think the child is having and identifying the reasons for the feeling (e.g., "That is a very *interesting* toy. When you are through, maybe you can show it to Johnny."; "You seem very excited about that. I'm excited too."; "I know you're *angry* because Johnny took the truck, but I can't let you hit him."; "It makes you *sad* that Daddy is not here to kiss you goodnight but you'll see him tomorrow and then you'll be *happy*.").	2. Prepare circle activities to elicit certain feelings. For example, put something very tiny in a great big box or put something in the box that is different from the picture on the box. Have the children guess what is in the box. When you pull out the contents, say "Surprise!"
2. Share you own feelings (e.g., "I'm crying because I'm *sad* that _____."; "I'm *angry* because _____."; "I'm *excited* because _____."; "You *surprised* me!").	
3. Call the child's attention to the feelings of other people and how they express them. Make it clear that all feelings are natural and alright, but that one is not allowed to act on negative feelings in a way that harms other people (e.g., "I know he's angry, but we do not allow hitting so he must go to time out.").	

Criterion: The child expresses feelings in a way that regular caregivers can identify them. The child must express at least 4 of the 6 feelings listed.

AREA: **12. Self-Concept**
BEHAVIOR: 12b. Knows age (e.g., tells or holds up fingers)

Materials: Normal home or classroom environment

Procedure	Group activities
Other adults frequently ask children their age. Instead of answering for a child, try to prompt the child to state their age (e.g., "Can you tell Mrs. Jones how old you are? Tell her you are 2 years old."; "Show Mrs. Jones how hold you are [and help the child hold up the correct number of fingers]."). Make a point of talking about age at the time of family and friends' birthdays. Although the child will have no real concept of the numbers associated with adults' birthdays he or she will learn that age is a part of who you are and will be more prepared to answer the question, "How old are you?"	In group care, birthdays are occurring quite frequently and give many opportunities to talk about age. Help children say the numbers and hold up the correct number of fingers to indicate their own age and the age of the "birthday boy" or "birthday girl."

Criterion: The child correctly responds to the question "How old are you?" 2 different times without prompts. The answer may be given either by holding up the correct number of fingers or by saying the age.

3

AREA: **12. Self-Concept**
BEHAVIOR: 12c. Makes positive statements about self

Materials: Normal home or classroom environment

Procedure	Group activities
Children will think positively about themselves and be more likely to say positive comments about themselves if they hear adults saying positive statements about them. It is important for children to hear specifics about themselves and what they are doing that pleases others (e.g., "You are such a good helper."; "I like the way you are sharing."; "You look so pretty in that dress."; "You're so smart to get that puzzle together."). Likewise, make positive statements about the child to other children and adults within the hearing of the child. Some children may feel good about themselves but do not make positive statements about themselves. Try to assess these feelings by asking a child a question such as, "Do you think you can do that by	1. It is particularly important in groups that *every child* gets to hear positive statements about him- or herself. Make it clear that every child has good qualities and behaviors. As soon as possible after a child is punished, look for something good to comment upon. Say it not only to the child but aloud so that the group will hear it. 2. Plan a circle activity in which you go around the group and tell each child one quality that you really liked about what they did in the time just preceding group. 3. Listen for positive statements that the children make about themselves. Let the child know you accept and appreciate such

(continued)

Procedure	Group activities
yourself?"; "Are you a good sharer today?"; or "Are you pretty in your new dress?"	statements (e.g., smile, nod, agree with them).

Criterion: The child makes 2 or more positive statements about him- or herself within a week's time. One of these statements may be in the form of responding "yes" to a question about a positive behavior or attribute.

3   AREA: **12. Self-Concept**
BEHAVIOR: 12d. Tells own first name

Materials: Normal home or classroom environment

Procedure	Group activities
Address the child by name frequently. When someone asks the child his or her name, prompt the child to answer (e.g., "Tell Mrs. Jones your name."; "Tell her your name is Billy."). Play games with puppets where the puppet says, "My name is Sally. What is your name?" Have the puppet ask the names of everyone in the room and have them answer, thereby showing the child what is expected. Let the child use the puppet and go around asking everyone their names and then responding when asked for his or her name.	Introduce "Mr. Mixup" to a group time. He can be a puppet, an animal, or a doll. He always gets information wrong and must be corrected. For example, he will say to Mary, "Oh, I remember you. You are Sally." All the children will probably laugh and then you can say for him, "You're not Sally. Well then, who are you?" Alternate Mr. Mixup's getting names incorrect, with getting other information incorrect. It is a good way to get children to listen and to think about what they have heard.

Criterion: The child will tell his or her first name when asked "What is your name?"; "Who are you?"; or the equivalent on 3 different occasions without prompting by an adult.

3   AREA: **12. Self-Concept**
BEHAVIOR: 12e. Shows pride in achievements

Materials: Normal home or classroom environment

Procedure	Group activities
Show excitement and praise a child for his or her accomplishments (e.g., clap your hands, hug him or her and say, "You made a beautiful picture, we'll hang it on the wall."). Praise the child and show off his or her accomplishments to other children or adults. Watch for the child to bring accomplishments	As the children work together in a group, note each child's accomplishments. Avoid comparing them with each other, but stress each child's progress. Have all the children give a cheer when one of them reaches a major milestone for him- or herself.

(continued)

Procedure	Group activities
to you for approval, to show them to others, and to repeat an accomplishment over and over.	

Criterion: The child shows accomplishment that he or she does or has made to other children or adults with smiles or other evidence of pride on 3 different occasions or repeats a difficult task several times after the first mastery while smiling or giving other indications of pride in the accomplishment.

3

AREA: **12. Self-Concept**
BEHAVIOR: 12f. Answers correctly when asked if he or she is boy or girl

Materials: Normal home or classroom environment

Procedure	Group activities
Talk about who is a girl and who is a boy. Refer to the child as a boy or a girl frequently (e.g., "You are a big girl."; "What a pretty girl you are today!"; "That's Mama's smart girl."). Play a game in which you ask, "Are you a girl?"; "Am I a girl?"; or "Is Daddy a girl?" Correct the child's errors.	1. Use Mr. Mixup (see item 12d.) to incorrectly identify whether children in the group are boys or girls and encourage them to make the correction. 2. Play games in which all the girls do one activity and all the boys do another. Have the children sort themselves in those 2 groups.

Criterion: The child answers correctly the questions, "Are you a boy?" *and* "Are you a girl?" on 2 different days.

3.⁵

AREA: **12. Self-Concept**
BEHAVIOR: 12g. Tells own first and last name

Materials: Normal home or classroom environment

Procedure	Group activities
Proceed as in item 12d., but work on whole name.	Proceed as in item 12d., but work on whole name.

Criterion: On several occasions the child tells first and last name when asked.

3.5

AREA: **12. Self-Concept**
BEHAVIOR: 12h. Calls attention to own performance

Materials: Normal home or classroom environment

Procedure	Group activities
This is very similar to item 12e. and should be encouraged in the same way (i.e., by praising the child and letting him or her know in many ways that you are proud of what he or she has accomplished or that what the child is doing is interesting). The difference between this item and item 12e. is that the child is more active in seeking attention and confident that what he or she is doing is worthy of that attention.	Proceed as in item 12e.

Criterion: The child requests an adult or other children to look at what he or she is doing or what he or she has accomplished on at least 3 occasions. It is important that the child exhibit real pride in his or her activity rather than just be seeking attention for its own sake.

3.5

AREA: **12. Self-Concept**
BEHAVIOR: 12i. Expresses enthusiasm for work or play

Materials: Normal home or classroom environment

Procedure	Group activities
There is no specific procedure for teaching enthusiasm for activities beyond modeling that enthusiasm yourself. Express enthusiasm for the child's choice of tasks and his or her accomplishments (e.g., "Wow, that's great!"; "Isn't that interesting!"; "Let's show Daddy what you made!"). Also, express enthusiasm for activities that you are doing.	1. Call the group's attention to activities of each individual child expressing your excitement or pleasure over these activities. 2. Have sharing time in the group when children show other children their favorite activities or toys.

Criterion: Children show enthusiasm in different ways. A child passes this item if he or she frequently shows enthusiasm for work or play activities by: 1) efforts to share the experience with adults or other children, 2) the vigor and/or happiness shown when engaged in the activities, 3) positive statements made about the activities, or 4) by other behaviors you can identify as a real investment in activities.

4

AREA: **12. Self-Concept**
BEHAVIOR: 12j. Identifies own feelings

Materials: Normal home or classroom environment

Procedure	Group activities
When you notice that the child is feeling angry, happy, sad, or excited, label the feeling for the child and respond appropriately (e.g., "It looks like you're feeling pretty sad. Do you need an extra hug?"). Also, make a point of labeling your own feelings for the child (e.g., "I'm too tired to do that now. I'll do it tomorrow."; "I am angry with you because ____."; "I'm crying because I'm sad that Grandma is leaving."). If the child does not begin to label his or her own feelings spontaneously, check out his or her ability to identify them by asking, "How are you feeling?"; "Are you angry?"; or "Are you sad because Daddy's gone?"	1. Help children in the group identify feelings by noticing, labeling, and responding to the feelings of each child. Use statements about feelings to describe and explain the behavior of the members of the group. As above, ask children how they are feeling or if they are experiencing a particular feeling. 2. Do a lesson one day in circle time about feelings. Make faces on paper plates or construction paper that demonstrate anger, sadness, or excitement. Describe a situation in 1 or 2 sentences and ask the children how the person would feel. Let them find the face that shows that feeling (e.g., "Jane had a dog she loved very much. One day the dog ran into the street and got run over. How would Jane feel?").

Criterion: The child identifies at least 3 different feelings either by labeling them or by responding appropriately (e.g., yes, no) to a question asking him or her about a specific feeling.

4

AREA: **12. Self-Concept**
BEHAVIOR: 12k. Can tell what eyes, ears, and nose are used for

Materials: Normal home or classroom environment

Procedure	Group activities
Talk to the child about the functions of the various parts of the body. As you help the child explore the environment, mention the parts of the body that aid in that exploration (e.g., "Smell this rose. Put your nose up closer so you can really smell it."; "Shut your eyes so you can't see. Now open your eyes. What do you see?"; "Use your ears. You have to listen."). When you look at books or read them to the child, comment on how the characters use their eyes, ears, and noses (e.g., "The fox smelled the gingerbread cooking and when the gingerbread boy started running away, the fox could smell him and chased him.").	1. For circle time, prepare "surprise sacks" that contain something that can be identified by sound or smell. Let each child listen or smell and try to guess what is inside. Talk about using the nose and ears for smelling and listening. Also, have something in a sack that you really can't identify by sound or smell, something you have to see. When the children can't identify it, show it to them and talk about having to use our eyes to see it in order to know what it is. 2. Look for songs or rhymes that can be used at group time that include references to eyes, ears, and nose, and what they are used for.

(continued)

Procedure	Group activities
Ask the child occasionally, "What do you smell with, look with, and listen with? When the child can answer these questions correctly, begin asking "What do you do with your ____?" or "Why do we have ____?"	

Criterion: The child answers questions about the use of eyes, ears, and nose. The child must be able to specify the use of all 3 and must be able to respond to questions in at least 2 different forms (e.g., "Why do we have ____"?; "What do you do with your ____?").

4.5

AREA: **12. Self-Concept**
BEHAVIOR: 12l. Talks about own feelings in relation to events

Materials: Normal home or classroom environment

Procedure	Group activities
Proceed as in item 12j. Talk about and respond appropriately to the child's feelings, your feelings, and the feelings of other people that the child is around. Also, ask the child questions about feelings.	Proceed as in item 12j.

Criterion: In a week's period, the child talks 2 or more times about his or her own feelings in relationship to something that happened. This can occur spontaneously or in response to questions (e.g., "What happened?"; "Why are you crying?") but the child must specify a feeling and an event associated with it.

4.5

AREA: **12. Self-Concept**
BEHAVIOR: 12m. Shows interest in own body—asks questions about its functions

Materials: Normal home or classroom environment

Procedure	Group activities
Talk to the child about his or her body when doing different activities. For example, when the child is eating, talk about the food going in his or her mouth and down into the stomach where it is ground up so that the body can get what it needs to grow and be strong. Act as if you are interested in how bodies work and be willing to answer any question the child has in an accurate, but simple way that he or she can understand.	1. In the science center in the classroom, have models of the body (e.g., the "visible man" or "visible woman") or pictures that show the digestive system, the ear, or other parts of the body. These will prompt questions by the children. 2. Plan a group activity around models or pictures of some part or system of the body. For example, you might show pictures

(continued)

Procedure	Group activities
Encourage the child to watch children's television shows that present simple ideas about science and the body.	of a duck's foot and a person's foot and talk about how the duck's foot makes it easier for it to swim and the person's foot makes it easier for him or her to walk and run. 3. Invite a nurse, a doctor, or a science teacher to visit the class and talk about why people sneeze and cough or something else that seems relevant to the children.

Criterion: The child asks at least 2 questions about his or her own body. These may be simple or complex questions. The issue is that the child is demonstrating an interest in his or her own body and how it works.

6

AREA: **12. Self-Concept**

BEHAVIOR: 12n. Answers questions about grooming or self-care
(e.g., "Why comb hair?")

Materials: Normal home or classroom environment

Procedure	Group activities
When going through the daily grooming routines, talk to the child about why these activities are done (e.g., "We need to wash our hands before we eat so that we don't eat the dirt or germs and get sick."; "We need to take a bath so that we will be clean and smell nice."; "We need to comb our hair so that we will look pretty."). Include grooming routines and explanations of them in pretend play with the child (e.g., comb the doll's hair, brush the bear's teeth). Occasionally check the child's understanding by asking him or her if he or she knows why you are doing one of these activities (e.g., "Why should you wash your hands?").	Bring some grooming materials (e.g., comb, toothbrush, washcloth) to circle time and have the children tell about what each is used for. Then ask why people brush their teeth or wash their hands. Correct incorrect responses.

Criterion: The child answers at least 3 questions related to grooming or self-care.

AREA: **12. Self-Concept**
BEHAVIOR: 12o. Seeks activities that challenge skills

Materials: Normal home or classroom environment

Procedure	Group activities
Observe the child to see if he or she routinely chooses activities that are very easy or if he or she frequently chooses ones that are somewhat difficult and require some effort. If the child always chooses easy ones, encourage him or her to try more difficult tasks and be particularly responsive to his or her successes on these. If the child gets discouraged quickly with difficult tasks, give him or her enough help to stay with the task to completion but *do not do it for the child*. If you provide help, *be sure that the child does the last step* so that he or she can have a sense of accomplishment. For example, on a difficult puzzle, you may need to turn the piece so it will readily go in the hole, but let him or her put the piece in; or if the child needs help getting on a t-shirt, help him or her get the arms and head in the correct holes, but let the child pull it on.	Select enough activities for the different centers so that there will be something easy and something that will challenge each child in the classroom. If the target child always chooses easy activities, you may remove that activity from the center before he or she enters it. Talk to the group about the importance of trying your best and be sure to pay special attention to children who try hard new activities whether they are fully successful or not.

Criterion: The child chooses at least 3 activities a week that present a challenge. The challenge may be mental, physical, or both (e.g., building a bigger tower than he or she has ever built before, choosing a puzzle that has given him or her trouble in the past, selecting a difficult picture to color).

13.

Interpersonal Skills

GETTING ALONG WITH OTHER people involves knowing how to join, share, help, and negotiate. It also involves a recognition of the rights, feelings, and needs of others. Because of their differences, children with special needs may be neglected by other children and thereby lose out on the experiences that teach them how to get along with others. It is important that adults try to teach appropriate skills and to arrange environments that will encourage children to play with and learn from one another. This sequence includes the major social skills that children learn in the preschool years that are the basis for interpersonal relationships throughout life.

Special efforts may have to be made to help children who are severely handicapped to develop these skills. Items will need to be modified to accommodate the effects of limited communication or limited physical skills.

13. Interpersonal Skills

a. Greets familiar adults spontaneously
b. Shares food or toys with familiar adults
c. Plays alongside other children without disruption for 15 minutes
d. Helps adults with activities such as picking up, dusting, or wiping the table
e. Expresses affection and/or preference for some peers
f. Expresses regret when another child is hurt or experiences unpleasantness
g. Converses with peers
h. Takes turn most of the time if reminded
i. Responds appropriately to social contact made by familiar adults
j. Separates easily from parent in familiar surroundings
k. Tries to comfort peers in distress
l. Plays group games with other children such as tag, hide-and-seek, without

constant adult supervision
m. Plays simple board or card games with other children with adult supervision
n. Asks permission to use other's belongings
o. Shows awareness of others' feelings (e.g., "He's mad."; "Are you sad?")
p. Uses such terms as "Thank you," "Please," and "You're welcome" appropriately
q. Recognizes another's need for help and gives assistance
r. Plays cooperatively with peers for extended periods without requiring adult intervention
s. Identifies special friends
t. Spontaneously takes turns and shares
u. Asserts self in socially acceptable ways

215

2·5

AREA: **13. Interpersonal Skills**
BEHAVIOR: 13a. Greets familiar adults spontaneously

Materials: Normal home or classroom environment

Procedure	Group activities
The child will probably learn to greet people by imitating your interactions with people. However, you may encourage the greetings by saying, "Say 'hello' to Mrs. Jones" (don't nag him or her if he or she doesn't respond; wait and try again another time). You can also encourage the greetings by practicing in pretend play with puppets, dolls, or stuffed animals.	Always greet each child as he or she joins the group and respond to each child who greets you. The children will learn from one another.

Criterion: The child greets familiar adults without prompting. This should occur fairly regularly (4 out of 5 opportunities). The greeting can be whatever the child has been taught or has observed (e.g., "Hello," "Hi," a wave of the hand with eye contact, a question).

2·5

AREA: **13. Interpersonal Skills**
BEHAVIOR: 13b. Shares food or toys with familiar adults

Materials: Normal home or classroom environment

Procedure	Group activities
Model sharing by sharing objects that you have with the child. Talk about sharing (e.g., "Maybe mother would like some of our popcorn. Shall we share with her?"). Always respond very positively to the child when he or she does share (e.g., "Thank you very much. It is good of you to share.").	1. Model and talk about sharing in the group (e.g., "We must share the crayons."; "Mary, it is time for you to let Jane have the puzzle, we need to share."). Share items that you have with the group (e.g., "I brought some cookies to share with you."). 2. At this age, children will be more likely to share with an adult than with another child. Be sure to respond positively to a child who tries to share with you. After you have instructed (or insisted) that children share with each other, be sure to pay attention to the sharing (e.g., "I like the way Mary is sharing the blocks.").

Criterion: The child shares food or toys with familiar adults, either spontaneously or when asked.

2·5

AREA: **13. Interpersonal Skills**

BEHAVIOR: 13c. Plays alongside other children without disruption for 15 minutes.

Materials: Normal home or classroom environment

Procedure	Group activities
Give the child opportunities to be with other children. Be present, but do not interact any more than necessary while they play. Comment on the good actions that you see happening, trying to give your attention to every child who is playing well. Some competition for toys is to be expected. If one child takes toys from another, attend to the "victim" by giving him or her another toy.	Provide opportunities for free play in the group setting. Concentrate on what is happening that is good and comment on it. Avoid giving too much attention to the disruptive child—it will increase disruptiveness!

Criterion: The child plays alongside other children with minimal adult supervision and without disruption for 15 minutes on 5 occasions.

2·5

AREA: **13. Interpersonal Skills**

BEHAVIOR: 13d. Helps adults with activities such as picking up,
dusting, or wiping the table

Materials: Normal home or classroom environment

Procedure	Group activities
Ask the child to help with simple activities and attend to him or her as he or she helps, making positive comments (e.g., "I like to have you helping me."; "You're a big help to Mommy.") and giving him or her hugs or other signs of affection. Brag on the child's helpfulness to other members of the family.	Always try to get everyone in the group to help in clean-up activities. Pay more attention to those children who are helping than those who are not (e.g., "Boy, I like the way Jerry is cleaning up the blocks!"). Make helping seem like a special reward (e.g., "Susan is the lunch helper today. She gets to wipe off the tables.").

Criterion: The child helps adults with activities such as picking up, dusting, or wiping the table when asked (most of the time).

3

AREA: **13. Interpersonal Skills**

BEHAVIOR: 13e. Expresses affection and/or preference for some peers

Materials: Normal home or classroom environment

Procedure	Group activities
Express affection for the child and model expressing affection toward other family members, visitors, and friends. Talk about liking other people and doing nice gestures for them.	Model expressing affection in the group. Give the children kisses, hugs, pats, or other indications of affection frequently. Encourage them to help each other, to comfort each other when hurt.

Criterion: The child expresses affection and/or preference for some peers. This should be a common occurrance; although, frequently it will vary according to the opportunities available. Some sign of affection or preference should be seen each time the child is with other children.

3

AREA: **13. Interpersonal Skills**

BEHAVIOR: 13f. Expresses regret when another child is hurt or experiences unpleasantness

Materials: Normal home or classroom environment

Procedure	Group activities
Model being sensitive to other people's misfortunes. Help the child when he or she gets hurt, be sympathetic when he or she is frustrated or unhappy, and help him or her find solutions to problems. Encourage the child to help other family members (e.g., "Johnny hurt his finger. Come help me kiss it and make it better.").	Model sympathy and help in the group setting. Encourage group members to comfort one another. Comment on this kind of helpfulness.
Engage the child in pretend play with dolls, animals, or puppets that involves 1 character caring for another when hurt.	

Criterion: The child expresses regret when another child is hurt or experiences unpleasantness, 5 or more times. At this level, the child need not spontaneously try to help the child, but should either tell the adult to help or will help when asked by the adult.

3 - 5

AREA: 13. Interpersonal Skills
BEHAVIOR: 13g. Converses with peers

Materials: Normal home or classroom environment

Procedure	Group activities
Spend a lot of time talking and listening to the child. Give him or her opportunities to be with peers for extended play periods.	Converse with the children and encourage them to do so with one another by providing opportunities for free play in the group setting. Set up centers that encourage group fantasy play (e.g., housekeeping, dress-up, construction). These will also encourage the children to talk among themselves.

Criterion: The child converses with peers with 3 or more exchanges on several occasions.

3 - 5

AREA: 13. Interpersonal Skills
BEHAVIOR: 13-h. Takes turn most of the time if reminded

Materials: Normal home or classroom environment

Procedure	Group activities
Emphasize and attend to sharing in general activities of the day. If the child is at home with adults only, it is easy to neglect the teaching of turn-taking. The adults should emphasize taking turns with them (e.g., "May I have a turn playing with your truck?"; "I get to choose the TV channel now; you'll have your turn to choose when this program is over.").	Taking turns is an essential part of group participation for young children. Focus on the positive aspects and attend to those children who take turns readily (e.g., thank them, give them a hug, comment about them to the other children), rather than on the negative points (e.g., scolding the child who doesn't share).

Criterion: The child takes turns with other children most of the time if reminded. He or she may make a face or otherwise look unhappy, but, nevertheless, complies with the request to take turns.

3 - 5

AREA: 13. Interpersonal Skills
BEHAVIOR: 13i. Responds appropriately to social contact made by familiar adults

Materials: Normal home or classroom environment

Procedure	Group activities
Model appropriate greetings and interactions with other adults and with children. Give the child opportunities to interact with your friends and visitors.	Invite visitors to the classroom or day care center. Have them move about the room talking to the children.

Criterion: The child responds appropriately to social contact made by familiar adults on most occasions (e.g., smiles when approached, answers or asks questions, shows the adult something interesting).

AREA: **13. Interpersonal Skills**
BEHAVIOR: 13j. Separates easily from parent in familiar surroundings

Materials: Normal home or classroom environment

Procedure	Group activities
When you separate from your child, always act confident that the child will do well without you. Tell the child that you are leaving and when you will return. Tell him or her to have fun, and then leave. *Do not* stress the good-byes. If the child cries, say something like, "I'll be back soon. You're going to have fun," and *leave*. Keep promises about your return. If the child cries for an extended period after you leave, you may need to work up to separations gradually (e.g., Leave the child for only 15 minutes several times, then 30 minutes, then 45 minutes, and then 60 minutes. At that point you can increase by 60 minute blocks.).	If a child cries when the parent leaves, ignore the crying as much as possible and try to distract the child with an interesting toy or activity. If the child will accept it, provide him or her with some physical contact as you try to distract him or her (e.g., hold the child on your lap, hold his or her hand). Be cheerful and do not act worried or distressed by the child's crying. Tell the child that you know he or she misses his or her parents but that they will come back and that while they are gone you're going to do a lot of fun things. If necessary, frequently reassure the child that the parents will return. Be specific about when they will return using terms the child will understand (e.g., "After we have our naps and go outside, your parents will return.").

Criterion: The child separates easily from parent in familiar surroundings. He or she does not cry and quickly becomes involved in activities.

4 AREA: **13. Interpersonal Skills**
BEHAVIOR: 13k. Tries to comfort peers in distress

Materials: Normal home or classroom environment

Procedure	Group activities
Model being sensitive to other people's misfortunes. Help the child when he or she gets hurt, be sympathetic when he or she is frustrated or unhappy, and help him or her find solutions to problems. Encourage the child to help other family members (e.g., "Johnny hurt his finger. Come help me kiss it and make it better."). Engage the child in pretend play with dolls, animals, or puppets that involves 1 character caring for another when hurt.	Model sympathy and help in the group setting. Encourage group members to comfort one another. Comment on this kind of helpfulness.

Criterion: The child tries to comfort peers in distress without being asked to do so by an adult. This should be observed at least 5 times.

4

AREA: **13. Interpersonal Skills**
BEHAVIOR: 13l. Plays group games with other children such as tag, hide-and-seek,
without constant adult supervision

Materials: Normal home or classroom environment

Procedure	Group activities
Play games with the child yourself so that he or she understands following rules and taking turns. Give the child opportunities to play with groups of children. Provide only as much supervision as needed to settle disputes and keep the children safe.	Plan simple group games for the children. Select games that have a limited number of rules such as tag, hide and seek, or dodge ball. Be available, but allow the children to play with as little supervision as necessary to keep them safe.

Criterion: The child plays group games with other children without constant adult supervision. That is, he or she participates, follows rules, and is not disruptive to the games. This must be observed at least 5 times.

4

AREA: **13. Interpersonal Skills**
BEHAVIOR: 13m. Plays simple board or card games with
other children with adult supervision

Materials: Simple board or card games (e.g., Candyland, Chutes and Ladders, Old Maid)

Procedure	Group activities
Play games with the child yourself. Do not always plan to lose or always plan to win. The child needs to learn that he or she will sometimes win and sometimes lose. When you lose, model being a "good loser." Make it fun, not serious! Make sure the child has opportunities to play games with other children. You may need to supervise in order to keep the rules intact and to help children resolve their disputes.	Plan simple board or card games for the group. Card games that require matching can be used to teach both matching and game playing. Board games teach counting in a much more enjoyable way than simple memorization. Build lesson plans around games.

Criterion: The child plays simple board or card games with other children with adult supervision. The child must follow the rules and engage in socially appropriate behavior. This should be observed on several different occasions.

AREA: **13. Interpersonal Skills**
BEHAVIOR: 13n. Asks permission to use other's belongings

Materials: Normal home or classroom environment

Procedure	Group activities
Model asking permission to use other's belongings in all of your interactions at home. It is especially important to respect the belongings of the child and to ask him or her if you can use (or move, or share) objects that belong to him or her. If the child takes something of yours without asking, explain that he or she must ask. Talk about the need to respect other people's property (e.g., "We can't take the gum without paying for it. It belongs to the store."; "Don't take Daddy's paper away until you ask him if he is through with it.").	1. Model respect for children's rights and property in your interactions with them. Insist that the children ask each other before taking toys from one another. If a child grabs a toy, say, "Johnny was playing with that. Please give it back. Now, ask him if you may play with it." If the other child says, "No," say, "He is not through with it yet. We'll wait until he is through," or, "I'll ask him to share in 5 minutes." 2. Notice when children do ask permission appropriately. Comment on their good behavior.

Criterion: The child usually asks permission before using other people's belongings.

4.5 AREA: **13. Interpersonal Skills**
BEHAVIOR: 13o. Shows awareness of others' feelings (e.g., "He's mad."; "Are you sad?")

Materials: Normal home or classroom environment

Procedure	Group activities
Model a sensitivity to the feelings of the child and other members of the family. Make comments like, "You look sad. What is making you sad?" or, "Mary's mad because I won't let her go outside now." Comment on the feelings of the characters in TV shows. Ask the child questions like, "How do you think he feels about that?"	As events occur in the group, talk about how people feel. Identify a child's feelings for another child (e.g., "I know you're angry that Bill will not let you have the truck, but you'll just have to wait."). When you read stories to the group, talk about how the different characters feel. Choose stories that will elicit a discussion of sadness, fear, anger, and happiness.

Criterion: The child shows an awareness of others' feelings by labeling those feelings. He or she should be observed to label at least 3 different feelings.

4. 5

AREA: **13. Interpersonal Skills**
BEHAVIOR: 13p. Uses such terms as "Thank you," "Please,"
and "You're welcome" appropriately

Materials: Normal home or classroom environment

Procedure	Group activities
Model these behaviors in your interactions with the child and with other members of the family. Ask the child to say, "Please" when he or she asks for something. Also, prompt the child to say, "Thank you" and "You're welcome," as appropriate. Attend to the child's efforts to use these terms and respond positively to them.	Proceed as in the "Procedure" section.

Criterion: The child frequently uses "Thank you," "Please," "You're welcome," and/or other terms commonly used in his or her culture appropriately. The child does not have to be reminded more than 2 times a day.

4-5

AREA: **13. Interpersonal Skills**
BEHAVIOR: 13q. Recognizes another's need for help and gives assistance

Materials: Normal home or classroom environment

Procedure	Group activities
Model providing help when the child or anyone else in the household is having difficulty (e.g., "Is that giving you trouble? May I help you?"; "Here, let me help you with that."). Ask the child for help when you need it. Praise him or her and display affection when he or she is helpful.	1. Model helpfulness within the classroom as you respond to the children. Encourage them to help one another (e.g., "Bill is having difficulty with the puzzle. Ask him if he would like some help."). 2. Sometimes plan a group time in which you ask, "What would you do if . . . ?" questions. Describe various situations in which people are in trouble (e.g., "What would you do if the eggs fell out of your mother's grocery sack and spilled all over the floor?"; "What would you do if the baby lost his ball under the couch?"). This is more fun if you can find pictures from magazines to illustrate the problems.

Criterion: The child recognizes another's need for help and gives assistance on at least 5 occasions. The child must do this without being asked to help.

4.5

AREA: 13. Interpersonal Skills
BEHAVIOR: 13r. Plays cooperatively with peers for extended periods without requiring adult intervention

Materials: Normal home or classroom environment

Procedure	Group activities
Give the child many opportunities to play with other children. Be available, but do not intervene unless necessary.	Give many opportunities for child-directed play. Attend to and reward cooperative play among the children.

Criterion: The child plays cooperatively with peers for extended periods (e.g., 15–30 minutes) without adult intervention. This should be a relatively common occurrence—at least once a day in group care settings.

5

AREA: 13. Interpersonal Skills
BEHAVIOR: 13s. Identifies special friends

Materials: Normal home or classroom environment

Procedure	Group activities
Talk to the child about the children with whom he or she plays. Let him or her talk freely about who he or she likes and does not like. Let the child choose who to have come to his or her house to visit. Also, talk to the child about the people you know. Stress the positive characteristics of people, but let him or her know that certain people are your special friends. Plan activities with those friends.	Observe the children playing. Allow preferences to be demonstrated in choices of playmates for activities, but try to arrange the environment to avoid the exclusion of the least liked children.

Criterion: The child identifies special friends, either through responding to a question about friends, or by requesting that particular children play with him or her.

5

AREA: 13. Interpersonal Skills
BEHAVIOR: 13t. Spontaneously takes turns and shares

Materials: Normal home or classroom environment

Procedure	Group activities
Model taking turns and sharing within the family. Praise the child or otherwise respond positively when he or she takes turns and shares.	Encourage taking turns and sharing in all activities in the classroom. Praise cooperation when it occurs.

Criterion: The child takes turns and shares without being told to do so by an adult. This should occur on a fairly regular basis, although occasional refusals to cooperate can be expected.

5

AREA: **13. Interpersonal Skills**

BEHAVIOR: 13u. Asserts self in socially acceptable ways

Materials: Normal home or classroom environment

Procedure	Group activities
Model self-assertion without being aggressive (e.g., "I would like to ____."; "I want ____."; "I would prefer it if you would.").	Proceed as in the section to the left.

Criterion: The child asserts self in socially acceptable ways (e.g., by asking directly for objects, by negotiating to get what he or she wants). The child rarely becomes involved in a fight or cries to get his or her needs met.

14-I.

Self-Help Skills:
Eating

INDEPENDENCE IN FEEDING skills represents an important achievement in the child's progress toward self-reliance. During the preschool period, feeding skills are refined as fine motor abilities develop. The child learns to eat in a socially acceptable manner. Simple food preparation, such as fixing a bowl of cereal or spreading jelly on a piece of toast, further heralds the child's emerging independence.

When children are learning to feed themselves, it is helpful to serve food that is easy to manage at first. Try to serve a variety of food, exposing the child to diverse tastes and textures. At the same time, avoid battles over eating. When the child refuses a food that has been served, just remove the food, leaving the child to wait until the next meal or snack that is served.

Children with developmental disabilities may demonstrate a variety of feeding difficulties that require intervention from an occupational or speech/language therapist. Difficulties may include:

1. Poor oral-motor control, leading to difficulty coordinating chewing and swallowing
2. Excessive drooling
3. Oral defensiveness, resulting in avoidance of many textures of food
4. Poor control of hands and arms, making utensil use poor

14. Self-Help Skills
I. Eating

a. Independently eats entire meal with spoon
b. Begins to use fork
c. Drinks from a small glass held with one hand
d. Gets drink unassisted (e.g., turns tap on and off)
e. Pours liquid from one container into another
f. Spreads with a knife

g. Cuts with edge of fork

h. Swallows food in mouth before taking another bite

i. Fixes bowl of dry cereal with milk independently

j. Holds fork in fingers

k. Drinks from water fountain independently

l. Fixes sandwich independently

2-5

AREA: **14-I. Self-Help Skills: Eating**
BEHAVIOR: 14-Ia. Independently eats entire meal with spoon

Materials: Bowl or plate, spoon, appropriate food

Procedure	Group activities
Place bowl with food and spoon in front of the child. If he or she is not yet using a spoon, snack time is a good opportunity to work on developing his or her skills. Tell the child to eat; if needed, remind him or her to use the spoon. If the child does not pick up the spoon, place it in one of his or her hands (if the child has demonstrated a hand preference, use that hand; otherwise, place in either hand). Give the child physical assistance as needed to scoop up the food and bring it to his or her mouth. Decrease physical assistance as quickly as possible. Use a bowl or plate with a lip to scoop food against to make feeding easier at first. Start with foods that adhere well to the spoon (e.g., mashed potatoes, pudding, mashed bananas). Practice is important; let the child feed him- or herself at all meals, once some success with a spoon has been achieved.	Children may need individual attention when learning to use a spoon.

Criterion: The child will feed him- or herself the entire meal with minimal spilling.

AREA: **14-I. Self-Help Skills: Eating**
2-5   BEHAVIOR: 14-Ib. Begins to use fork

Materials: Fork, plate, easily speared food (e.g., cut-up pancakes, scrambled eggs, casseroles)

Procedure	Group activities
Place plate with food on it and a fork in front of the child. Show him or her how to stab food with the fork and to place it in his or her mouth. Tell the child that it is now his or her turn to eat with the fork. If the child does not pick up the fork, place it in one of his or her hands (if child has demonstrated a hand preference, use that hand; otherwise, place in either hand). At this age, most children will hold a fork in a gross grasp with forearm pronated (i.e., palm down). Give the child physical assistance as needed to stab the food and to bring it to his or her mouth. Decrease your physical assistance as quickly as possible. Practice is important; let the child feed him- or herself with a fork for a number of consecutive meals once some success has been achieved. Be sure to serve the child foods that are easy to eat with a fork.	Children may need individual attention when learning to use a fork.

Criterion: The child will eat some foods with a fork.

2·5

AREA: **14-I. Self-Help Skills: Eating**
BEHAVIOR: 14-Ic. Drinks from a small glass held with one hand

Materials: Small glass (e.g., juice size), liquid that the child enjoys

Procedure	Group activities
Fill a small glass about ⅓ of the way full. Place it in front of the child at a time when he or she is likely to be thirsty (e.g., meal or snack time). Encourage the child to pick up the cup and to take a drink. If needed, place the cup in the child's hand and help him or her to bring it to his or her mouth. Children often learn to pick up a cup and to bring it to their mouth before they learn to set the cup back on the table. It may be necessary to "catch" the child's hand before he or she removes the cup from his or her mouth to help the child guide the cup to the table and set it down. Pair this with a verbal command (e.g., "Put the cup on the table."). Then fade the physical prompt while still using the verbal command.	Children may need individual attention when learning this task.

Criterion: The child will drink from a small glass held with one hand.

5

ℬ˙

AREA: **14-I. Self-Help Skills: Eating**
BEHAVIOR: 14-Id. Gets drink unassisted (e.g., turns tap on and off)

Materials: Accessible sink (e.g., child size or standard with sturdy stepstool), small cup

Procedure	Group activities
Show the child how to turn on the cold water tap, to fill up a cup, and then to turn off the water. Have the child practice this activity, providing any assistance needed. Children who have difficulty turning on the tap may need practice with activities in *Fine Motor Skills: Manipulation*. Before children are allowed to get a drink independently, the hot water tap should be inactivated or the water temperature reduced to avoid accidental burns. As the child demonstrates success, fade any verbal or physical cues that you may have been using.	Children may need individual instruction with this task.

Criterion: The child will get a drink of water unassisted, turning tap on and off.

3

AREA: **14-I. Self-Help Skills: Eating**
BEHAVIOR: 14-Ie. Pours liquid from one container into another

Materials: Small pitcher with liquid, cup

Procedure	Group activities
Place a pitcher with liquid and a cup in front of the child. Show him or her how to pour liquid into the cup. Usually, children will need to hold the pitcher handle in one hand and support it from underneath with the other hand as they pour. At first, only put the amount of liquid in the pitcher that will fit in the cup. Later, the child can learn to stop pouring before the cup is full. When older, the child can hold the pitcher with one hand and the cup with the other.	1. Practice pouring skills by pouring sand or beans from one container into another. 2. Have a different child in charge of pouring juice for snack each day.

Criterion: The child will pour liquid from one container into another.

AREA: **14-I. Self-Help Skills: Eating**
 BEHAVIOR: 14-If. Spreads with a knife

Materials: Toast or firm bread, soft margarine, knife, plate

Procedure	Group activities
Place a piece of toast on a plate with a knife and margarine on table in front of the child. With a second piece of toast, show the child how to spread on the margarine, covering its entire surface. Encourage the child to spread the margarine on his or her piece of toast. Teach the child to stabilize the toast with one hand, while his or her other hand uses the knife for spreading. Give the child physical assistance as needed.	1. Have children fix crackers by spreading peanut butter or jelly on top. 2. Decorate cookies by spreading soft frosting on top of them.

Criterion: The child will use a knife for spreading.

AREA: **14-I. Self-Help Skills: Eating**
BEHAVIOR: 14-Ig. Cuts with edge of fork

Materials: Easy-to-cut food (e.g., pancakes), fork, plate

Procedure	Group activities
Place a pancake on a plate with a fork on table in front of child. With the fork, show the child how to cut the pancake with the edge of his or her fork. Position the fork sideways in the child's hand. Help him or her to cut the pancake by pushing down with the edge of the fork and then pulling the fork away. Then ask the child to do the activity independently. Encourage him or her to keep his or her index finger on top edge of the fork to apply pressure.	Have the children practice cutting Play-Doh that they have made into snakes or have rolled out flat.

Criterion: The child will cut with the edge of his or her fork.

AREA: **14-I. Self-Help Skills: Eating**
BEHAVIOR: 14-Ih. Swallows food in mouth before taking another bite

Materials: Food normally served at meal or snack time

Procedure	Group activities
Observe the child eating. If he or she swallows food in his or her mouth before taking a next bite, no intervention is needed. If the child tends to cram food into his or her mouth, try serving food that requires the use of a utensil and ask the child to put the utensil down on the table after each bite. Serving small amounts of food at one time may also help.	Observe each child in the group.

Criterion: The child will swallow food in his or her mouth before taking another bite.

4

AREA: **14-I. Self-Help Skills: Eating**
BEHAVIOR: 14-Ii. Fixes bowl of dry cereal with milk independently

Materials: Small pitcher or carton of milk, box of cereal, bowl

Procedure	Group activities
Show the child how to pour cereal into a bowl, filling the bowl about half-way full. Then add milk, teaching the child to stop pouring at about 1–2 inches before reaching the top of the bowl. It is much easier to begin with controlled amounts; for instance use a little box of cereal and have the child pour milk from his or her glass of milk. The box of cereal may need to be preopened for the child since many boxes are difficult for young children to manage.	Serve a breakfast or snack of cereal and milk using little boxes of cereal. Each child is responsible for fixing his or her own.

Criterion: The child will fix a bowl of cereal independently, pouring the milk and cereal by him- or herself.

4

AREA: **14-I. Self-Help Skills: Eating**
BEHAVIOR: 14-Ij. Holds fork in fingers

Materials: Fork, plate, appropriate food (e.g., meat, casseroles, pancakes)

Procedure	Group activities
Place a plate with food on it and a fork in front of the child. Observe how he or she holds the fork. If the child does not hold the fork between his or her thumb and first 2 fingers (i.e., similar to the pencil grip), help reposition in his or her hands. If the child reverts to his or her old pattern, give occasional verbal reminders (e.g., "Turn your hand the other way."). Children who have a lot of difficulty with this may need further skill development in *Fine Motor Skills: Tool Use*.	Monitor all children in the group, giving assistance as needed.

Criterion: The child will consistently hold a fork in his or her fingers.

AREA: **14-I. Self-Help Skills: Eating**
BEHAVIOR: 14-Ik. Drinks from water fountain independently

Materials: Accessible water fountain (e.g., child size or standard with sturdy stepstool)

Procedure	Group activities
Show the child how to turn on the water fountain and to keep it on while taking a drink. If the child has difficulty, break this task into steps. First, teach the child to take a drink while you hold on the water. Then, teach the child to turn on the water for you to get a drink or to fill a water cup. When the child is able to perform both of these steps, have him or her try to get his or her own drink. Have the child practice this activity, providing any assistance that is needed. Children who have difficulty turning handles may need practice with activities in *Fine Motor Skills: Manipulation*. As the child demonstrates success, fade any verbal or physical cues that you may have been using.	Children may need individual instruction with this task.

Criterion: The child will drink from a water fountain independently.

AREA: **14-I. Self-Help Skills: Eating**
BEHAVIOR: 14-Il. Fixes a sandwich independently

Materials: Knife, plate, firm bread, appropriate ingredients (e.g., soft margarine or mayonnaise, lunch meats, peanut butter and jelly)

Procedure	Group activities
Show the child how to make a sandwich, using spreading skills taught in item 14-If. Teach the child to put different ingredients on different pieces of break to make the process easier (e.g., peanut butter on one slice and jelly on the other). Encourage the child to spread the ingredients to the edges of the bread. Show him or her how to cut sandwich in half (some children may not have success with cutting).	1. Have children fix crackers, spreading peanut butter or jelly on top of them. 2. Decorate cookies by spreading soft frosting on top of them.

Criterion: The child will use a knife for spreading to make his or her own sandwich.

14-II.

Self-Help Skills: Dressing

B Y THE AGE OF 5, MOST children have learned to dress and undress themselves, including handling simple fasteners. Children should be encouraged to be as independent as possible, even when the process may be initially very slow. When children are learning to dress, it is recommended that they wear simple clothing that is easy to put on and remove (e.g., pants with elastic waistbands, pullover shirts). As the child demonstrates success and confidence, more difficult clothing can be introduced. Encourage children to make their own selections in what clothing they want to wear on a particular day, or at least allow them to pick between 2 or 3 choices.

In the classroom, dressing skills can be reinforced through the use of dress-up clothes and simple costumes for pretend play.

Dressing skills depend to some extent on the development of skills in the Fine Motor Skills: Manipulation section; particularly, learning to handle fasteners. By focusing specifically on the development of those skills, the foundation for greater success in dressing skills will be set. Children with significant coordination difficulties may need clothing adaptations such as the use of Velcro closures rather than buttons or snaps. An occupational therapist can assist in developing the dressing skills and finding adaptations for children with motoric limitations.

14. Self-Help Skills
II. Dressing

a. Removes shoes
b. Removes coat
c. Puts on simple clothing (e.g., hat, pants, shoes, socks)
d. Puts on all clothes unaided, except for fasteners
e. Undoes fasteners (e.g., large buttons, snaps, shoelaces)
f. Buttons coat or dress
g. Dresses and undresses with little assistance
h. Zips front-opening clothing such as jacket

2.5   AREA: **14-II. Self-Help Skills: Dressing**
BEHAVIOR: 14-IIa. Removes shoes

Materials: Shoes that are easy to remove

Procedure	Group activities
Ask the child to remove his or her shoes (ideally at a natural time [e.g., before nap]). If the child has difficulty, slip one of the shoes off his or her heel, and ask the child to finish removing the shoe. Repeat this process with the other shoe. Assist the child as needed in removing his or her shoes, and then gradually fade assistance. If the child has difficulty, start with loose fitting shoes such as slippers or moccasins.	1. Have children remove shoes at naptime. 2. Use a variety of shoes and boots for dress-up.

Criterion: The child will independently remove his or her shoes.

2.5   AREA: **14-II. Self-Help Skills: Dressing**
BEHAVIOR: 14-IIb. Removes coat

Materials: Coat that child typically wears (should fit the child or be slightly large)

Procedure	Group activities
Ask the child to remove his or her coat (ideally at a natural time [e.g., when coming into the classroom]). Undo any fasteners if the child is not able to undo them yet. If the child has difficulty, slip the coat down slightly past his or her shoulders, and ask the child to finish removing it. If the child still has difficulty, help him or her remove 1 arm and then ask him or her to finish taking off the coat. Gradually fade the assistance that you are giving to the child.	Have hooks marked with child's picture and name in the classroom. Encourage each child to remove his or her coat and to hang it on his or her hook.

Criterion: The child independently removes his or her coat.

AREA: **14-II. Self-Help Skills: Dressing**

BEHAVIOR: 14-IIc. Puts on simple clothing (e.g., hat, pants, shoes, socks)

Materials: Hat, pants with elastic waistbands, tube socks, slip-on shoes

Procedure	Group activities
Place an article of clothing in front of the child and ask him or her to put it on. If the child does not know how to put on a piece of clothing, teach the child by sitting behind him or her and physically assisting in putting it on. Provide simple verbal descriptions as you help the child (e.g., "First put one leg in, now the other leg, now pull your pants up."). Teach the child by putting the clothing halfway on and then asking him or her to finish (e.g., roll up a sock and place it over the toes, ask the child to finish pulling the sock on).	Have loose-fitting dress-up clothing for the children to wear in pretend games. Have them practice dressing up.

Criterion: The child will independently put on simple clothing (e.g., hat, pants, shoes, socks).

3

AREA: **14-II. Self-Help Skills: Dressing**

BEHAVIOR: 14-IId. Puts on all clothing unaided, except for fasteners

Materials: Simple, loose-fitting clothing (e.g., shirt, dress, sweater)

Procedure	Group activities
Place an article of clothing in front of the child and ask him or her to put it on. If the child does not know how to do this, teach the child by sitting behind him or her and physically assisting in putting it on. Provide simple verbal descriptions as you help the child put the clothing on (e.g., "First put the shirt over your head, now put one arm in one sleeve, now the other arm in the other sleeve."). Have the child do as much of the process as possible, gradually fading your assistance (e.g., the child may be able to pull shirt over head, but will need help getting arms in).	Have loose-fitting dress-up clothing for children to wear in pretend games. Have them practice trying them on.

Criterion: The child will independently put on all clothing (e.g., shirt, dress, sweater).

AREA: **14-II. Self-Help Skills: Dressing**
BEHAVIOR: 14-IIe. Undoes fasteners (e.g., large buttons, snaps, shoelaces)

Materials: Clothing; dressing doll; dressing boards with large, easy-to-handle fasteners

Procedure	Group activities
Ask the child to unbutton buttons. If he or she does not know how to approach this task, slowly demonstrate it 2 or 3 times. Then, try to physically assist the child. He or she should hold and lightly pull cloth next to hole with one hand, and with other hand, grasp the button and push it through the hole (see *Fine Motor Skills: Manipulation* for further suggestions). Repeat procedure with other types of fasteners. If the child has difficulty unzipping a zipper, try attaching a bead with yarn to the zipper to pull, providing the child with something easier to grasp.	1. Play dress-up with very simple clothing that has easy-to-handle fasteners. At this age, the goal would be for children to undo fasteners and to remove clothing independently. In another year, the focus will be on independently fastening the clothing. 2. Button boards that can have a surprise picture hidden under the material can be fun to use with a group of children who can then share what they "found."

Criterion: The child independently undoes fasteners (e.g., large buttons, snaps, shoelaces).

AREA: **14-II. Self-Help Skills: Dressing**
BEHAVIOR: 14-IIf. Buttons coat or dress

Materials: Coat, dress, or shirt with easy-to-handle front buttons (can use dressing vest for practice)

Procedure	Group activities
Have the child put on an appropriate garment and ask him or her to button it. Start with the button at bottom of the garment that will be easier for the child to see while manipulating. If the child does not know how to button, demonstrate the task slowly 2 or 3 times. Physically assist the child, then gradually fade your assistance. It is generally easier to stand behind the child when giving assistance so that your hands and arms are moving in the same direction as his or hers (see *Fine Motor Skills: Manipulation* for further suggestions).	Play dress-up with simple clothing that has front buttons.

Criterion: The child buttons his or her coat, dress, or shirt that has easy-to-handle buttons.

4.5

AREA: 14-II. Self-Help Skills: Dressing
BEHAVIOR: 14-IIg. Dresses and undresses with little assistance

Materials: Clothing that the child typically wears

Procedure	Group activities
Place an article of clothing in front of the child and ask him or her to put it on. At this point the child should be familiar with most of the tasks required for dressing. Show the child how to tell the front of his or her clothes from the back (e.g., tag in back). When the child is first dressing independently, select clothes that are easy to put on. The child should be encouraged to dress and undress independently at home. It is often easiest for the child to begin by taking off and putting on pajamas. Gradually add more complex clothing such as those with various fasteners.	1. Children can dress up in various clothing and costumes for pretend play. 2. Let children dress dolls in simple clothing.

Criterion: The child dresses and undresses with little assistance and can tell the difference between front and back. The child is able to undo and fasten buttons, snaps, and zippers.

5

AREA: 14-II. Self-Help Skills: Dressing
BEHAVIOR: 14-IIh. Zips front-opening clothing such as jacket

Materials: Jacket with front zipper

Procedure	Group activities
After the child puts on his or her jacket, ask him or her to zip it up. Show the child how to hold the bottom of the zipper with one hand and to guide the other side of the zipper in with the other hand. If the child has difficulty with this task, try stabilizing the bottom of the jacket for him or her, while the child inserts the zipper. Remind the child to hold the bottom of the zipper with one hand while pulling up the tab with the other. Practice this task with the child when he or she is not wearing the jacket.	This activity is best done with individual children.

Criterion: The child zips front-opening clothing such as a jacket.

14-III.

Self-Help Skills: Grooming

GOOD GROOMING SKILLS AND habits of cleanliness are important to establish during the preschool period. Children who are not encouraged to develop these skills before the age of 6, often have difficulty ever incorporating these habits into their daily routine. Good grooming is particularly important for children with developmental disabilities, due to society's tendency to judge people by their appearances. The child with special needs, who appears clean and well groomed, is seen to have one less strike against him or her when trying to fit into a "normal" peer group.

At school, mealtime provides a good opportunity for the child to develop and reinforce good grooming skills. Children can be expected to wash their hands before and after eating. Regular hand washing is also an important practice for reducing the spread of germs, which is problematic in groups of small children. By having personalized toothbrushes, children can brush their teeth after meals. For some children, this may be the only time their teeth are brushed.

14. Self-Help Skills
III. Grooming

a. Dries hands
b. Washes own hands
c. Washes and dries hands and face without assistance

d. Brushes teeth
e. Runs brush or comb through hair
f. Blows nose independently upon request

AREA: **14-III. Self-Help Skills: Grooming**
BEHAVIOR: 14-IIIa. Dries hands

Materials: Water, towel

Procedure	Group activities
Hand the child a towel and ask him or her to dry his or her hands. Show the child how to rub the towel over the front and back of his or her hands. It may be easier for the child to use a small, lightweight towel, such as a dishtowel or even a washcloth, at first. Also, show the child how to dry his or her hands by using part of a towel that is hanging up. Give the child physical assistance as needed, then gradually fade your assistance.	After snack or mealtime, give each child 1 wet cloth and 1 dry cloth to wash and dry his or her hands.

Criterion: The child independently dries his or her hands.

AREA: **14-III. Self-Help Skills: Grooming**
BEHAVIOR: 14-IIIb. Washes own hands

Materials: Water, soap

Procedure	Group activities
Model hand washing for the child (e.g., get hands wet, rub soap on, then rinse hands). Ask the child to wash his or her hands. Give the child verbal directions and physical assistance if needed. It is generally better to stand behind the child when giving physical assistance, then gradually fade your assistance. Liquid soap may be easier than a bar of soap for a child who is learning to wash his or her hands.	Wash dolls, doll clothes, or plastic dishes with a group of children in an activity center.

Criterion: The child independently washes his or her own hands.

AREA: **14-III. Self-Help Skills: Grooming**
BEHAVIOR: 14-IIIc. Washes and dries hands and face without assistance

Materials: Water, soap, towel

Procedure	Group activities
Model washing your face for the child (it may be best to teach face washing without soap, to avoid accidentally getting soap in eyes). Ask the child to wash his or her hands and face. The child may wash his or her face with wet hands or with a wet cloth. Give the child verbal directions and physical assistance in washing his or her face and hands as needed. Remind the child to dry his or her hands and face, giving assistance as needed. After child progresses, gradually fade assistance. Expect the child to wash his or her own hands and face whenever needed; however, touch-up and/or supervision may still be needed.	Hand and face washing, occurring at regularly scheduled times, offers practice for all children in the group.

Criterion: The child independently washes and dries hands and face most of the time.

AREA: **14-III. Self-Help Skills: Grooming**
BEHAVIOR: 14-IIId. Brushes teeth

Materials: Water, toothbrush, toothpaste

Procedure	Group activities
Model brushing your teeth for the child. Ask the child to brush his or her teeth. Put toothpaste on a brush for the child at first. Give him or her physical assistance and verbal directions as needed throughout the activity. Gradually fade your assistance. The child will often need some assistance or follow up for some time. For the child who is having a lot of difficulty, an electric toothbrush can be useful. Expect the child to brush his or her own teeth whenever needed; however, touch-up and/or supervision may still be needed.	Have personalized toothbrushes so children can brush after each meal.

Criterion: The child brushes his or her teeth most of the time.

4.5   The Carolina Curriculum

AREA: **14-III. Self-Help Skills: Grooming**
BEHAVIOR: 14-IIIe. Runs brush or comb through hair

Materials: Comb or brush, mirror

Procedure	Group activities
Model brushing your hair for the child. Ask the child to brush his or her hair. Give the child physical assistance and verbal directions as needed, then gradually fade your assistance. The child will often need some assistance or follow up for some time. An easy-to-care-for haircut can be useful for promoting independence in caring for the child's hair. Expect the child to brush his or her own hair whenever needed; however, touch-up and/or supervision may still be needed.	Have children keep a personalized hairbrush in their cubbies for hairbrushing practice.

Criterion: The child brushes his or her own hair most of the time.

5   AREA: **14-III. Self-Help Skills: Grooming**
BEHAVIOR: 14-IIIf. Blows nose independently upon request

Materials: Facial tissue

Procedure	Group activities
Demonstrate how to blow air out through nostrils. Hand the child a tissue and ask him or her to blow nose. If the child has difficulty in doing this task, try holding the tissue to the child's nose for him or her, and then again demonstrate blowing out through nostrils. Remind the child to close his or her mouth, if needed. Gradually fade any physical assistance. Teach the child to throw the tissue away after use.	This task needs to be done on an individual basis.

Criterion: The child blows his or her nose independently upon request.

14-IV.

Self-Help Skills: Toileting

THE NORMAL TIMETABLE FOR achieving toilet training is highly variable, with some children being fully trained by 2 years, while others are not trained until 3–3½ years. Boys are often somewhat older than girls before they have the physical maturation for toilet training. Nighttime wetting may persist throughout the preschool period in some children.

Children with developmental disabilities are often delayed in toilet training. A developmental psychologist can be helpful in establishing a toilet training program for an older child who is still in diapers. The child who is physically handicapped may need adaptive equipment for toileting. An occupational or physical therapist can assist in determining what would be useful. Note that in some conditions, such as spina bifida, toilet training may not be an appropriate goal due to the lack of bowel and bladder sensation and control.

14. Self-Help Skills
IV. Toileting

a. Usually indicates need to toilet; rarely has bowel accidents

b. Uses toilet by self, except for cleaning after a bowel movement

c. Seldom has toileting accidents; may need help with difficult clothing

d. Cares for self at toilet (may need assistance wiping after bowel movement)

e. Tears toilet tissue and flushes toilet after use

f. Wipes self after bowel movement

$2.^5$

AREA: 14-IV. Self-Help Skills: Toileting
BEHAVIOR: 14-IVa. Usually indicates need to toilet; rarely has bowel accidents

Materials: Child-size toilet or potty chair

Procedure	Group activities
A child is generally ready for toilet training when his or her diapers are dry for longer periods of time, bowel movements occur on a fairly regular schedule, and the child is interested in copying other children who use the toilet. Give positive reinforcement when the child is successful. In addition to the "regular" times for toileting, it is important to pay attention to a child's physical or verbal cues that he or she might need to go to the bathroom. By taking him or her at these times, the child will begin to associate the physical signs with the need to use the toilet. Encourage the child to tell you when he or she needs to go to the bathroom.	Often in group settings, there are logical time periods for children to use the toilet (e.g., after a meal, before and after nap time). The modeling effect of other children using the potty will be helpful for a child who is just beginning to toilet train.

Criterion: The child usually indicates the need to toilet and rarely has bowel accidents.

3

AREA: 14-IV. Self-Help Skills: Toileting
BEHAVIOR: 14-IVb. Uses toilet by self, except for cleaning after a bowel movement

Materials: Child-size toilet or potty chair, pants that are easy to remove

Procedure	Group activities
After the child is having some regular success in toileting, keep him or her in training pants and easy to pull down outer pants. When the child is not rushed to go to the toilet, encourage him or her to pull down his or her own pants. After using the toilet, hand him or her several pieces of toilet tissue and ask him or her to wipe him- or herself. Children usually need assistance in wiping after bowel movements for some time. When finished, encourage the child to pull his or her pants up and then wash the hands. Gradually fade any physical assistance you have been giving after a while. When the child is demonstrating some independence, encourage him or her to go alone, having you come in when he or she is finished to assist with cleanup.	Children need individual attention when learning to toilet. Modeling by other children may be helpful.

Criterion: The child uses the toilet by him- or herself, except cleaning after bowel movement.

AREA: **14-IV. Self-Help Skills: Toileting**

BEHAVIOR: 14-IVc. Seldom has toileting accidents; may need help with difficult clothing

Materials: Child-size toilet or potty chair, pants that are easy to remove

Procedure	Group activities
Following procedures in item 14-IVb., the child will gradually demonstrate greater success and consistency with toileting. Continue to remind the child to toilet before outings.	Proceed as in item 14-IVb.

Criterion: The child seldom has toileting accidents.

4

AREA: **14-IV. Self-Help Skills: Toileting**

BEHAVIOR: 14-IVd. Cares for self at toilet (may need assistance wiping after bowel movement)

Materials: Child-size toilet or potty chair, easy-to-remove pants

Procedure	Group activities
Proceed as in item 14-IVb. The child at this stage is fairly independent in toileting, although, he or she may need assistance with difficult clothing and wiping.	This task is best taught on an individual basis.

Criterion: The child cares for him- or herself at toilet; however, he or she may still need some assistance wiping after bowel movement.

4.5

AREA: **14-IV. Self-Help Skills: Toileting**

BEHAVIOR: 14-IVe. Tears toilet tissue and flushes toilet after use

Materials: Toilet that is accessible to child (some children may be able to use a regular toilet, while others may need an adapter seat on the toilet)

Procedure	Group activities
Show the child how to tear off a few sheets of toilet paper at a time. Flatten the toilet paper roll before hanging it so that the roll's rolling ability will be slowed down and the child won't end up with a large amount of toilet paper. Show the child how to flush the toilet. Remind him or her to only flush once. If needed, give the child physical assistance, and then fade that assistance as soon as possible.	This task is best taught on an individual basis.

Criterion: The child tears toilet tissue and flushes toilet after use.

AREA: **14-IV. Self-Help Skills: Toileting**
BEHAVIOR: 14-IVf. Wipes self after bowel movement

Materials: Toilet, toilet paper

Procedure	Group activities
After a bowel movement, tell the child to take some toilet paper and wipe him- or herself. It is best to teach the child to reach his or her hand around back to wipe (to avoid any possibility of urinary tract infection). Child may have best success if he or she stands up to wipe. Encourage the child to wipe several times, using new pieces of toilet paper. Have some type of wet wipe available for final wiping.	This task is best taught on an individual basis.

Criterion: The child successfully wipes him- or herself after a bowel movement.

15.

Fine Motor Skills: Hand use

THE DEVELOPMENT OF fine motor skills has been divided into four areas, each representing different aspects of development. During the preschool period, children refine their manipulative skills and establish a hand dominance. They learn to use simple tools as an extension of their body. The development of more advanced fine motor skills allows increasingly sophisticated mastery of the environment.

Hands-on learning is an integral part of the preschool curriculum. Children who are poorly coordinated may need to have some tasks simplified in order to be successful. If a child is having significant difficulty, an occupational therapist can help in adapting this program to met that child's particular needs. For children with severe motor impairment, development of fine motor skills may not be a realistic goal.

15. Fine Motor Skills: Hand use

a. Plays with messy materials such as clay —patting, pinching, and fingering
b. Demonstrates a hand preference (typically in eating)
c. Identifies an object by feeling it
d. Builds a tower of 8–10 blocks

e. Demonstrates hand preference by picking up most materials with the same hand; will cross midline in body
f. Places ¼″ pegs in a pegboard
g. Places 10 pellets in a bottle in 30 seconds

AREA: 15. Fine Motor Skills: Hand use
BEHAVIOR: 15a. Plays with messy materials such as clay—patting, pinching, and fingering

Materials: Play-Doh, plasticine, fingerpaint

Procedure	Group activities
Present material to the child for free exploration. If he or she does not spontaneously engage, demonstrate play, providing positive descriptions (e.g., "This feels good."; "It's fun to squeeze this."). You may need to provide some assistance, but do not push if the child is very resistive. (See information regarding Tactile Defensiveness, pp. 26–27.) Children who are hesitant may do best by beginning with a dry substance such as a tray of lentils or beans.	1. Try making figures with Play-Doh in a group activity. Children can help mix together and work color into their own piece. 2. Sand/water tables are nice for group messy play, and a good way to integrate children who are in wheelchairs.

Criterion: The child spontaneously plays with messy materials with no avoidance responses.

AREA: 15. Fine Motor Skills: Hand use
BEHAVIOR: 15b. Demonstrates a hand preference (typically in eating)

Materials: Spoon, food

Procedure	Group activities
Present the child with a plate of food, placing a spoon at midline above his or her plate. Observe the child eating on several occasions and note if he or she has a preference for either hand (may also be evident during other activities). If a preference is demonstrated, continue to support that hand as dominant, and encourage consistent use. If a preference is not clear, consistently present materials at midline to offer the child free choice.	Proceed as in the left column with all children.

Criterion: The child regularly uses the same hand for a skilled task (e.g., eating with spoon at lunch).

Note: There is a large variation in age regarding achievement of hand dominance with complete dominance establishment generally not expected until 5–6 years of age. Exclusive use of one hand at a very early age (e.g., before one year) is suspect and may be indicative of motor difficulties with the child's other hand. Children do not necessarily need to have established a dominant hand until approaching school age (5–6 years). If a hand preference has not emerged at this age, consultation with an occupational therapist should be sought.

AREA: **15. Fine Motor Skills: Hand use**
BEHAVIOR: 15c. Identifies an object by feeling it

Materials: A variety of small familiar items (e.g., cup, toothbrush, toy car, crayon, block, spoon)

Procedure	Group activities
Place 1 object in a small bag. Ask the child to reach in and tell you what is in the bag without looking. If the child has difficulty, present the objects visually first and review each object's name. Then remove all objects from view and repeat activity. Begin with objects that are very different from each other (e.g., cup, toothbrush). If the child has difficulty or has limited language, use a duplicate set of objects. Place 1 set of objects on the table in front of the child. Then, ask the child to point to the one on the table that is the same as the one in the bag. Use descriptive words to assist the child in identifying the objects' differences (soft, hard, rough, smooth).	1. Give each child a bag with 1 or 2 objects in it. Ask, "Who has a ____?" (several children may have the same object to help maintain interest). 2. Place a large object under a blanket. Have the children reach their hands under the blanket and try to guess what the object is (e.g., chair, pillow, broom, basket, ball).

Criterion: The child correctly identifies 4 out of 5 objects that are presented, by feeling or touching the items.

AREA: **15. Fine Motor Skills: Hand use**
BEHAVIOR: 15d. Builds a tower of 8–10 blocks

Materials: Ten 1-inch blocks

Procedure	Group activities
Place 10 blocks on the table in front of the child. Ask the child to build a tower (or tall building). If needed, demonstrate building a tower and then knock it down (or let the child knock it down). Ask the child to make a tower (or tall building) like you did. Start with larger blocks and a smaller tower if child has difficulty. For the child experiencing difficulty in motor control, try magnetic blocks or blocks with small Velcro spots attached. Beginning stacking games can also be done with bean bags.	1. Encourage a small group of children to build roads and buildings with a large selection of blocks. 2. Build towers of blocks (or small boxes) to knock down with bean bags.

Criterion: The child builds a tower of at least 8 blocks.

AREA: 15. Fine Motor Skills: Hand use
BEHAVIOR: 15e. Demonstrates hand preference by picking up most materials with the same hand; will cross midline in body

Materials: Ten 1-inch blocks

Procedure	Group activities
Scatter 10 blocks in front of the child. Ask the child to place the blocks in a container or to build a tower. Observe which hand he or she uses each time to pick up a block. Some children may tend to pick up blocks near the right side of the body with the right hand, and blocks near the left side with the left hand. In this case, continue offering materials generally at midline to avoid influencing hand choice. When a child has begun to demonstrate a clear hand preference for certain tasks (e.g., eating), encourage him or her to consistently use that hand for other skilled tasks. Sometimes a watch or bracelet on the child's preferred hand can be used as a visual cue for him or her and may encourage consistent use of the child's preferred hand.	Children should be observed individually.

Criterion: The child demonstrates a hand preference by picking up 8 out of 10 blocks with the same hand on several occasions.

Note: See information regarding hand dominance under item 15b.

AREA: 15. Fine Motor Skills: Hand use
BEHAVIOR: 15f. Places ¼″ pegs in a pegboard

Materials: ¼″ beaded pegs, hard plastic or wooden pegboard

Procedure	Group activities
Place pegs and a pegboard in front of the child and ask him or her to put the pegs in the holes. If the child does not respond, demonstrate the activity. If the child has difficulty, try placing a peg correctly in the child's hand (in pincer grasp). Sometimes just holding each peg out to the child by the opposite end will encourage him or her to grasp it correctly. Provide physical assistance if needed. If the task is too difficult for the child, try using larger pegs and pegboard initially. Then try dropping the ¼″ pegs into a small opening.	1. Making picture mosaics with various beans will help reinforce the child's use of the pincer grasp (make sure that no children in the group are still at a mouthing stage). 2. Playing bank or store during which children place pennies in a piggy bank or through a slotted lid is a good preparatory or related activity.

Criterion: The child places ten ¼″ pegs in a pegboard.

AREA: **15. Fine Motor Skills: Hand use**
BEHAVIOR: 15g. Places 10 pellets in a bottle in 30 seconds

Materials: Ten small pellets (or beads, pegs, beans, raisins, Cheerios), small bottle with a small opening (e.g., about 1″)

Procedure	Group activities
Give the child a bottle with pellets inside. Ask him or her to open and pour out the bottle's contents. Then ask the child to put the contents back in, one at a time, as fast as he or she can. If the child has difficulty, try practicing the activity with a larger container at first to work just on speed. Later, add the accuracy component of placement in a small opening.	See suggestions in item 15f.

Criterion: The child places 10 pellets in a bottle in 30 seconds on 3 separate occasions.

16.

Fine Motor Skills: Manipulation

16. Fine Motor Skills: Manipulation

a. Turns doorknob with forearm rotation
b. Unscrews cap from small bottle
c. Unbuttons large buttons (e.g., $3/4''$)
d. Screws on lids
e. Makes simple forms with Play-Doh (e.g., balls, snakes)
f. Turns wind-up key 90° in one turn
g. Removes bottle cap in 30 seconds
h. Holds one small object in palm of hand and then moves forward to pincer grasp without assistance from other hand
i. Buttons $1/2''$ buttons
j. Places paper clips on paper

AREA: **16. Fine Motor Skills: Manipulation**
BEHAVIOR: 16a. Turns doorknob with forearm rotation

Materials: Classroom door with easy-to-turn doorknob

Procedure	Group activities
When entering or leaving room, wait for the child to open the door. If the child does not spontaneously do this task, ask him or her to open the door. If the child has difficulty, give him or her verbal cues such as turn (physically prompting in the correct direction), then push (or pull). It is usually easier to open doors that need to be pushed. If the child is unsuccessful, practice with other activities involving turning would be useful (e.g., nested barrels, Kitty in the Keg, plastic nuts and bolts, unscrewing loosely fastened lids from various jars). Incorporating supination (i.e., palm up) patterns into activities may also be useful (e.g., using one hand to drop small objects into the other hand (palm up)—trying to see how many small objects the child can hold before dropping any.	1. Have the children take turns opening the door when going out. 2. Have a sign on the door requesting that all visitors knock and wait for a child to answer, giving each child further natural opportunity for practice.

Criterion: The child can open a doorknob using forearm rotation.

2.5   AREA: **16. Fine Motor Skills: Manipulation**
BEHAVIOR: 16b. Unscrews cap from small bottle

Materials: Small bottle with screw-on cap, small edibles or toys

Procedure	Group activities
Present the child with a bottle and ask him or her to remove the cap—a tiny edible or toy inside may provide motivation. If the child is unsuccessful, provide a demonstration, then give physical assistance as needed. For related activities, see activities suggested in item 16a. In general, children may have more success starting with a larger jar and lid (e.g., 2″ in diameter) that is only loosely fastened. Give verbal cues for the child to turn the lid the other way, if needed. Make sure that the fingers on the hand on the lid are only touching the lid. Some children tend to hold on to the lid and the jar, making turning impossible. By playing with radio knobs and music boxes with a turn dial, the child can practice the coordination of finger movements that are needed to unscrew a jar lid.	1. Have the children take turns opening a jar that contains the group snacks. 2. Provide various materials as described to the left and in item 16a. with which children can play. A basket of various-sized jars and bottles with lids is a nice option.

Criterion: The child is able to unscrew and remove the lid from a small bottle.

AREA: **16. Fine Motor Skills: Manipulation**
BEHAVIOR: 16c. Unbuttons large buttons (e.g., $^3/_4''$)

Materials: Cloth strip (or dressing vest or doll) with $^3/_4''$ buttons and button holes that are slightly
loose

Procedure	Group activities
Present the cloth strip with buttons buttoned and ask the child to unbutton it. If he or she does not know how to approach this task, slowly demonstrate 2 or 3 times. Then, try to physically assist the child. He or she should hold and lightly pull cloth next to the hole with one hand and with other hand grasp the button and push it through the hole. If this task is too difficult for the child, a good preliminary activity is pushing coins or checkers through a slit cut into a plastic jar. The slit should provide a tight fit, so that the child has to exert some effort to push the coin through.	1. Play dress-up with very simple clothing that has large buttons. At this age, the goal would be for the children to undo fasteners and remove clothing independently. In another year, the focus will be on independently putting on and fastening the clothing. 2. Button boards that can have a surprise picture hidden under the material can be fun to use with a group of children who can then share what they "found." 3. Playing bank or store during which children place pennies in a piggy bank or through a slotted lid is a good preparatory activity.

Criterion: The child can unbutton three $^3/_4''$ buttons.

AREA: **16. Fine Motor Skills: Manipulation**
BEHAVIOR: 16d. Screws on lids

Materials: Small bottles or jars of various sizes with matching lids

Procedure	Group activities
After doing the activities in item 16b., ask the child to put the lid back on, perhaps as part of cleanup. If the child has difficulty with this task, demonstrate screwing on the lid and then physically assist the child. Show him or her how to hold the lid in overhand fashion with his or her fingers around the edge of the rim. Give verbal cues as to which direction the child should turn.	1. Have the children hide tiny surprises for each other in opaque jars. Close the lids and then exchange the jars. 2. After opening a snack jar as described in item 16b., have a child replace the lid, giving different children a turn on various days.

Criterion: The child can screw on lids on various type jars or bottles.

AREA: **16. Fine Motor Skills: Manipulation**
BEHAVIOR: 16e. Makes simple forms with Play-Doh (e.g., balls, snakes)

Materials: Play-Doh

Procedure	Group activities
First place some Play-Doh in front of the child and allow him or her an opportunity for free play and exploration. You may need to provide some prompting and demonstration, but do not push this activity if the child is very resistive (see information on Tactile Defensiveness, pp. 26–27). Starting with snakes, show the child how to roll out a long thin roll using his or her hands and fingers. Then, give the child a piece of Play-Doh that you have already begun to roll out and ask him or her to make it into a long snake. Try giving the child an unshapen piece of Play-Doh and asking him or her to make a snake without assistance. When the child has achieved good success making a snake, introduce making a ball (this requires a more complicated motor pattern). Show the child how to move his or her hand in a circle, rolling the Play-Doh around on the table or between both hands. Balls are more difficult for most children to make and may not be achieved until the child is a little older.	Have the children make Play-Doh together, mixing in various colors of their choice. Then, have the children make snakes or bracelets perhaps in conjunction with a story read earlier.

Criterion: The child independently rolls out Play-Doh with his or her hands to form snakes and balls.

AREA: **16. Fine Motor Skills: Manipulation**
BEHAVIOR: 16f. Turns wind-up key 90° in one turn

Materials: Small action toys with wind-up key or knob

Procedure	Group activities
Wind up toy and then place it before the child on a table. When it has finished moving, ask the child to wind it up so that the toy will go again. This is generally a very motivating activity for children and needs little instruction. Encourage the child to make "big turns." If the child has difficulty with this activity, try a variety of toys, selecting one that is very easy to turn (e.g., key protrudes well away from toy and is large and easy to grasp). If needed, provide physical assistance, helping the child to hold the toy still with	Have a basket filled with a variety of wind-up toys available for free play.

(continued)

Procedure	Group activities
one hand and turn the key with the other (preferred hand). If the child is still unsuccessful, use a large toddler toy, such as a wind-up radio, to teach the motion that is required.	

Criterion: The child turns a wind-up key 90° in one turn.

AREA: **16. Fine Motor Skills: Manipulation**
BEHAVIOR: 16g. Removes bottle cap in 30 seconds

Materials: Small bottle with screw-on cap (e.g., 1–1½″ in diameter), small toys or edibles

Procedure	Group activities
Present a bottle to the child and ask him or her to remove the lid. Motivation may be increased by providing a tiny toy or edible treat inside. If the child has difficulty with this activity, check the tightness of the cap to make sure that the task is not too difficult. Encourage the child to open the bottle quickly. If he or she is not successful, return to item 16b. to develop the required motor control.	See item 16b.

Criterion: The child unscrews and removes the lid from a small bottle within 30 seconds.

AREA: **16. Fine Motor Skills: Manipulation**
BEHAVIOR: 16h. Holds one small object in palm of hand and then moves forward to pincer grasp without assistance from other hand

Materials: Pennies and bank, or ¼″ pegs and pegboard

Procedure	Group activities
Place a penny in the palm of your hand and demonstrate moving it forward to pincer grasp it through finger and thumb movements. Then, drop it in the bank. Place a penny in the palm of the child's hand and ask him or her to put it in the bank like you did. Hold the child's other hand, if necessary, to encourage manipulation of the object within one hand. If the child is not successful, begin by placing the penny in his or her palm near the index finger so that very little movement will be needed to bring it forward to pincer grasp. If the child still has difficulty,	Have each child select a small item (e.g., penny, peg, bead, button) to hold "secretly" in the palm of his or her hand. Then, call out each item in turn for the children to drop into a container (e.g., "Does anyone have a _____?").

(continued)

Procedure	Group activities
try a larger object, such as a 1″ block. When the child is successful with pennies, try alternative objects such as ¼″ pegs and pegboard.	

Criterion: The child holds a small object in the palm of his or her hand and then moves forward to a pincer grasp without assistance from the other hand.

4.5

AREA: 16. Fine Motor Skills: Manipulation
BEHAVIOR: 16i. Buttons ½″ buttons

Materials: Cloth strip (or dressing vest, or dressing doll) with ½″ buttons and button holes that are slightly loose

Procedure	Group activities
Present the cloth strip with its buttons buttoned and ask the child to unbutton them. Then ask the child to button them back together. If he or she does not know how, demonstrate the activity slowly, 2 or 3 times. Show the child how to hold the cloth with one hand and the button with the other hand. After pushing the button through the hole, grasp the button with the other hand and pull it through the hole. If the child has difficulty, he or she can practice passing a large button, checker, or poker chip through a slit cut into a plastic lid. The button should be passed from one hand to the other hand.	1. Play dress-up with simple clothing that has front buttons. 2. Play with dressing dolls such as "Dapper Dan." Pretend it is cold and he needs to button up to stay warm.

Criterion: The child is able to button ½″ buttons.

5

AREA: 16. Fine Motor Skills: Manipulation
BEHAVIOR: 16j. Places paper clips on paper

Materials: Paper, several standard-size metal paper clips

Procedure	Group activities
Demonstrate how to place paper clips on paper. Point out the difference in the 2 ends of the paper clip. The child should hold the paper clip in his or her preferred hand with the paper clip's double loops directed toward the paper. Have the child rest the edge of the large loop on the edge of the paper held in the other hand. Press down slightly (which will open clip) and slide the clip forward. If the child has difficulty, have the child place paper clips on index cards.	1. Give each child several paper clips of one color, with each child having a different color. Ask the children to find cards of the same color as their clips, from a mixed pile, and then put a paper clip on each card. 2. Give each child a card with a picture on it. Ask the children to find a matching card from the pile and to clip them together with the paper clip.

(continued)

Procedure	Group activities
Large plastic paper clips will also facilitate the task. For some children, it is easier, at first, if you hold the paper taut for them.	

Criterion: The child places 3 paper clips on a piece of paper.

17.

Fine Motor Skills: Bilateral skills

17. Fine Motor Skills: Bilateral skills

a. Strings large beads
b. Pulls apart large popbeads
c. Holds bowl and stirs
d. Strings small beads (e.g., $1/2''$)
e. Ties single knot

f. Laces 2 holes in shoes
g. Does simple sewing on lacing card or cloth
h. Folds 8 $1/2'' \times 11''$ paper in half (no demonstration)

2.6

AREA: **17. Fine Motor Skills: Bilateral skills**
BEHAVIOR: 17a. Strings large beads

Materials: 1–1 ½″ beads (kindergarten beads of various shapes and colors); lace with stiff tip, knotted at one end

Procedure	Group activities
Place several beads and a lace in front of the child. Ask him or her to string some beads. With a second string, demonstrate how to hold the bead in one hand and use the other hand to push the string through the hole, and then grasp it on the other side to pull it through. Physically assist the child as needed. If he or she has difficulty, try teaching the child to place the beads on a stiff object such as a swizzle stick or aquarium tubing first.	Place a large number of beads in various colors in the center of the table. Give each child a lace and encourage him or her to make a necklace (or snake).

Criterion: The child is able to string several large beads on a lace.

2.5

AREA: **17. Fine Motor Skills: Bilateral skills**
BEHAVIOR: 17b. Pulls apart large popbeads

Materials: Large (e.g., 1 ½–2″) popbeads of various shapes and colors

Procedure	Group activities
Place a string of 4–5 popbeads in front of the child. Ask him or her to pull the popbeads apart. If he or she does not do this, demonstrate pulling them apart and then push the beads back together. If needed, give physical assistance. (Different brands of pop beads require differing degrees of strength to pull apart. Begin with easy to pull apart beads, gradually increasing difficulty, as child demonstrates competence.) Expand the child's skills through play with other toys that involve pulling apart and putting together.	Proceed with the activity described to the left, but with a group of children.

Criterion: The child pulls apart a strand of 4 large popbeads.

2.5

AREA: 17. Fine Motor Skills: Bilateral skills
BEHAVIOR: 17c. Holds bowl and stirs

Materials: Bowls, large spoons

Procedure	Group activities
Place 1 bowl and 1 spoon in front of the child. With second set, demonstrate stirring. Ask the child if he or she can help you do some cooking. Pretend to mix together the ingredients for a soup or cake. Prompt the child to keep 1 hand on the bowl while stirring with the other. A bowl with a handle may make this activity easier.	1. Play in a housekeeping or kitchen center to facilitate this type activity. 2. With a small group of children, prepare a simple dish, such as pudding, giving each child an opportunity to stir.

Criterion: The child stabilizes a bowl with one hand and uses his or her other hand to stir with a spoon.

AREA: 17. Fine Motor Skills: Bilateral skills
BEHAVIOR: 17d. Strings small beads (e.g., $\frac{1}{2}''$)

Materials: Bowl with a number of small beads, lace with one stiff end and a knot on the other end

Procedure	Group activities
Place a bowl of beads and lace in front of the child and ask him or her to make a necklace or a snake. Demonstrate the procedure with a second lace. In general, beads with straight sides, such as a square, may be easier for child to hold and string than round or oval beads. If the child has difficulty, check first to be sure he or she can string large beads (see item 17a.). If the child passes 17a., but still can not do this task, he or she may need more practice handling small objects (e.g., putting pennies in a bank, placing $\frac{1}{2}''$ pegs in a pegboard; finger feeding small pieces of cereal or raisins).	1. Have the children string wheel-shaped macaroni to decorate the classroom or a Christmas tree. 2. Place several bowls containing beads of various shapes, colors, and sizes in the center of the table for the children to make necklaces or snakes.

Criterion: The child strings several small beads (e.g., $\frac{1}{2}''$)

AREA: 17. Fine Motor Skills: Bilateral skills
BEHAVIOR: 17e. Ties single knot

Materials: Laces; laced shoe, board with holes, or similar item used to hold laces

Procedure	Group activities
Present a laced shoe to the child. Sitting next to the child, with a similar shoe, show him or her how to tie the ends into a simple overhand knot. Hold the lace in one hand and bring the lace across the other lace, held in the other hand (forming and "X"). Hold the "X" with one hand, while taking the first lace behind and through the loop under the "X". Then, pull the laces tight, holding the ends of laces. This task is much easier for the child to follow when laces of 2 contrasting colors are used. This also makes it easier to give the child verbal cues (e.g., "Pull the yellow lace"). Some people use a simple story to cue the child. The child is told that one end is a rabbit and that the rabbit must go around the tree (the other end), and then down the hole. Knot tying can also be taught by using a single lace or string without a shoe or similar holder that anchors the middle.	Two longer pieces of colored yarn or string that are anchored to a hook can be used by children to repeatedly tie knots. The resulting strand can be used to make a necklace or bracelet.

Criterion: The child ties a single knot.

AREA: 17. Fine Motor Skills: Bilateral skills
BEHAVIOR: 17f. Laces 2 holes in shoes

Materials: Shoes with laces

Procedure	Group activities
Place a shoe before the child with the first 2 holes laced. Ask the child to finish lacing the shoe. You may want to have a second shoe for you so that you can demonstrate lacing. Show the child how to push the lace through the hole with one hand, then grasp and pull it the rest of the way with the other hand. At this age, following an appropriate lacing pattern is not expected.	Use simple lacing cards with a group of children.

Criterion: The child laces at least 2 holes in his or her shoes.

AREA: **17. Fine Motor Skills: Bilateral skills**
BEHAVIOR: 17g. Does simple sewing on lacing card or cloth

Materials: Simple sewing cards, lace or easy-to-sew cloth (e.g., burlap), and large blunt needle with yarn

Procedure	Group activities
Give the child a sewing card and lace. On second card, demonstrate how to sew the card. Typically, the child would hold the card in his or her nondominant hand. With the dominant hand, push the lace through the hole and then reach under card with same hand to grasp lace and pull it through. Provide physical assistance as needed. If the child is sewing on cloth, it may be easier if the cloth is stabilized in a small embroidery hoop.	1. Make simple greeting cards for parents by sewing a simple design onto a piece of cardboard (pre-punch sewing holes for children). 2. Have the children create their own designs using various colors and weights of yarn, sewn onto burlap. 3. Children who enjoy sewing can create simple pillows by sewing together 2 pieces of felt and stuffing it with batting.

Criterion: The child sews at least 8 stitches on a sewing card or piece of cloth.

AREA: **17. Fine Motor Skills: Bilateral skills**
BEHAVIOR: 17h. Folds 8 ½″ × 11″ paper in half (no demonstration)

Materials: Sheets of 8 ½″ × 11″ paper

Procedure	Group activities
Place a sheet of paper in front of the child and ask him or her to fold the paper in half. If the child does not know what to do, demonstrate folding a second sheet of paper and then ask him or her to fold his or her sheet. Help the child bring the edges of the paper close together and show him or her how to crease it by pushing down with his or her fingers. On a different occasion, again ask the child to fold the paper in half without providing a demonstration.	1. Have the children fold napkins for snack or lunch time. 2. Have the children make simple cards by folding a piece of paper in half and then decorating it.

Criterion: The child folds an 8 ½″ × 11″ paper in half without a demonstration.

18.

Fine Motor Skills:
Tool use

18. Fine Motor Skills: Tool use

a. Transfers material with a spoon
b. Uses small wooden hammer to pound in objects
c. Uses rolling pin to flatten material

d. Uses wooden tongs to transfer materials
e. Uses hammer and pegs or nails
f. Uses clothespin to transfer small objects

AREA: **18. Fine Motor Skills: Tool use**
BEHAVIOR: 18a. Transfers material with a spoon

Materials: Two bowls, teaspoon, loose material such as small stones, lentils, rice, or sand (if mouthing is a problem, use Cheerios)

Procedure	Group activities
Fill 1 bowl with lentils and set it in front of the child with an empty bowl next to it. With a spoon, demonstrate scooping the lentils and dumping them into the second bowl. Then, give the spoon to the child and ask him or her to fill up the second bowl. Give physical assistance as needed. Use of heavy bowls that will not tip over easily may offer the child greater success. If the child tends to lose most of the material before reaching the second bowl, let him or her use a long handled measuring cup at first.	1. Scooping and filling containers is an easy activity to encourage during group play at a sand table or sand box. 2. Have children serve themselves a snack (e.g., dry cereal, raisins) from a large bowl using a spoon or scoop. 3. Use shovels to fill up pails when building a sand castle.

Criterion: The child uses a spoon to scoop and transfer material to a second container.

AREA: **18. Fine Motor Skills: Tool use**
BEHAVIOR: 18b. Uses small wooden hammer to pound in objects

Materials: Wooden hammer, pegs and pounding bench or golf tees and styrofoam

Procedure	Group activities
Present a toy and hammer to the child. Demonstrate how to hammer in pegs. Reset the pegs and give the hammer to the child. Tell him or her to hammer the pegs all the way in. (There are a variety of pounding toys available commercially. Some are much easier to use than others. If a child has difficulty with this activity, try a set that is easier to hammer. A well-used wooden set allows easy hammering.) Golf tees are fairly easy to hammer in; however, somewhat greater eye-hand accuracy is required. You may need to start the pegs or tees for the child to finish.	Children should not be encouraged to play close to each other when hammering due to the potential risk of accidentally hitting someone. Proceed with a similar activity as in the "Procedure" section.

Criterion: The child uses a wooden hammer to pound in several objects.

AREA: **18. Fine Motor Skills: Tool use**
BEHAVIOR: 18c. Uses rolling pin to flatten material

Materials: Rolling pin, Play-Doh or cookie dough

Procedure	Group activities
Give the child a ball of Play-Doh and show him or her how to flatten it slightly with his or her hands. Then, give the child the rolling pin and ask him or her to roll out the Play-Doh to make a big cookie. Demonstrate how to do this activity with a second rolling pin and piece of Play-Doh. If needed, physically take the child through the activity, encouraging him or her to both roll and push at the same time. Children may find it easier to use a rolling pin that has handles that allow the body of the rolling pin to turn independently (vs. a solid piece of wood). Brio and Galt toys both make child-size rolling pins with independent handles; however, most children can use a standard-sized pin.	Make cookies or biscuits, giving each child a small portion of the dough to roll out.

Criterion: The child uses a rolling pin to flatten a small ball of Play-Doh or cookie dough.

AREA: **18. Fine Motor Skills: Tool use**
BEHAVIOR: 18d. Uses wooden tongs to transfer materials

Materials: Wooden toaster tongs, container, small objects (e.g., $\frac{1}{2}''$ cubes, Legos, shells)

Procedure	Group activities
Place several small objects on the table in front of the child. Using wooden tongs, demonstrate how to pick up the objects and to drop them into a container. Tongs should be held in the hand similarly to how a fork or pencil is held. Place the tongs in the child's hand correctly and ask him or her to pick up the objects and to drop them into the container. A low container with a large opening will be easier for the child to manage at first.	Proceed with the activity in the "Procedure" section but with a group of children who are filling up one large container.

Criterion: The child uses wooden tongs to pick up at least 5 small objects and drop them into a container.

4.5

AREA: **18. Fine Motor Skills: Tool use**
BEHAVIOR: 18e. Uses hammer and pegs or nails

Materials: Lightweight hammer, nails or pegs, wood

Procedure	Group activities
Start several nails in a piece of wood. Demonstrate to the child how to hammer in 1 nail. Then give the hammer to the child and ask him or her to hammer in the rest of the nails. Encourage the child to hold the hammer toward the end of the handle and to raise the hammer several inches above the nail before hitting each time. Give physical assistance, if needed, to help the child establish a hammering rhythm. If the child has successfully passed item 18b., but still has difficulty with this task, try hammering the nails into a very soft piece of wood, such as balsa, first.	Have the children hammer nails into several stumps that are set up in the play yard. Children should not be encouraged to play near each other when hammering due to the potential risk of accidentally hitting someone.

Criterion: The child uses a hammer to pound in several nails.

5

AREA: **18. Fine Motor Skills: Tool use**
BEHAVIOR: 18f. Uses clothespin to transfer small objects

Materials: Standard-size spring-type clothespins, pennies, Play-Doh, container

Procedure	Group activities
Slightly flatten a ball of Play-Doh. Stand several pennies on end in the Play-Doh. Show the child how to use the clothespin to pick up a penny and drop it into a container. Then ask the child to use the clothespin to pick up the pennies and to drop them into the container. After the child picks up a penny, remind him or her not to squeeze the clothespin again until it is over the container. If the child has difficulty, allow him or her time to practice using clothespins by clipping them onto a piece of cardboard. After he or she gains good control of the clothespins, return to using the clothespin as a tool. This activity can also be done with small beaded pegs placed in a pegboard.	Do the activity in the "Procedure" section with a small group of children.

Criterion: The child uses a spring-type clothespin to pick up at least 5 small objects and to transfer them to a container.

Visual-Motor Skills: Pencil control and copying

VISUAL-MOTOR SKILLS REFERS to the development of drawing and cutting skills. The emergence of visual-motor skills requires integration of visual-perceptual and fine motor skills. There is considerable normal variability in visual-motor development during the preschool period, with girls often demonstrating a developmental advantage.

Children who have difficulty with drawing and coloring often avoid these activities. As a result, lack of practice and experience further compromises their difficulties or delays. In addition to teaching specific drawing and coloring skills, it is important to find materials and/or methods that will encourage the child to practice and develop visual-motor control.

When children demonstrate significant lags or difficulty with drawing and cutting skills, an occupational therapist should be consulted. Mastery of basic pencil control and shape production is an important foundation for the future development of writing skills.

19. Visual-Motor Skills
I. Pencil control and copying

a. Makes a crayon rubbing
b. Imitates vertical stroke
c. Imitates horizontal stroke
d. Copies a circle with a circular scribble
e. Copies a circle
f. Copies a cross
g. Traces a 6″ × ¼″ line with no more than one deviation
h. Holds marker with fingers in tripod position
i. Copies a square
j. Traces outline of simple stencil
k. Copies asterisk (*)

2.5

AREA: 19-I. Visual-Motor Skills: Pencil control and copying
BEHAVIOR: 19-Ia. Makes a crayon rubbing

Materials: Paper, crayons, textured surfaces

Procedure	Group activities
Tape a piece of paper over a textured surface (e.g., plastic needlepoint canvas, large leaf, template). Show the child how to rub a crayon back and forth repeatedly over paper so that the design of the textured surface can be seen. Then ask the child to color the paper like you did. Hold the child's hand and give him or her physical assistance in coloring, if needed.	1. Have the children collect leaves, bark, and grass from outside. Glue the collection onto pieces of cardboard. After drying, have the children place paper over the cardboard and make crayon rubbings. 2. Have the children take paper outside and make crayon rubbings against trees or rocks.

Criterion: The child uses a crayon to make a rubbing on a piece of paper.

2.5

AREA: 19-I. Visual-Motor Skills: Pencil control and copying
BEHAVIOR: 19-Ib. Imitates vertical stroke

Materials: Large pieces of paper, crayons or markers

Procedure	Group activities
Place paper in front of the child and demonstrate how to make vertical strokes. While doing so, say to the child, "Watch me. I am making lines that go up and down." Try adding a sound as you make each line (e.g., "Zip!"). Then ask the child to make a line like you did. If he or she does not, take his or her hand and help him or her make several vertical lines. Then ask the child to make one by him- or herself. If the child is having a lot of difficulty, make a cardboard guide to help him or her. Cut a slot in a piece of cardboard about $1/2'' \times 8''$. Place the cardboard over the paper and guide the child's hand in making the lines using the slot. Then, see if the child can do this activity independently.	1. Try finger painting and encourage the children to make vertical lines. 2. Make vertical strokes in sand, either in a sand box or in a small amount of sand on a cookie sheet.

Criterion: The child imitates a vertical stroke.

AREA: **19-I. Visual-Motor Skills: Pencil control and copying**
BEHAVIOR: 19-Ic. Imitates horizontal stroke

Materials: Large pieces of paper, crayons or markers

Procedure	Group activities
Place a piece of paper in front of the child and demonstrate making several horizontal strokes. While doing so, say to the child, "Watch me. I am making lines that go back and forth." Try adding a sound as you make each line (e.g., "vroom!"). Then ask the child to make a line like you did. If the child does not, take his or her hand and help him or her make several horizontal lines. Then ask the child to make one by him- or herself. If the child is having a lot of difficulty, make a cardboard guide as in item 19-Ib. Place the cardboard over the paper and guide the child's hand in making lines using the slot. Then, see if the child can do the activity independently.	1. Try finger painting and encourage the children to make horizontal lines. 2. Make horizontal strokes in sand, either in a sand box or in a small amount of sand on a cookie sheet.

Criterion: The child imitates a horizontal stroke.

AREA: **19-I. Visual-Motor Skills: Pencil control and copying**
BEHAVIOR: 19-Id. Copies a circle with a circular scribble

Materials: Paper, crayons or markers

Procedure	Group activities
At top of a piece of paper draw several circles. Then ask the child to make a circle like yours. Talk to the child about going "around" and making circles on the paper. If needed, guide the child's hand several times in making a circular scribble (going around several times).	1. Try finger painting and encourage the children to make circular scribbles. 2. Draw circular scribbles in the sand, either in a sand box or in a small amount of sand on a cookie sheet.

Criterion: The child produces a circular scribble when attempting to copy a circle.

AREA: **19-I. Visual-Motor Skills: Pencil control and copying**
BEHAVIOR: 19-Ie. Copies a circle

Materials: Paper, crayons or markers

Procedure	Group activities
At the top of a piece of paper draw several circles. As you make each circle, tell the child, "Go around and stop." Then ask the child to make a circle like yours. If the child has difficulty, guide his or her hand several times in making a circle. Then ask the child to do the activity independently. Try making circles of different sizes. See if the child can make big and small circles. He or she may enjoy making circles for you to turn into happy faces.	1. Try finger painting and encourage the children to make circles. 2. Draw circles in the sand, either in a sand box or in a small amount of sand on a cookie sheet.

Criterion: The child copies a circle.

AREA: **19-I. Visual-Motor Skills: Pencil control and copying**
BEHAVIOR: 19-If. Copies a cross

Materials: Paper, crayons or markers

Procedure	Group activities
At the top of a piece of paper draw several crosses. As you make each cross, tell the child, "Line down, line across." Then ask him or her to make a cross like yours. If the child has difficulty, guide his or her hand several times in making a cross. Then ask the child to do the activity independently. Some children may need extra verbal cues at first (e.g., "Make a line down, pick your hand [crayon] up, now make a line across").	1. Try finger painting and encourage children to make crosses. 2. Draw crosses in the sand, either in a sand box or in a small amount of sand on a cookie sheet.

Criterion: The child copies a cross.

AREA: **19-I. Visual-Motor Skills: Pencil control and copying**
BEHAVIOR: 19-Ig. Traces a 6″ × ¼″ line with no more than one deviation

Materials: Paper, wide marker, pencil

Procedure	Group activities
Draw a straight line about 6″ long using the marker. Ask the child to trace over your line using a pencil. To make the task more interesting and goal directed, try drawing a small car at the beginning of the line and a garage at the end. Ask the child to "drive" the car to the garage, making sure he or she stays on the road. If the child has difficulty, physically assist him or her in tracing the line several times. For some children, placing masking tape on either side of the line is helpful in providing an extra clue to stay on the line. A cut-out guide as described in item 19-Ib. can also be used.	This may be done with a small group of children; however, children may need individual attention.

Criterion: The child traces a 6″ × ¼″ line with no more than one deviation.

AREA: **19-I. Visual-Motor Skills: Pencil control and copying**
BEHAVIOR: 19-Ih. Holds marker with fingers in tripod position

Materials: Paper, marker

Procedure	Group activities
Ask the child to draw a picture. Observe how the child holds the marker. A mature grasp consists of the marker being held between the thumb and the index finger, resting on the middle finger, with the last 2 fingers loosely flexed in palm of the hand. Also acceptable at this age is holding the marker between thumb and first 2 fingers. The marker should be held within 1″ of the tip to provide good control. If the child is holding the marker awkwardly, try to reposition his or her hand in a more mature grasp. Often, an immature grasp is a reflection of poorly developed hand and finger skills. The child may need more work on manipulation skills before he or she is ready to consistently use a mature grasp.	Observe children writing as described in the "Procedure" section.

Criterion: The child consistently holds a marker with fingers in a tripod position (e.g., thumb and 1 or 2 fingers).

4. 5

AREA: 19-I. Visual-Motor Skills: Pencil control and copying
BEHAVIOR: 19-Ii. Copies a square

Materials: Paper, crayons or markers

Procedure	Group activities
At the top of a piece of paper draw a square. Then hold the child's hand and help him or her make several large squares. There are several different approaches to making squares and you may need to experiment to see which approach works best for a particular child. After doing squares together, ask the child to draw a square by him- or herself.	1. Try finger painting and encourage the children to make squares.
	2. Draw squares in the sand, either in a sand box or in a small amount of sand on a cookie sheet.
If a child is having limited success, it may be helpful initially to draw part of square, and ask the child to complete it (e.g., Draw 3 sides of the square and ask the child to draw the fourth side. Then draw only 2 sides, asking him or her to add the other 2 sides. It is easier at first, if you draw 2 vertical lines and the child adds the 2 horizontal lines. When he or she is successful with this, try drawing a right angle and asking the child to complete it by adding the other right angle.)	

Criterion: The child copies a square on 3 different occasions.

5

AREA: 19-I. Visual-Motor Skills: Pencil control and copying
BEHAVIOR: 19-Ij. Traces outline of simple stencil

Materials: Paper, stencils, markers or pencil

Procedure	Group activities
Secure 2 pieces of paper (1 for you and 1 for the child) to the table with tape. Place a stencil on top of your paper. Show the child how to trace around the stencil, while stabilizing it with the nondominant hand. Then, ask the child to trace the stencil on his or her paper. Encourage the child to keep the point of his or her pencil against the edge of the stencil. If the child is having difficulty, physically assist him or her in tracing the stencil several times. Then ask him or her to do the activity alone. If necessary, secure the stencil onto the paper with tape.	1. Have the children make stencils appropriate to the season or holiday to use to decorate the classroom.
	2. Have the children make name tags by tracing a simple shape and cutting it out.
	3. Try having the children trace simple pictures using tracing paper.

Criterion: The child traces a simple stencil, maintaining his or her pencil in contact with the stencil 75% of the time.

AREA: **19-I. Visual-Motor Skills: Pencil control and copying**
BEHAVIOR: 19-Ik. Copies asterisk (*)

Materials: Paper, crayons or markers

Procedure	Group activities
At the top of a piece of paper draw several asterisks. Then ask the child to make an asterisk like yours. If the child has difficulty, guide his or her hand several times in making one. Then, ask him or her to do the activity independently. Some children may need extra work initially on making diagonal lines. Try making dots for the child to connect that will produce diagonal lines. Also, draw squares for the child and ask him or her to make an "X" inside of it by connecting the corners with diagonal lines. When the child can make an "X" independently, have him or her add the third line to complete the asterisk.	1. Try finger painting and encourage the children to make asterisks. 2. Draw asterisks in the sand, either in a sand box or in a small amount of sand on a cookie sheet. 3. Make nighttime pictures drawing asterisks in the "sky" to represent stars.

Criterion: The child copies an asterisk.

Visual-Motor Skills:
Representational drawing

19. Visual-Motor Skills
II. Representational drawing

a. Draws a person with a head and 1 feature

b. Draws a person with a head and 4 features

c. Draws simple pictures of things seen or imagined

d. Draws a person with a head and 6 features

e. Draws a person with a head and 8 features

3. 5

AREA: **19-II. Visual-Motor Skills: Representational drawing**
BEHAVIOR: 19-IIa. Draws a person with a head and 1 feature

Materials: Paper, pencil (or markers or crayons)

Procedure	Group activities
Ask the child to draw a picture of him- or herself. If the child does not produce anything recognizable, suggest that he or she draw a circle for a head. (Child should be able to draw a circle before attempting this item.) Then ask the child what else the picture needs. Try having him or her look in a mirror (preferably full length). Encourage the child to add something else to his or her picture (e.g., eyes, mouth, lines to represent legs). If the child does not think of something to add, suggest that he or she add the eyes, mouth, or legs to his or her picture since those are usually the first "body parts" to be added. On a different occasion, ask him or her to draw a picture of him- or herself, without providing any cues initially. If he or she has little success, repeat the teaching procedure.	This may be done with small groups; however, some children may need individual attention.

Criterion: The child draws a head and 1 other feature when asked to draw a picture of him- or herself.

4

AREA: **19-II. Visual-Motor Skills: Representational drawing**
BEHAVIOR: 19-IIb. Draws a person with a head and 4 features

Materials: Paper, pencil (or markers or crayons)

Procedure	Group activities
Ask the child to draw a picture of him- or herself. If the child does not produce anything recognizable, return to item 19-IIa. Typically, the child will draw a circle for the head and perhaps 1 or 2 other features. Then, ask him or her what else the picture needs. Try having him or her look in a mirror (preferably full length). Encourage the child to add more parts to his or her picture. If the child does not think of something to add, suggest features or body parts that he or she might add. Draw a simple drawing of a person on a separate piece of paper as an example. On a different occasion, ask the child to draw a picture of him- or herself, without providing any cues initially. If he or she has little success, repeat the teaching procedure.	1. Have the children work on body puzzles to help enhance their visual awareness of body parts and where they are in relationship to each other. 2. Use a flannel board at group time with cutouts of a person. Have the children take turns adding body parts.

Criterion: The child draws a head and 4 other features when asked to draw a picture of him- or herself.

AREA: **19-II. Visual-Motor Skills: Representational drawing**
BEHAVIOR: 19-IIc. Draws simple pictures of things seen or imagined

Materials: Paper, crayons, markers, pencils

Procedure	Group activities
Ask the child to draw a picture. If he or scribbles or makes little response, suggest something that he or she might draw, particularly something you know in which he or she is interested. Often it is helpful to suggest and demonstrate easy to draw pictures (e.g., rainbow, car, house, flower). Draw a very simple picture and ask the child to make one like yours. The goal is not that the child reproduce yours exactly, but rather to give him or her some ideas on how to draw simple objects; a foundation upon which he or she can expand. When the child does draw spontaneous pictures, ask him or her to tell you about the picture.	1. Ask the children to draw pictures related to a topic being explored that week or to a favorite story. 2. Have the children use a flannel board to construct a scene.

Criterion: The child draws simple pictures of things he or she has seen or imagined.

AREA: **19-II. Visual-Motor Skills: Representational drawing**
BEHAVIOR: 19-IId. Draws a person with a head and 6 features

Materials: Paper, pencil (or markers or crayons)

Procedure	Group activities
Ask the child to draw a picture of him- or herself. This item expands on the skills demonstrated in item 19-IIb. Try having the child look in a mirror (preferably full length). Encourage the child to add a body to his or her picture, if he or she has not done this already. Show the child how arms and legs are attached to the body. Ask him or her what else is on the body that is not part of his or her picture. Draw a simple drawing of a person on a separate piece of paper as an example. On a different occasion, ask the child to draw a picture of him- or herself, without providing any cues initially. If he or she has limited success, repeat the teaching procedure.	1. Make body tracings of children by having them lie on a large piece of paper while you trace around them. Then, have the children fill in the details by looking in a mirror for clues. 2. Draw incomplete pictures of a person for the children to complete by adding the missing body parts.

Criterion: The child draws a head and 6 other features when asked to draw a picture of him- or herself.

AREA: **19-II. Visual-Motor Skills: Representational drawing**
BEHAVIOR: 19-IIe. Draws a person with a head and 8 features

Materials: Paper, pencil (or markers or crayons)

Procedure	Group activities
Ask the child to draw a picture of him- or herself. This item expands on the skills demonstrated in item 19-IId. Typically, the child will already be producing a head, body, arms, legs, and 2 facial features. Encourage the child to expand his or her picture, looking in a mirror (preferably full length) as needed. Ask the child what else he or she could add, giving suggestions if the child is unable to think of any more body parts. On a different occasion, ask the child to draw a picture of him- or herself, without providing any cues initially. If he or she has limited success, repeat the teaching procedure.	1. Ask the children to draw pictures of each other or the teacher. 2. Try making people out of Play-Doh.

Criterion: The child draws a head and 8 other features when asked to draw a picture of him- or herself.

19-III.

Visual-Motor Skills: Cutting

19. Visual-Motor Skills
III. Cutting

a. Snips with scissors
b. Makes continuous cut across paper
c. Cuts straight line, staying within $1/2''$ of guideline
d. Cuts a $5''$ circle (at least three-fourths of the circle)

e. Cuts a $5''$ square
f. Cuts out pictures following general shape

AREA: 19-III. Visual-Motor Skills: Cutting
BEHAVIOR: 19-IIIa. Snips with scissors

Materials: Paper, safety scissors

Procedure	Group activities
Place a piece of paper and scissors in front of the child. Ask him or her to cut the paper. If he or she does not know how, place the scissors in his or her preferred hand. For best control, place his or her thumb and middle fingers in handle holes, with the index finger on the handle next to the hole. Hold the paper taut between your hands and ask the child to cut. Verbal cues such as open or squeeze may be useful. If the child is having a lot of difficulty, use small squeeze scissors or training scissors that have extra handle holes for your hand. When the child is successful in making cuts, encourage him or her to hold the paper. Use stiff paper or index cards to make the activity easier.	Have the children make place mats, cutting "fringe" around the edge of the paper

Criterion: The child snips paper with scissors several times.

AREA: 19-III. Visual-Motor Skills: Cutting
BEHAVIOR: 19-IIIb. Makes continuous cut across paper

Materials: 6-inch square pieces of paper, safety scissors

Procedure	Group activities
Place a piece of paper and scissors in front of the child. Ask him or her to cut the paper in half or to cut all the way across the paper. Give him or her verbal cues (e.g., open, squeeze, open, squeeze) as well as physical assistance, if needed, to maintain continuous cutting. It may be helpful if you initially hold the paper for the child. Then, when he or she is having some success cutting, have him or her hold the paper. Use stiff paper or index cards initially to make the activity easier.	Have the children make simple puzzles by cutting a picture that is glued on cardboard into several pieces

Criterion: The child makes several continuous cuts across a piece of paper.

3 5

AREA: 19-III. Visual-Motor Skills: Cutting
BEHAVIOR: 19-IIIc. Cuts straight line, staying within ½″ of guideline

Materials: 6-inch square pieces of paper, wide-tip marker, safety scissors

Procedure	Group activities
Draw a line about ¼″ wide across a piece of paper. Place the paper and scissors in front of the child. Ask him or her to cut on the line. Encourage the child to look at the paper while he or she is cutting and to stay on the line. Use stiff paper or index cards initially to make the activity easier. If the child is having a lot of difficulty staying on the line, try placing a piece of tape on either side of the line to encourage the child to stay on the line. Try rolling out a piece of Play-Doh and drawing a line in the dough for the child to cut on. The Play-Doh will be thinner where the line was drawn and will encourage him or her to stay on the line.	Have the children cut paper into strips to make paper chains

Criterion: The child cuts on a straight line, staying within ½″ of the guideline.

4

AREA: 19-III. Visual-Motor Skills: Cutting
BEHAVIOR: 19-IIId. Cuts a 5″ circle (at least three-fourths of the circle)

Materials: 6–8-inch square pieces of paper, wide-tip marker, safety scissors

Procedure	Group activities
Draw a circle about 5″ wide on a piece of paper. Place the paper and scissors in front of the child. Ask him or her to cut out the circle. Encourage the child to look at the paper while cutting and to stay on the line. Help the child use his or her other hand to rotate the paper as he or she cuts. Note that right-handed children should cut counter-clockwise and left-handed children should cut clockwise around the circle. Try rolling out a piece of Play-Doh and drawing a circle in the dough for the child to cut out. The Play-Doh will be thinner where the circle was drawn and will encourage him or her to stay on the line.	This may be done in small groups; however, some children may need individual attention.

Criterion: The child cuts out a circle at least three-fourths of the way around the circle.

4.5

AREA: 19-III. Visual-Motor Skills: Cutting
BEHAVIOR: 19-IIIe. Cuts a 5″ square

Materials: 6–8-inch square pieces of paper, wide-tip marker, safety scissors

Procedure	Group activities
Draw a square about 5″ wide on a piece of paper. Place the paper and scissors in front of the child. Ask him or her to cut out the square. Encourage the child to look at the paper while cutting and to stay on the line. Help the child use his or her other hand to rotate the paper as he or she cuts. Encourage him or her to cut all the way to the end of each line before turning the corner. Try rolling out a piece of Play-Doh and drawing a square in the dough for the child to cut out. The Play-Doh will be thinner where the square was drawn and will encourage him or her to stay on the line.	This may be done in small groups; however, some children may need individual attention.

Criterion: The child cuts out a square on 3 different occasions.

5

AREA: 19-III. Visual-Motor Skills: Cutting
BEHAVIOR: 19-IIIf. Cuts out pictures following general shape

Materials: Variety of simple pictures, wide-tip marker, safety scissors

Procedure	Group activities
Place a picture and scissors in front of the child. Ask him or her to cut out the picture. It may be helpful for you or the child to trace around the outline of the picture with a Magic Marker before cutting it out. Encourage the child to stay on the line and not cut into the picture. Select easy pictures initially with gentle curves and no significant angles to maneuver. Increase the complexity as the child's competence grows.	1. Have the children make collages by cutting their favorite pictures out of magazines. 2. Make a scrap book for the year, each week cutting out pictures that are relevant to what is being studied that week.

Criterion: The child cuts out a picture following its general shape.

20-I.

Locomotion: Walking

THE ITEMS IN THE LOCOMOTION sequence presume that the child is already able to walk alone without falling and to stoop to retrieve objects. Early items relating to walking and running are important for daily life; children tend to do them naturally, and they should be developed in every child if possible. Falling is a natural part of learning how to cope with different surfaces and can not be entirely prevented. Note whether a child uses his or her arms to catch him- or herself when falling. If the child does not do this, or if he or she allows his or her head to strike the ground, the activity should be discontinued and a physical therapist consulted.

Galloping, hopping, and skipping are not necessary life skills, but are part of childhood games, dancing, and sports. You will note on the Developmental Progress Chart that a child needs to be able to hop and gallop before skipping can be learned. Most preschools restrict running and other fast locomotion patterns to specific times and places.

If you see a child having difficulty with the basic walking skills or with learning the higher level skills, consult a physical or occupational therapist for guidance. A therapist should also be consulted regarding a child who walks on his or her tiptoes a great deal of the time.

20. Locomotion
I. Walking

a. Walks backward 10 feet
b. Walks on all types of surfaces, rarely falling

c. Uses heel-toe walking pattern, arms swinging at side or free to carry objects

AREA: **20-I. Locomotion: Walking**
BEHAVIOR: 20-Ia.   Walks backward 10 feet
BEHAVIOR: 20-Ib.   Walks on all types of surfaces, rarely falling
BEHAVIOR: 20-Ic.   Uses heel-toe walking pattern,
          arms swinging at side or free to carry objects

Materials: Pull toys, large empty boxes, small carts or wagons with wide handles, a variety of
surfaces to walk on (e.g., smooth floors, rugs, grass, gravel)

Procedures	Group activities
For walking backward, encourage the child to take backward steps by pulling a wheeled toy backward, giving a ride to a friend in a small wagon or cart, or pulling a cardboard box backward. You can also play, "I'm going to get you," while facing the child, or simply move the child gently backward with your hands. For walking on uneven surfaces, encourage the child to walk on different types of surfaces, indoors and outdoors. Include sloping and irregular terrain. Mature walking pattern will emerge naturally as a result of adequate strength, balance, and practice with walking. The static and dynamic balance activities in the *Balance* sequence will help to improve the child's strength and balance. If a child persists in holding one or both arms up in the air while walking, habitually walks on the toes, or has an awkward appearing gait, consult a physical therapist for further guidance.	All of the activities described to the left can easily be done in small groups, either indoors or out. Walking on uneven terrain can be done as part of a nature hike.

Criteria: The child passes this sequence when he or she can:
a. Walk backward 10 feet
b. Walk on all types of surfaces, rarely falling
c. Use a heel-toe walking pattern with his or her arms either swinging at the side or free to carry objects

20-II.

Locomotion:
Tiptoe walking

20. Locomotion
II. Tiptoe walking

a. Walks 3–4 steps with heels off the ground
b. Walks 5 steps on tiptoes with hands on hips or carrying an object with both hands
c. Walks 10 feet on tiptoes on a 1″ line

AREA: **20-II.   Locomotion: Tiptoe walking**
BEHAVIOR: 20-IIa.   Walks 3–4 steps with heels off the ground
BEHAVIOR: 20-IIb.   Walks 5 steps on tiptoes with hands
on hips or carrying an object with both hands
BEHAVIOR: 20-IIc.   Walks 10 feet on tiptoes on a 1″ line

Materials: Any toys or materials that will induce reaching high overhead, footprints or lines of different widths taped or painted on the floor, boards that can be placed on the floor

Procedures	Group activities
Encourage the child to rise onto tiptoes while holding onto a support to reach objects on shelves. This can be made a part of a routine by selectively placing favorite toys just out of reach. Then, encourage tiptoe standing away from a solid support. At first, offer one of your hands for support. You can also ask the child to imitate you as you walk on tiptoes. Once the child can walk several feet at a time on tiptoes, start doing activities in which the arms are held in a stable position so that the balancing must be done with the trunk and legs. Carrying objects in the hands or keeping the hands in pockets while tiptoe walking will achieve this goal. Walking with hands on hips can also be practiced. Work on narrowing the base of support while on tiptoes, thus challenging and improving balance. Have the child walk a specified distance (e.g., 10–15 feet) on tiptoes. Start with a 6″ wide walking base and gradually bring it down to 1″. This can be done in several ways. Lines of different widths can be painted or taped to the floor, boards can be laid side-by-side, or other available objects can be placed on the floor.	1. Have the children practice walking "quietly." 2. Construct an obstacle course in which tiptoe walking is part of the game. 3. Practice counting while walking on tiptoe.

Criteria: The child passes this sequence when he or she can:
a.   Walk 3–4 steps with his or her heels off the ground
b.   Walk 5 steps on his or her tiptoes with hands on hips or while carrying an object in both hands
c.   Walk 10 feet on his or her tiptoes on a 1″ wide line

20-III.

Locomotion: Galloping/skipping

20. Locomotion
III. Galloping/skipping

a. Gallops 5 cycles
b. Skips 5 steps
c. Skips 5–10 steps, with coordinated step-hop

d. Skips 10+ steps with rhythmical weight transfer, landing on toes

AREA: 20-III. Locomotion: Galloping/skipping

3.5 BEHAVIOR: 20-IIIa. Gallops 5 cycles
BEHAVIOR: 20-IIIb. Skips 5 steps
4.5 BEHAVIOR: 20-IIIc. Skips 5–10 steps, with coordinated step-hop
5 BEHAVIOR: 20-IIId. Skips 10+ steps with rhythmical weight transfer, landing on toes

Materials: Open space to move in, a drum or recorded music with a pounding beat.

Procedures	Group activities
Begin galloping instruction with a slow-motion demonstration. Show the child how to step forward with one leg and draw the other up to it. Then, string together a number of these movements and gradually speed up the tempo. Teach the child to lead with both the right and the left foot.	1. Have the children pretend to be horses and gallop across the floor or in a circle.
Sideways sliding is a variation of the galloping movement that is used in many sports and dance activities. It can be taught once the forward progression is mastered.	2. Do galloping or skipping in a circle, keeping time to music or acting out a story.
Many variations of galloping can be devised by altering speed, direction, or body configuration. Galloping on uneven surfaces provides an extra challenge.	
Begin skipping instruction with a slow-motion demonstration. Show the child how to step and hop on the same foot, then step and hop on the other foot. Then, help the child to string a number of these sequences together, either by visual demonstration or by holding the child's hand and skipping alongside. As the child practices, skipping will become smooth and coordinated. At that point, you can introduce skipping at different speeds, in different directions, and with partners.	

Criteria: The child passes this sequence when he or she can:
a. Gallop 5 cycles
b. Skip 5 steps, frequently leading with the same foot on subsequent skips (The pattern looks choppy and uncoordinated.)
c. Skips 5–10 steps with coordinated step-hop (The arms are used rhythmically. Hopping height is exaggerated and the child lands on flat feet.)
d. Skips at least 10 steps with rhythmical weight transfer, landing on toes. (Hopping height is not exaggerated and the arms can be engaged in carrying or hand-holding.)

20-IV.

Locomotion: Running

20. Locomotion
IV. Running

a. Runs 5–10 feet without falling
b. Spontaneously avoids large obstacles when running
c. Runs with some periods of flight (i.e., both feet off ground)

d. Runs fast
e. Runs, changing direction 180° within 4–8 steps

AREA: **20-IV.   Locomotion: Running**
BEHAVIOR: 20-IVa.   Runs 5–10 feet without falling
BEHAVIOR: 20-IVb.   Spontaneously avoids large obstacles when running
BEHAVIOR: 20-IVc.   Runs with some periods of flight (i.e., both feet off ground)
BEHAVIOR: 20-IVd.   Runs fast
BEHAVIOR: 20-IVe.   Runs, changing direction 180° within 4–8 steps

Materials: Open space with a few large obstacles, 8″–10″ diameter ball

Procedures	Group activities
Early running should take place indoors on a smooth surface. Use verbal commands to "go fast," accompanied by hand-clapping and a simple demonstration of running. Most children enjoy kicking a ball and chasing it. At this stage, the child should not be competing with others, following rules, or using equipment.	1. Run in a circle as part of imaginative play or while listening to music. Incorporate sudden starts and stops.
Watch to see if the child runs around large obstacles rather than bumping into them. If instruction is needed, run near the child and instruct him or her to look ahead toward obstacles and to change direction of running. If a child is having difficulty learning this activity, there may be a visual or motor problem and a physical or occupational therapist should be consulted.	2. Practice running around obstacles by playing follow-the-leader. 3. Have small groups of children take turns running at different speeds, or imitating different animals. 4. Older children can learn to play tag. Teach them to tag lightly and not push.
The maturation of the running pattern will take place naturally as the child practices in a variety of activities. Three-year-olds can begin to use their running abilities in chasing and fleeing games that incorporate rules and simple equipment. Listening skills, sudden stops, and direction changes can all be incorporated into games. Children should be taught beginning sports etiquette such as not pushing and abiding by rules.	
Four-year-olds can benefit from specific instruction about movement. Demonstrate leaning forward with the trunk, keeping the elbows flexed and pumping the arms, landing on the heels and pushing off with the balls of the feet. From this age onward, children can participate in games that have formal rules and that incorporate equipment.	

Criteria: The child passes this sequence when he or she can:
a.   Run 5–10 feet without falling, landing on flat feet, keeping trunk upright, and showing little arm movement
b.   Spontaneously avoid large obstacles when running
c.   Run with some periods in which both feet are off the ground (Arms swing back and forth but look awkward.)
d.   Run fast, pumping with the arms and leaning into the run
e.   Change running direction 180° within 4–8 steps

Locomotion: Hopping

20. Locomotion
V. Hopping

a. Hops once in place
b. Hops up to 3 times on preferred foot
c. Hops forward 6″ on preferred foot
d. Hops 5 times on preferred foot; 3 times on nonpreferred foot
e. Hops forward 8 times with each foot
f. Hops forward 16″ on preferred foot; 12″ on nonpreferred foot

AREA: **20-V. Locomotion: Hopping**

3.5 BEHAVIOR: 20-Va. Hops once in place

4 BEHAVIOR: 20-Vb. Hops up to 3 times on preferred foot

4 BEHAVIOR: 20-Vc. Hops forward 6″ on preferred foot

4.5 BEHAVIOR: 20-Vd. Hops 5 times on preferred foot; 3 times on nonpreferred foot

4.5 BEHAVIOR: 20-Ve. Hops forward 8 times with each foot

5 BEHAVIOR: 20-Vf. Hops forward 16″ on preferred foot; 12″ on nonpreferred foot

Materials: Open space; lines or other designs, such as footprints, painted on the floor

Procedures	Group activities
Begin by having the child follow a demonstration. It may be helpful to build up strength by having the child jump on 1 foot on a trampoline. Throughout the development of hopping abilities, the following guidelines can be used:	1. Incorporate hopping into circle games or obstacle courses. 2. Teach simple dances that incorporate hopping.
There will be a preferred leg that will show the most advanced abilities	
Work on hopping in place before hopping forward	
Work on developing a controlled pattern before working on speed or distance	
Encourage exploration of different kinds of hopping before incorporating hopping into structured games	

Criteria: The child passes this sequence when he or she can:

a. Hop once in place (There is very little height; the arms do not participate and the trunk remains upright.)

b. Hop up to 3 times on the preferred foot (The trunk is still upright and the arms are held high.)

c. Jump forward 6″ at once on the preferred foot (There is some forward leaning of the trunk and the arms are moved vigorously up and down as the hop occurs.)

d. Hop 5 times on the preferred foot and 3 times on the nonpreferred foot (Body movements as described in "3" above.)

e. Hop forward at least 8 times with each foot (The arms lift smoothly and rhythmically to assist in movement.)

f. Hop forward at least 16″ at once on the preferred foot and 12″ on nonpreferred foot (Body movements as described in "5" above.)

21-I.

Stairs:
Up stairs

WHILE CHILDREN ARE developing their stair-climbing abilities, they will use different patterns, depending upon how secure they feel, how deep or high the steps are, and whether there is a person or railing to hold onto. The height of the child is an additional factor—shorter children will tend to place both feet on the same step because their legs cannot easily reach the next step. In general it is more important to have a safe and functional way to use stairs than to have a fast, mature way.

Young children who are physically handicapped are usually carried up and down stairs, but a physical therapist should be consulted to see when instruction on independent use of stairs can begin.

21-I. Stairs
I. Up stairs

a. Walks up 3 steps, using same-step placement, holding railing

b. Walks up 10 steps, using same-step placement, holding railing

c. Walks up 4 steps, using alternate-step placement, holding railing

d. Walks up 10 steps, using alternate-step placement, holding railing

e. Walks up 3 steps, using alternate-step placement, without holding railing

f. Walks up 10 steps, using alternate-step placement, without holding railing

AREA: **21-I.   Stairs: Up stairs**

2⁶ BEHAVIOR: 21-Ia. Walks up 3 steps, using same-step placement, holding railing

2⁵ BEHAVIOR: 21-Ib. Walks up 10 steps, using same-step placement, holding railing

2⁵ BEHAVIOR: 21-Ic. Walks up 4 steps, using alternate-step placement, holding railing

3 BEHAVIOR: 21-Id. Walks up 10 steps, using alternate-step placement, holding railing

3 BEHAVIOR: 21-Ie. Walks up 3 steps, using alternate-step placement, without holding railing

3 .5 BEHAVIOR: 21-If. Walks up 10 steps, using alternate-step placement, without holding railing

Materials: Staircases with and without railings, stairs of different heights and depths, other materials that can be stacked (e.g., large books, large flat blocks)

Procedures	Group activities
Expose the child to steps with and without railings. While the children are developing their stair-climbing skills, they will use different patterns, depending on how secure they feel, how deep and high the steps are, and whether there is a railing or person to hold onto. An additional factor is the height of the child—shorter children will use more same-step placement because their legs cannot reach easily to the next step. Observe the child's natural way of going up stairs. The child who is moving up easily and briskly is probably ready to start learning a more advanced method. If you are teaching a child to go up stairs without a railing, use a staircase without railings or use the center portion of a staircase with railings. Stand behind the child and give light physical support along with verbal encouragement. Gradually withdraw the help as the child becomes more confident. The same-step pattern will be used for a long time before an alternate-step pattern emerges. Another way to encourage letting go of the rail is to give the child a medium-sized object to carry. You may have to drop back to a lower step at first. If you are teaching a child to go up stairs using an alternate-step pattern, start with a staircase with railings. Stand next to the child and hold his or her free hand as you encourage stepping all the way up. Gradually withdraw this help as the child begins to use the alternate-step pattern. Whichever new pattern you are teaching, you may be more successful if at first you ask for more advanced performance on only the first few or last few steps of a staircase.	Small flights of portable stairs or stacks of blocks or books can be incorporated into obstacle courses. Teaching the child to use longer flights of stairs is best done on an individual basis if a child is having problems.

(continued)

Criteria: The child passes this sequence when he or she can:
a. Walk up 3 steps, using same-step placement, holding onto a wall or railing
b. Walk up 10 steps, using same-step placement, holding onto a wall or railing
c. Walk up 4 steps, using alternate-step placement, holding onto a wall or railing
d. Walk up 10 steps, using alternate-step placement, holding onto a wall or railing
e. Walk up 3 steps, using alternate-step placement, without holding railing
f. Walk up 10 steps, using alternate-step placement, without holding railing.

Note: These criteria are based on the use of standard steps (i.e., 6½″ high × 10″ deep).

21-II.

Stairs: Down stairs

21. Stairs
II. Down stairs

a. Walks down 3 steps, using same-step placement, holding railing

b. Walks down 3 steps, using same-step placement, without holding railing

c. Walks down 10 steps, using same-step placement, without holding railing

d. Walks down 3 steps, using alternate-step placement, holding railing

e. Walks down 10 steps, using alternate-step placement, holding railing

f. Walks down 3 steps, using alternate-step placement, without holding railing

g. Walks down 10 steps, using alternate-step placement, without holding railing

AREA: 21-II. Stairs: Down stairs

2.5 BEHAVIOR: 21-IIa. Walks down 3 steps, using same-step placement, holding railing

3 BEHAVIOR: 21-IIb. Walks down 3 steps, using same-step placement, without holding railing

3.5 BEHAVIOR: 21-IIc. Walks down 10 steps, using same-step placement, without holding railing

4 BEHAVIOR: 21-IId. Walks down 3 steps, using alternate-step placement, holding railing

4.5 BEHAVIOR: 21-IIe. Walks down 10 steps, using alternate-step placement, holding railing

4-5 BEHAVIOR: 21-IIf. Walks down 3 steps, using alternate-step placement, without holding railing

5 BEHAVIOR: 21-IIg. Walks down 10 steps, using alternate-step placement, without holding railing

Materials: Same as in sequence 21-I.

Procedures	Group activities
Use the same general procedures as in sequence 21-I. It is usually more successful to stand in front of the child who is learning a new way of coming down stairs, in order to keep their confidence. Children are more likely to use a more advanced method of going down stairs if you ask for it at first on the lowest step(s).	Use the same general group activities as found in sequence 21-I.

Criteria: The child passes this sequence when he or she can:

a. Walk down 3 steps, using same-step placement, without holding railing.
b. Walk down 10 steps, using same-step placement, without holding railing
c. Walk down 3 steps, using alternate-step placement, using a rail or wall for support
d. Walk down 10 steps, using alternate-step placement, using a rail or wall for support
e. Walk down 3 steps, using alternate-step placement, without holding railing
f. Walk down 10 steps, using alternate-step placement, without holding railing

Note: These criteria are based on use of standard steps (i.e., 6½" high 10" deep).

Jumping:
Jumping up

JUMPING IS A SKILL that comes into play in many games and sports, including Special Olympics. It should be developed whenever possible in order to maximize social integration of children with handicapping conditions. However, depending on your setting, you may or may not want to teach children to jump from heights! If you do teach it, set firm rules about when and where this can be done. Children whose physical abilities are much higher than their mental abilities, or children who have very poor judgment, should not be taught to jump from heights. Children who have fragile bones or joints should, likewise, not be taught this skill. The parents will know if these activities are allowed.

22. Jumping
I. Jumping up

a. Jumps off floor with both feet
b. Jumps 2″ off ground or over 2″ hurdle
c. Jumps 8″ off ground or over 8″ hurdle
d. Jumps rope for 2 cycles

e. Jumps over several 8″ obstacles in succession
f. Jumps up 3″ beyond arms' reach
g. Jumps, completing a half-turn in 1 jump

AREA: **22-I. Jumping: Jumping up**

5 BEHAVIOR: 22-Ia. Jumps off floor with both feet

3 BEHAVIOR: 22-Ib. Jumps 2″ off ground or over 2″ hurdle

3.5 BEHAVIOR: 22-Ic. Jumps 8″ off ground or over 8″ hurdle

4 BEHAVIOR: 22-Id. Jumps rope for 2 cycles

4 BEHAVIOR: 22-Ie. Jumps over several 8″ obstacles in succession

4.5 BEHAVIOR: 22-If. Jumps up 3″ beyond arms' reach

5 BEHAVIOR: 22-Ig. Jumps, completing a half-turn in 1 jump

Materials: Rope, low obstacles, trampoline, tape or chalk

Procedures	Group activities
Jumping up requires considerable strength and speed of movement. Children who are having difficulty learning to jump will experience success first on spring-like surfaces such as a trampoline or mattress. Initially, they will need to hold on as they jump. During early attempts at jumping, the child will not use his or her legs together, little height will be achieved, the arms will not assist the movement, and the legs will be "pulled" off the floor rather than used to propel the body upward. With practice, the legs will flex and extend simultaneously, a preparatory crouch will emerge, and the arms will move upward with the body. When teaching jumping on the floor, follow these guidelines:	1. Incorporate various patterns of jumping into songs, nursery rhymes, or circle games. 2. Mark lines on the floor and have the children pretend to jump "over the river" or "into the house." 3. Include a variety of jumping activities into an obstacle course, making sure that each child can succeed at something.
Ask for a single jump before asking for a succession of jumps	
When teaching jumping over obstacles, grade the demands by having the child jump over a rope or hula hoop held gradually higher off the floor	
When teaching the child to jump for height, use a target such as a chalk mark or piece of tape on the wall	

Criteria: The child passes this sequence when he or she can:

a. Jump off the floor with both feet

b. Jump 2″ off the ground or over a 2″ hurdle

c. Jump 8″ off the ground or over an 8″ hurdle

d. Jump rope for 2 cycles

e. Jump over several 8″ obstacles in succession

f. Jump up 3″ beyond arms' reach

g. Jump, completing a half-turn in 1 jump

Jumping:
Jumping down

22. Jumping
II. Jumping down

a. Jumps from 8″ height, 1 foot leading

b. Jumps from 16″–18″ height, 1 foot leading

c. Jumps from 18″–24″ height with feet together on take-off and landing

d. Jumps from 24″–30″ height with feet together on take-off and landing

e. Jumps from 32″ height, possibly leading with 1 foot

AREA: 22-II. Jumping: Jumping down

3 BEHAVIOR: 22-IIa. Jumps from 8" height, 1 foot leading
3 BEHAVIOR: 22-IIb. Jumps from 16"–18" height, 1 foot leading
3.5 BEHAVIOR: 22-IIc. Jumps from 18"–24" height with feet together
on take-off and landing
4 BEHAVIOR: 22-IId. Jumps from 24"–30" height with feet together take-off and landing
4.5 BEHAVIOR: 22-IIe. Jumps from 32" height, possibly leading with 1 foot

Materials: Large stable objects of varying heights (e.g., boxes, stairs, tables), medium-size stable
objects (e.g., books, pieces of wood to stack)

Procedures	Group activities
Teach jumping down by starting with low objects. For each child, determine the highest object from which he or she can jump. Place a mat on the floor. Hold the child's hand at first, then gradually move off to the side. First attempts will be little more than stepping down, with no real flight. As skill and confidence increases, the take-off will be 2-footed but landing will be on 1 foot; some real flight will also be present. At this stage, the child will frequently touch the floor at landing. Finally, both take-off and landing will be 2-footed, with definite flight and the arms out at the side for balance. As the child goes through the stages and skills, more mature patterns will always be evident when he or she jumps from lower heights.	Incorporate jumping down into obstacle courses, with objects of varying heights.

Criteria: The child passes this sequence when he or she can:

a. Jump from 8" height, 1 foot leading, without assistance
b. Jump from 16"–18" height, leading with 1 foot, without assistance
c. Jump from 18"–24" height, with feet together on take-off and landing, without assistance
d. Jump from 24"–30" height, with feet together on take-off and landing, without assistance
e. Jump from 32" height, possibly leading with 1 foot, without assistance

22-III.

Jumping: Broadjumping

22. Jumping
III. Broadjumping

a. Broadjumps 4″–14″

b. Broadjumps 14″–23″

c. Broadjumps 24″–35″

d. Broadjumps 36″ or more

AREA: **22-III. Jumping: Broadjumping**
3   BEHAVIOR: 22-IIIa. Broadjumps 4″–14″
3.5 BEHAVIOR: 22-IIIb. Broadjumps 14″–23″
4   BEHAVIOR: 22-IIIc. Broadjumps 24″–35″
4.5 BEHAVIOR: 22-IIId. Broadjumps 36″ or more

Materials: Lines or other markers on the floor, carpet squares

Procedures	Group activities
Observe the child's attempts at broadjumping and determine how far he or she can presently jump. Initial attempts will be short jumps with 1-foot take-off, with the trunk upright and slight upward arm movement. Later, the arms are held in front of the body and are used to initiate the jump; a preparatory crouch is evident but is not deep, and the legs are flexed during flight. In the mature broadjump, the child prepares by crouching deeply and bringing the arms behind the body. The arms are moved forward forcefully and the trunk leans forward during the jump.	1. Imitate animal movements that involve broadjumping. 2. Incorporate broadjumping into an obstacle course, using carpet squares placed at varying distances from each other.
Early instruction should focus on getting the child to take off with both feet together. The child may be better able to get this idea if you have him or her jump *down* a short distance with his or her feet together, then repeat the broadjump. Once the 2-foot take-off is established, you can encourage the child to get more distance, using marks on the floor. Finally, if more mature arm movements are not emerging, the child can be instructed in that area.	

Criteria: The child passes this sequence when he or she can:
a.   Broadjump 4″–14″ with 2-foot take-off
b.   Broadjump 14″–24″ with 2-foot take-off
c.   Broadjump 24″–34″ with 2-foot take-off
d.   Broadjump 36″ or more with 2-foot take-off

23-I.

Balance:
Static balance

THE BALANCING SEQUENCES contain a wide variety of skills relating to steady body control while standing still or moving. The items assume that the child is able to walk independently and safely, and is ready to be prepared for more challenging exploration of his or her environment. The skills learned here will also prepare the children to participate in sport and recreational activities. Children should develop the ability to perform these activities without a lot of body sway or extra arm movement. If you have questions about a child's balance, consult with a physical or occupational therapist.

23. Balance
I. Static balance

a. Stands on 1 leg for 1–2 seconds
b. Stands with both feet on balance beam
c. Balances on preferred leg, with hands on hips and opposite knee bent for 3 seconds
d. Balances on preferred leg, with hands on hips and opposite knee bent for 5 seconds
e. Stands on tiptoes, with arms overhead for 2 seconds

f. Stands on each leg, with hands on hips and opposite knee bent for 6 seconds
g. Stands on tiptoes, with hands overhead for 8 seconds
h. Stands on each leg, with hands on hips and opposite knee bent for 10 seconds each

AREA: **23-I.   Balance: Static balance**

2.5   BEHAVIOR: 23-Ia.   Stands on 1 leg for 1–2 seconds

2.5   BEHAVIOR: 23-Ib.   Stands with both feet on balance beam

3   BEHAVIOR: 23-Ic.   Balances on preferred leg, with
hands on hips and opposite knee bent for 3 seconds

3.5   BEHAVIOR: 23-Id.   Balances on preferred leg with
hands on hips and opposite knee bent for 5 seconds

4   BEHAVIOR: 23-Ie.   Stands on tiptoes, with arms overhead for 2 seconds

4   BEHAVIOR: 23-If.   Stands on each leg, with hands
on hips and opposite knee bent for 6 seconds

4.5   BEHAVIOR: 23-Ig.   Stands on tiptoes, with arms overhead for 8 seconds

5   BEHAVIOR: 23-Ih.   Stands on each leg, with hands
on hips and opposite knee bent for 10 seconds each

Materials: Balance beam that is 2 ½″ wide, boards that can be placed on the floor

Procedures	Group activities
Since static balance activities are not particularly fun, children will not generally practice them spontaneously, as they will with many other gross motor activities. They are best practiced by taking advantage of naturally occurring activities or by embedding them in games that force their practice.	1. Set up a "circus" in which the children can perform a variety of static and dynamic balance activities.
For beginners, use dressing time to force the child to stand on 1 leg when putting on shoes or pants. Walking up and down stairs without a rail also demands a 1-leg stance. These young children can also be encouraged to initate static balance activities for short periods.	2. Act out stories in which the children pretend to be statues, trees, or crossing bridges.
From about 3 years old and up, children will be more interested in challenging themselves to maintain static postures for longer periods. Use of visual imagery, such as pretending to be a tree or statue, is successful with older children as well. In order to develop these abilities, children should be practiced in a variety of situations and on a variety of surfaces.	3. In an outdoor area, set up targets to be used for ball-kicking.
For all static balance activities, the child should show reasonable body control, without marked swaying or excessive arm movements. If you see these, consult with a physical or occupational therapist.	

(continued)

Criteria: The child passes this sequence when he or she can:

a. Stand on 1 leg for 1–2 seconds
b. Stand with both feet on a balance beam
c. Balance on a preferred leg, with his or her hands on hips and the opposite knee bent for 3 seconds
d. Balance on a preferred leg, with his or her hands on hips and the opposite knee bent for 5 seconds
e. Stand on tiptoes, with his or her arms overhead for 2 seconds
f. Stand on each leg, with his or her hands on hips and the opposite knee bent for 6 seconds
g. Stand on tiptoes, with his or her hands overhead for 8 seconds
h. Stand on each leg, with his or her hands on hips and the opposite knee bent for 10 seconds each

23-II.

Balance:
Dynamic balance

23. Balance
III. Dynamic balance

a. Walks along 10′ line in a general direction

b. Walks with 1 foot on balance beam, other foot on floor

c. Kicks a ball a few feet

d. Walks 3 steps on balance beam with both feet

e. Walks along a 10′ line, keeping feet on line

f. Kicks a ball 4′–6′

g. Kicks a ball 6′–12′

h. Kicks a ball 12′–15′

i. Walks 4–5 steps on balance beam

j. Does 1 somersault

k. Walks full length of balance beam

l. Walks full length of balance beam while carrying something in both hands or with hands on hips

m. Does 2 somersaults in a row

n. Kicks ball 6′–12′ in the air

AREA: **23-II. Balance: Dynamic balance**

2.5 BEHAVIOR: 23-IIa. Walks along a 10' line in a general direction

2.5 BEHAVIOR: 23-IIb. Walks with 1 foot on balance beam, other foot on floor

2.5 BEHAVIOR: 23-IIc. Kicks a ball a few feet

3 BEHAVIOR: 23-IId. Walks 3 steps on balance beam with both feet

3 BEHAVIOR: 23-IIe. Walks along a 10' line, keeping feet on line

3 BEHAVIOR: 23-IIf. Kicks a ball 4'–6'

3.5 BEHAVIOR: 23-IIg. Kicks a ball 6'–12'

4 BEHAVIOR: 23-IIh. Kicks a ball 12'–15'

4.5 BEHAVIOR: 23-IIi. Walks 4–5 steps on balance beam

4.5 BEHAVIOR: 23-IIj. Does 1 somersault

4.5 BEHAVIOR: 23-IIk. Walks full length of balance beam

5 BEHAVIOR: 23-IIl. Walks full length of balance beam while carrying something in both hands or with hands on hips

5 BEHAVIOR: 23-IIm. Does 2 somersaults in a row

5 BEHAVIOR: 23-IIn. Kicks ball 6'–12' in the air

Materials: 10' line, 1" wide, on floor; balance beam 2 ½" wide, 4" off floor, 6' long; boards of various widths that can be placed on the floor or raised up from the floor at various heights; balls of various sizes; open floor space for play

Procedures	Group activities
For balance beam:	1. Proceed with activities listed in the "Group activity" section of sequence 23-I.
Provide graduated opportunities for walking on narrowed and raised surfaces. Start with wide boards on the floor and as the child masters walking on the board, place supports under each end. Then, start using a narrower board, first on the floor and then raised up. A selection of board widths and heights in the play space will encourage experimentation.	2. In an outdoor area, set up targets for ball-kicking.
If a child needs your support for physical or emotional reasons, start by holding his or her hand on the beam. Then, as confidence is gained, walk behind the child, holding on lightly to the shirt.	
Never force a fearful child to perform balance beam activities. Gentle encouragement combined with imitation will gradually convince the reluctant child.	
Children enjoy using imagery such as walking over a bridge.	
At first, allow the child to use the arms for balance; later have the child keep his or her hands on hips or in pockets, or carry objects to the end of the beam.	
For ball-kicking:	
Watch for changes in performance. Early kicking will be carried out with an upright trunk, little backswing of the nonkicking leg, and use of arms	

(continued)

Procedure	Group activities
to maintain balance. Later, the knee of the kicking leg will be bent and the leg will pull back just after kicking. At this intermediate stage, the child will be able to take a few steps toward the ball before kicking it. The mature kicking pattern is started at the hip, and the leg follows through rather than being withdrawn. The arm opposite to the kicking leg is swung forward with that leg. At this mature level, the child can also run toward the ball before kicking it. Use balls about the size of a soccer ball; for beginning kickers, a ball of the same size but lighter weight will get a better result. In order to get a more mature pattern, stress increasing distance rather than improving accuracy. Once the mature pattern is achieved, accuracy can be improved by incorporating kicking into simple stationary target-kicking, and later into simple drills. The mature kicking pattern will be achieved first on the preferred side. After this occurs, work on the nonpreferred side. For somersault: Before working on somersaults, be sure the child understands about taking weight on the hands and is able to do it at least briefly. Wheelbarrow walking is a good way of practicing this skill. Learning how to hold a curled-up position in sideways rolling will help prepare the child for holding a curl in a forward roll. Use a padded surface for practicing somersaults. To teach this skill, provide an example yourself, or use another child as a model. Then, physically assist the child in the movement, withdrawing assistance as soon as you can. First stress taking weight on the hands rather than the head. Later stress holding the curled posture and repeating the movement.	

Criteria: The child passes this sequence when he or she can:

a Walk along a 10' line, following the general direction but not keeping his or her feet on the line
b. Walk with 1 foot on the balance beam and 1 on the floor
c. Kick a ball a few feet
d. Walk 3 steps on a balance beam, keeping both feet on the beam
e. Walk along a 10' line, keeping both feet on the line
f. Kick a ball 4'–6', deviating only slightly from a straight line
g. Kick a ball 6'–12', deviating only slightly from a straight line
h. Kick a ball 12'–15', deviating only slightly from a straight line
i. Walk 4–5 steps on a balance beam

(continued)

j. Do 1 somersault; some weight is taken on the arms and 1 leg may lead
k. Walk full length of the balance beam
l. Walk full length of the balance beam while carrying something in both hands or keeping his or her hands on the hips
m. Do 2 somersaults without pausing; weight is taken on the arms and the legs take off together
n. Kick a ball so that it becomes airborne and travels 6'–12'

24-I.

Balls:
Throwing balls

$\mathbf{T}$HROWING AND CATCHING balls is one of the basic play skills of early childhood. The skills in the following 2 sequences are intended to lay the basis for more advanced games that use equipment, such as baseball, basketball, and volleyball. Children in the 2–5-year age range should be getting comfortable with throwing and catching, using a variety of objects. These skills should be stressed as much with girls as with boys.

For children with handicapping conditions, there are many adaptations that can be made. Children who are visually impaired can use very brightly colored balls or noise-making balls. Children who are motor impaired should try different types of balls to find the one that works best (e.g., soft balls that can be grasped in a fist, large balls that are easier to hold, balloons, suspended balls). Some children can use "ball scooopers" made from bleach bottles. Games involving rolling balls, such as "bowling" with empty plastic bottles, are also fun.

24. Balls
I. Throwing balls

a. Throws 8″ ball to an adult, underhand, 5′

b. Throws 3″ ball to an adult, underhand, 7′

c. Throws 3″ ball to an adult, underhand, 9′

d. Throws 8″ ball to an adult, 2-handed underhand, 9′

e. Throws 3″ ball to an adult, overhand, 10′

f. Throws 8″ ball to an adult, overhand, 10′

AREA: **24-I.   Balls: Throwing balls**

2 5   BEHAVIOR: 24-Ia.   Throws 8″ ball to an adult, underhand, 5′
2 5   BEHAVIOR: 24-Ib.   Throws 3″ ball to an adult, underhand, 7′
3   BEHAVIOR: 24-Ic.   Throws 3″ ball to an adult, underhand, 9′
3 5   BEHAVIOR: 24-Id.   Throws 8″ ball to an adult, 2-handed underhand, 9′
4 4 5   BEHAVIOR: 24-Ie.   Throws 3″ ball to an adult, overhand, 10′
4, 5   BEHAVIOR: 24-If.   Throws 8″ ball to an adult, overhand, 10′

Materials: Soft balls of various sizes, beanbags, targets on the wall

Procedures	Group activities
Provide different sizes of balls to throw; the balls should be soft in order to avoid possible injury. Structure the activity and restrict throwing to certain times and places. Observe each child to see what type of throwing pattern is being used. These vary depending on the size of the ball being thrown and the size of the child's hands. In general, an early thrower will have mostly back and forth movement and will not throw very far. With structured practice, twisting motions appear in the trunk and the child takes a forward step with the leg on the same side as the throwing arm. A mature thrower will show rotation before and during the throw and will step out with the leg opposite the throwing arm. Most 5-year-olds will not achieve the most mature form of throwing. When teaching throwing, work first on throwing for *distance*, then for *speed*, and finally for *accuracy*. To work on distance, start by standing close, as the child throws a ball to you. Each time the ball is thrown far enough to reach you, take 1 step back. Another method is to have the child throw a ball to hit a wall, and to move back 1 step with each successful throw. To work on speed, use verbal instructions. To work on accuracy, use a variety of targets, first larger and closer, then smaller and farther away. Hula hoops, waste baskets, wall targets, and low basketball hoops all make good stationary targets. Moving targets are generally beyond the limits of this age group. If a child who is motor handicapped has trouble releasing a ball to throw, hold the ball in your hand and allow the child to strike it.	1. Form a circle of children around a target such as a wastebasket or hula hoop. The target can be as large or small as you want. Let the children take turns throwing the ball, and award "points" for their performance. 2. Targets can be laid on the floor or mounted on the wall for the children to throw balls toward. 3. Older preschoolers can learn the rules involved in throwing balls to each other (e.g., not throwing too hard, aiming the ball accurately).

(continued)

Criteria: The child passes this sequence when he or she can:

a.   Throw an 8″ ball to an adult, underhand, 5′
b.   Throw a 3″ ball to an adult, underhand, 7′
c.   Throw a 3″ ball to an adult, underhand, 9′
d.   Throw an 8″ ball to an adult, 2-handed, underhand, 9′
e.   Throw a 3″ ball to an adult, overhand, 10′
f.   Throw an 8″ ball to an adult, overhand, 10′

24-II.

Balls:
Catching balls

24. Balls
II. Catching balls

a. Catches 8″ ball from 5′, arms straight in front of body

b. Catches 8″ ball from 5′, elbows bent

c. Catches 3″ ball from 5′, elbows bent

d. Catches 8″ ball from 6′, elbows bent and arms held at sides

e. Catches 3″ ball from 7′, elbows bent and arms held at sides

AREA:　**24-II.　Balls:　Catching balls**

3　BEHAVIOR:　24-IIa.　Catches 8″ ball from 5′, arms straight in front of body

3.5　BEHAVIOR:　24-IIb.　Catches 8″ ball from 5′, elbows bent

4　BEHAVIOR:　24-IIc.　Catches 3″ ball from 5′, elbows bent

4.5　BEHAVIOR:　24-IId.　Catches 8″ ball from 6′, elbows bent and arms held at sides

5　BEHAVIOR:　24-IIe.　Catches 3″ ball from 7′, elbows bent and arms held at sides

Materials:　Soft balls of various sizes, beanbags, yarnballs

Procedures	Group activities
Soft balls of different sizes should be available for practice. For early catchers, beanbags may be useful since they are easier to grasp.	1.　Place a group of children in a line or circle, and throw a ball to each in turn, modifying your technique as needed according to the guidelines in the "Procedure" section.
Observe the child to see what type of pattern is being used. Early catchers will extend their arms in front with palms up; they scoop the ball with their arms and trap it against the chest. At this stage, the child may avoid the ball by turning his or her face away. Later, the arms are held at the side, with elbows bent at right angles and palms facing each other; the ball is trapped by the bent arms. Children at this stage may close their eyes as the ball approaches. The mature catcher will adjust to the flight of the oncoming ball and catch it only with his or her hands.	2.　Use the situation in the above activity to help teach concepts: say you will throw the ball to each girl, or to somebody wearing red; let the children tell you where to throw the ball.
Use verbal preparation such as "ready, catch" before each throw to the child.	
Begin by standing very close to the child and throwing gently and accurately to insure a successful catch. Then, gradually increase the distance between yourself and the child as long as catching remains successful. Start with larger balls and move gradually to smaller ones in order to promote more mature catching patterns.	

Criteria:　The child passes this sequence when he or she can:

a.　Catch an 8″ ball from 5′, with his or her arms straight in front of the body

b.　Catch an 8″ ball from 5′, with his or her elbows bent

c.　Catch a 3″ ball from 5′, with his or her elbows bent

d.　Catch an 8″ ball from 6′, with his or her elbows bent and arms held at the sides

e.　Catch a 3″ ball from 7′, with his or her elbows bent and arms held at the sides

25.

Outdoor Equipment

THIS SEQUENCE CONTAINS a combination of indoor and outdoor activities. When the group is outdoors, close and constant supervision is necessary. Children should wear shoes that will stay on their feet, not thong sandals or loose, untied shoes. Pieces of equipment should be spaced well apart in the play area, and should be well maintained. Wooden pieces need to be sanded regularly to prevent splinters, and there should be no sharp edges on equipment.

A selection of outdoor equipment would include riding toys, balls of various sizes, swings, and a variety of climbing equipment. Most of the climbing equipment should be stable, but movable, and unsteady surfaces, such as wiggling bridges or tires lashed together, should also be available.

Every effort should be made to integrate children who are handicapped into playground activities. They need vigorous activity as much as other children, and much of children's social bonding takes place on the playground.

25. Outdoor Equipment

a. Propels riding toy with feet, 10′
b. Climbs ladder on low slide (e.g., 3′–6′)
c. Climbs on low jungle gym bars and will drop several inches to ground
d. Pedals tricycle at least 10′
e. Enjoys unsteady surfaces and tries to make them move
f. Pumps swing
g. Rides bicycle with training wheels

326

The Carolina Curriculum

AREA: 25. Outdoor Equipment

2.5 BEHAVIOR: 25a. Propels riding toy with feet, 10′
2.5 BEHAVIOR: 25b. Climbs ladder on low slide (e.g., 3′–6′)
3 BEHAVIOR: 25c. Climbs on low jungle gym bars and will drop several inches to ground
3.5 BEHAVIOR: 25d. Pedals tricycle at least 10′
4 BEHAVIOR: 25e. Enjoys unsteady surfaces and tries to make them move
4.5 BEHAVIOR: 25f. Pumps swing
5 BEHAVIOR: 25g. Rides bicycle with training wheels

Materials: Slides, swings, riding toys, tricycles, bicycles, jungle gym with variety of surfaces and climbing opportunities

Procedures	Group activities
Outdoor free play activities do not generally require instruction; however, if a particular child is not participating in age-appropriate activities, some gentle encouragement and assistance is necessary. Sometimes children are afraid of heights or unstable surfaces. If this happens, do not force a child to try. Carrying a child through an activity, or letting him or her do just part of it may ease the fears, and generally, within a few weeks, he or she will attempt the activities alone. A physical or occupational therapist should be consulted if any adaptations to playground equipment are needed in order to allow a child who is handicapped to use them, or if a child displays extreme or long-lasting fear of heights or unstable surfaces. Children who are motor impaired are often frightened of slides because they feel out of control. Never impose this activity on such a child: If the slide is big enough, you may hold the child on your lap and slide down. You can also ride the child on the last 2 or 3 feet of the slide.	Proceed as in the section to the left with a group of children.

Criteria: The child passes this sequence when he or she can:
a. Propel a riding toy with his or her feet at least 10′
b. Climb a ladder on a low slide (e.g., 3′–6′)
c. Climb on the low jungle gym bars and will drop several inches to the ground
d. Pedal a tricycle at least 10′
e. Enjoy unsteady surfaces and try to make them move
f. Pump the swing on which he or she is playing
g. Ride a bicycle with training wheels

Index